*The Skin Diver's Travel Guide*

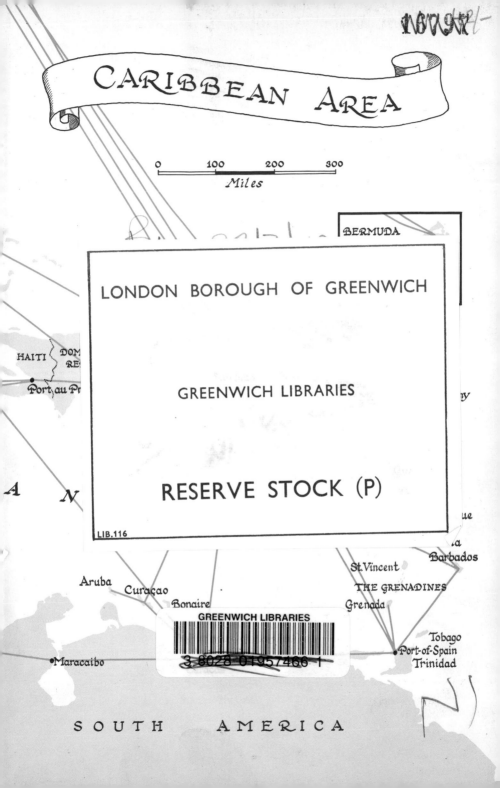

CARIBBEAN AREA

0     100     200     300
*Miles*

BERMUDA

HAITI   DOM
RE

Port au Pr

A    N

Barbados

Aruba    St.Vincent
Curaçao    THE GRENADINES
Bonaire    Grenada

Tobago
Port-of-Spain
Trinidad

Maracaibo

SOUTH     AMERICA

# THE
# SKIN DIVER'S
# TRAVEL GUIDE

PAM AM's guide to Snorkeling and Scuba Diving
in Bermuda, the Bahamas, the Caribbean, and the
Mediterranean *by* **GENE TINKER**

Doubleday & Company, Inc., Garden City, New York, 1967

*This one is for*
NICK STANFORD

# PREFACE

The information presented here was accumulated during a unique and exciting trip to the many countries described on the following pages. In the course of my diving tour I was able to see, and record, diving conditions in places as culturally and geographically diverse as Saba and Cyprus. It was a rare opportunity to travel and to meet some wonderful and unusual people and I enjoyed it immensely.

The many language barriers I encountered were minimized by our intense enthusiasm about diving. Language problems disappear underwater anyway, and that is where we spent a good deal of time. In this preface I want to offer my thanks to these extraordinarily helpful people who share my enthusiasm about a guidebook written by a diver for divers.

My journey could not have been made without wholehearted assistance from Pan American World Airways and I want to thank the company for this support. I am also grateful to the many Pan Am representatives in overseas ticket offices who patiently and efficiently acted as information centers, translators, advisors, even mailmen. They are too numerous to be listed individually, but I hope each of them will accept this as an expression of my gratitude.

I want to thank John Nelson of Barbados for the invaluable advice he gave me at the very beginning of this project.

James Dugan's advice and encouragement was given freely and was exceptionally helpful. Paul Tzimoulis of *Skin Diver* magazine and Arnold Post of Richard's Aqua Lung Center in New York helped me to get this project off the ground.

I also want to thank the following European divers who, in one way or another, have contributed to this book: Frédéric Dumas, Jean-Albert Foëx, Pierre Marie, Christian Berjonneau, Barry Blair, Claude Vidal-Revel, Claude Arzillier, François Clouzot, and Maurice Braud of France; Eduardo Admetlla and Roberto Díaz of Spain; Jorge Albuquerque and Dr. Luiz Saldanha of Portugal; Tony Kruse of Tangier; Corporal N. Atkinson of Gibraltar; Miguel Juliá of Mallorca; Honor Frost of England; Luigi Ferraro, Duilio Marcante, Dr. Sergio Scuderi, Raniero Maltini, and Bruno Vailati of Italy; Joe Grech of Malta; Josip Medur and Sreten Babic of Yugoslavia; Peter Throckmorton, George Legakis, and Dr. Bob Sholz of Greece; Cüneyd M. Dosdoğru, Dr. Zaréh Magar, and Sergeant Dick Lawyer of Turkey; Youssef Ali of Syria; André Cointet of Lebanon; Edmundo Branco, "Oscar" Wilde, and Fred Tordoff of Cyprus; Chaim Stav, Elisha Linder, Arthur Gross, Gideon Shor, Dov Neumann, and Morris Greenberg of Israel.

Divers on this side of the world were equally helpful and enthusiastic. I would like especially to thank Park Breck, Harry Cox, and Ross Doe of Bermuda; Dave Woodward, Harry Kline, Gardner Young, Howard Adamson, Jack and Dick Birch, and Peter Lloyd of the Bahamas; Sarita Robertson and Ramón Zapata of Cozumel; Bobby Soto and Tom Hubbell of the Cayman Islands; Kent Eldemire, Ian Champion, and the members of the Jamaica Sub-Aqua Club of Jamaica; Gaston Baussan, George Demorenschildt, Dick Forgham, and Bill Hansen of Haiti; Chuck Bangert, Jim Wilson, and Walt Hendricks of Puerto Rico; Tim Ireland, Jack Grubel, John Hamber, and Joe Vogel of St. Thomas; Jack McDonough of St. Croix; Dick Stewart of St. John; Claude Lake, Charles Oberle, Fritz Halley, and Jeff Adams of St. Maarten; Calvin Holm of Saba; Captain J. L. Wigley of St. Kitts; Mrs. Mary Pomeroy of Nevis; Lee Westcott and Tony Johnson of Antigua; Dr. Brian Blatcher of Dominica; Rick Jeary of Trinidad; and Bob Schouten, Ole Hansen, and Dick Hoogerwerf of Curaçao.

A list of my wife's contributions to this project would cover several pages. I just want to voice my gratitude to her again; this time, publicly.

# CONTENTS

Contents xi

Part Two: THE MEDITERRANEAN

# ILLUSTRATIONS

# INTRODUCTION

Whether you are trying on a mask and snorkel for the first time or are an experienced diver planning a foreign diving vacation, this guide can help you derive maximum diving enjoyment from your holiday. You may be interested in shallow-water snorkeling, spearfishing, underwater photography, or deep-water scuba diving. Whatever your underwater interest, this book will show you the places to visit that are best suited to you.

Chapter 1 is a brief explanation of how to select and use snorkeling equipment. Chapter 2 and succeeding chapters describe the diving spots in Bermuda, the Bahamas, the Caribbean, and the Mediterranean. Each island or country is the subject of a separate chapter.

Each chapter is divided into two parts: general information and skin diving information. The part giving general tourist information is organized as follows:

**How to Get There:** It is assumed in this section that you will be traveling direct from the United States. Bear in mind that it is possible to visit several places along a given route at little or no additional cost.

**Customs Regulations:** Few customs officials will search a tourist's luggage. A verbal declaration is usually all that is required. The allowances on liquor, tobacco, etc., are listed in each chapter.

**Travel Documents Required:** You must have a smallpox vaccination certificate issued within three years to return to the United States and, in a few cases, to enter a foreign country.

Unless otherwise indicated, you will need valid proof of identity and nationality such as a birth certificate or a passport. Driver's licenses and social security cards are not acceptable.

**Currency:** Before you leave the United States, change a few dollars into the currency used at your destination. This is helpful when paying taxi fares, tips, etc., on arrival. Foreign currency can be obtained from Foreign Exchange Brokers. One such broker, Perera Company, maintains an office at the John F. Kennedy International Airport, New York (Tel. OL 6-8444).

**Hotels:** Individual rates are not quoted. Instead, the variety and price range are shown. Hotel lists, with current rates, can be obtained from the Tourist Boards of each country.

**Transportation:** Unless otherwise indicated, traffic keeps to the right, as in the United States. *Always* settle the fare in advance before entering an unmetered taxi.

The second part of each chapter, skin diving information, is organized to provide the information necessary to evaluate the desirability of a given area for diving. When the word "Visibility" is used, I have indicated the average horizontal visibility. Visibility is reduced by rainfall, nearby silty rivers, a muddy bottom, even strong winds.

In each chapter the section on skin diving information is presented in the following order:

**Laws:** All laws which restrict, prohibit, or regulate any underwater activity are listed.

**Diving Gear for Sale:** Stores offering either snorkeling or scuba equipment for sale are listed in this paragraph.

**Diving Gear for Rent:** If you are a beginner, it may make sense first to rent snorkeling equipment before investing in your own. Scuba equipment for rent is also listed.

**Guides, Boats, Instruction:** Professional diving guides know their area thoroughly and can make your trip thoroughly enjoyable. Most of them also have boats for rent and offer instruction in scuba diving. Wherever boats are available, the places will be listed in this paragraph.

**Compressed Air:** Sources of compressed air for scuba diving are listed here.

**Currents, Winds:** Information on ocean and tidal currents is listed in this paragraph because of their importance to diving. Ocean current is a term describing the general direction of the movement of seawater. Currents are also caused by winds; for example, a sustained easterly wind is likely to cause a current which sets to the westward. The term "tide" is used to describe the movement of seawater caused by the gravitational pull of the sun and the moon. When the tide is rising, it is said to be flowing, or flooding. When it is falling, it is said to be ebbing. The ebb and flow of the tide will be in opposite directions; the tide will ebb to the east and flow to the west, for example.

You should know in advance the direction and strength of the current in the diving area you use. If the current is strong, the best system is to enter the water from a boat "upstream" and float along with the current. Make sure your boat accompanies you.

Winds not only create surface currents, they can cause rough seas which may be dangerous to divers. One advantage of island diving is that there is always a lee (sheltered) shore where calm-water diving can be enjoyed.

*The Skin Diver's Travel Guide*

# Chapter 1

# HOW TO SNORKEL

Snorkeling is easy. It is not necessary to be an expert swimmer to enjoy this fast-growing sport, provided you know your physical limitations and do not exceed them. Snorkeling is one of the few sports that can be enjoyed on an equal basis by all members of the family. If you are in good health and can swim, you can snorkel; however, the more at home you feel in the water, the easier it will be to learn diving techniques. If you have a history of heart, respiratory, or sinus trouble, be sure to consult your doctor before putting on diving gear. You should never go diving if you have a cold or infected sinuses.

## WHAT IS A SKIN DIVER?

As used in this book, the designation "skin diver" includes both snorkelers who enjoy lazing over shallow reefs while observing the always-changing life underwater and the more venturesome, deeper diving snorkelers and scuba divers. It includes those who have their own scuba diving gear and dive at every opportunity as well as those who enjoy puttering around in shallow water while on vacation in a warm-water area. By this definition there are over ten million skin divers in the United States.

A snorkeler is a skin diver who uses only mask, fins, and snorkel. Use of the snorkel permits breathing on the surface while your face is in the water. Mask, fins, and snorkel are referred to collectively as basic equipment. This chapter is a summary of the basic techniques of snorkeling.

Scuba divers use basic equipment plus a "self-contained underwater breathing apparatus" which provides the submerged diver with compressed air at the ambient pressure.

The term scuba is an unfortunate one since it also includes oxygen rebreathing devices which are extremely dangerous and should be used only by specially trained military divers. Aqua Lung is a more descriptive term; however, this term is a trade name owned by La Spirotechnique in France and can only be used by this company and its subsidiaries, such as U. S. Divers in this country. Clearly, other lung manufacturers had to use some other term to refer to their compressed air underwater breathing devices. Their choice was scuba, formed from the initial letters of "self-contained underwater breathing apparatus." When used in this book, the word scuba refers only to an underwater breathing device using compressed air, not oxygen. Scuba divers are also sometimes referred to as free divers or lung divers.

A discussion of the techniques of lung diving is outside the scope of this guidebook. If you are interested in learning, be sure to seek qualified instruction, such as that offered by the diving instructors listed in this book.

## CHOOSING YOUR EQUIPMENT

Diving gear can be bought almost anywhere: in sporting goods stores, variety stores, department and discount stores, even through mail order catalogues. The best place to buy equipment is from a professional dive shop. The selection will be wide, the equipment will be of good quality, and the dive shop owner (a diver himself) can offer valuable tips on selection of proper equipment. Dive shops are also an excellent source of information on scuba instruction classes, diving clubs, and diving trips.

Don't try to save money by buying cheap equipment. The rubber will be poor in quality and performance and the useful life will be short.

### THE MASK

A mask creates an air space between your eyes and the water, permitting clear vision underwater. There are dozens of different masks on the market in various price ranges. The important features of a mask are a soft skirt (the part that comes into contact with your face) that will mold itself comfortably to the contours of your face, a shatterproof safety glass lens, and a corrosion-resistant metal rim to hold the lens securely in place. Some models have a nose pinching device which permits you to equalize pressure easily. Others have a built-in purging (one-way) valve which allows water to be expelled simply by exhaling through your nose. These last two features are not absolutely necessary, but they will make your introduction to diving easier and more comfortable.

When buying a mask, try on several until you find the one which gives you the greatest field of vision and fits most comfortably on your face. To find out if the mask will seal out the water, fit it on your face without placing the mask strap around your head. Inhale through your nose. The mask should stay in place by suction, and you should not feel any air leaking into it. If air does come into the mask, it means that this mask will also leak water when in use. Discard it and try another mask.

Do not buy a mask with a plastic lens. Plastic lenses get scratched easily and become misted over, or fogged, when used in the water.

Do not buy a mask with a built-in snorkel. The valves used to keep the water out of these combination masks usually do not work, with the result that the mask is constantly flooded. The valves also have a way of closing up just when you want a breath of air.

Do not buy goggles. Unless the two lenses are on exactly the same plane, you will see double underwater.

FINS

Fins are used to increase the length of time you can stay in the water without becoming tired, to free your hands for other important tasks such as holding a camera or spear gun, and to provide increased speed. The important considerations in buying fins are comfort, blade stiffness, and foot pocket design.

A stiff blade will produce more thrust than a limber blade, if you are in good physical condition. If you are out of shape, stiff fins will give you a leg cramp. Most beginners use fins with a blade of medium stiffness, most of which are patterned after the Cressi Rondine fins. Many, but not all, competition divers use stiff, high thrust fins such as Duck Feet.

Your fins must be comfortable and fit your foot snugly but not too tightly; otherwise, your foot will become tired and, probably, blistered.

The three types of foot pocket designs are open heel, full foot, and adjustable. The open heel is limited almost exclusively to Duck Feet and other stiff fins which produce great thrust. The disadvantage of this design is that your heel is unprotected and may become cut by coral or stones when entering or leaving the water. To overcome this problem, the use of flipper slippers (neoprene socks) is necessary.

Full foot fins such as the Cressi Rondine are excellent for all-around use. As the name suggests, your entire foot is enclosed and, thus, protected.

Adjustable fins are usually less expensive than the other kinds. They are generally used by those who want to keep their investment in equipment to a minimum.

Fins that float are easier to retrieve than nonfloating fins. Make sure to find out whether the fins you choose will float.

Fin sizes correspond with shoe sizes. Try several kinds on your bare feet until you find the most comfortable fit. Leave them on your feet for a few minutes to make certain that they are comfortable.

## SNORKEL

The best kind of snorkel is the all-rubber, flexible, J-shaped design. Select a model with a comfortable mouthpiece. Stay away from snorkels with a valve built into the opening at the top. These gadgets are supposed to keep water out, but they seldom work properly. When water does enter your J-shaped snorkel, just blow sharply through it and the water will spurt out.

## USING YOUR EQUIPMENT

Find a diving site with shallow, clear, calm water. Before putting on your mask, rinse it out in the water, spit on the inside of the lens, rub the saliva around on the entire inner lens, then rinse the mask again. The saliva will prevent the lens from fogging. Fit the mask to your face and secure the strap around your head. The strap should be tight enough to hold the mask securely and comfortably on your face.

The snorkel can be fastened to the mask strap by a rubber snorkel tab or can just be slipped under the strap. It should be adjusted so the mouthpiece rests comfortably in your mouth, without pulling. The first time you use the snorkel, it is a good idea to take a few deep breaths through it before entering the water, just to become used to the volume of air you can obtain through it.

Put on your fins by inserting your foot into the pocket and pushing back with a hand on each side of the blade. If you pull back sharply on the heel, the rubber might tear, especially with some full foot fins.

If you enter the water from a boat you can use the backward roll entry or the giant stride entry. To use the backward roll, squat at the edge of the boat, hold your mask firmly in place, and roll backward into the water. The giant stride method consists of simply taking a big step off the side of the boat while holding your mask firmly in place. Either method is satisfactory if you are in a small boat. If you are entering the water from a large boat, use a boarding ladder. Never dive in headfirst while wearing a mask.

Practice snorkeling in chest- or waist-deep water. If you feel uncomfortable, you can stand up. Lie facedown in the water, arms at your sides. Move your legs slowly up and down, with your toes pointing back. You will now be gliding across the surface. Make sure that, when you are in this facedown position, your snorkel is pointed straight up. Hold the snorkel mouthpiece firmly enough to prevent water from getting into your mouth.

The proper leg stroke is one which uses all the muscles in your leg, including your upper thigh. You can bend your knee a little with each stroke, but not as much as you would if you were using a regular swimming flutter kick. Use long, slow, rhythmic strokes instead of short, choppy ones as used in regular surface swimming.

After you have practiced for a while and are more confident in your ability, make an effort to keep your fins under the water instead of allowing them to break the surface on the "up" stroke. This splashing is undesirable for two reasons: it wastes your energy (because your fins are not doing you any good while they're flapping in the air), and the splashing scares away the fish.

To make a surface dive, stretch out flat on the surface with your arms hanging straight down. Bend at the waist so your head and arms are both pointing toward the bottom, then raise your legs straight into the air. Your entire body is now pointed toward the bottom, and your descent will be started. Now, use your hands to help pull you under. Wait until your fins are completely underwater before starting a slow, rhythmic kick.

When you are a few feet underwater you will feel pressure on your eardrums, similar to the feeling you get when descending in a fast-moving elevator. To relieve this feeling, push your mask firmly against your face and snort sharply through your nose. If your mask has an equalizing device, pinch your nostrils together and snort through your nose. This process is referred to as clearing your ears. The pressure on your eardrums was caused by the increased pressure of the water, which increases at the rate of .445

pounds per square inch for each foot of depth. You may have to clear your ears more than once on deep dives. The more you practice diving the easier it will be to clear your ears.

If you have a cold or sinus problems it will be difficult to clear your ears and you should not dive. If you persist in diving with blocked sinuses or Eustachian tubes, an infection may result.

Another thing you will notice when descending is that your mask lens will push against your face. This is referred to as mask squeeze. To relieve this, simply exhale gently through your nose until the mask is again in proper position.

If your mask has a purging device, any water that enters can be expelled by snorting through your nose. If your mask does not have a purging device, come to the surface, raise your head, lift the skirt of the mask slightly, and the water will run out. Alternatively, turn your head so that one side is lower than the other. Press in slightly on the "high" side and snort through your nose. The water will be blown out.

When ascending to the surface remember the rule, "look up before you come up." It will help you to avoid bumping your head on the keel of your boat, or another diver.

As soon as your head comes out of the water, blow sharply through your snorkel to clear it of water.

## SOME DIVING TIPS

Never dive alone. Make sure you and your partner stay together so you can help each other, if necessary.

Wash off your equipment as soon as possible after it has been in the sea. Salt water is extremely corrosive and will shorten the life of your gear unless washed off.

Wear an ordinary work glove, or two. Gloves permit you to hold onto rocks and coral or handle fish without damage to your hands.

Do not dive in areas with heavy boat traffic. Water ski boats are especially dangerous to divers.

When swimming out from the shore, take along a float, such as an inner tube. Should you become tired, you can rest on it.

Use a diver's flag. It is a red rectangle with a diagonal white stripe. It can be attached to your boat or float and is used to warn boatmen away from your diving site.

Remember that the sun can burn your back while you are snorkeling, although you probably won't feel it until you leave the water. Unless you have a good tan, wear protective clothing for at least the first few days of tropical snorkeling.

If your snorkeling area is very far offshore, hire a boat to take you there and back and stand by while you're in the water. When you're tired and are trying to return to shore, you will appreciate having one. If you are spearing fish, they can be boated immediately, not strung around your waist.

Rocky headlands, capes, and points are usually subject to stronger currents than the rest of the shoreline. Exercise caution when exploring such areas and make sure you have a boat with you.

Don't wear earplugs. If you do, and you dive under the surface, the pressure will drive them deep into your outer ear, perhaps hard enough to break your eardrum.

## UNDERWATER PHOTOGRAPHY

One of the most satisfying and challenging underwater activities is underwater photography. Long after the spearfisherman has proudly dined off his catch, you can show your awed friends what an unbelievably intrepid chap you are.

The Nikonos is a 35-mm amphibious camera capable of taking excellent black and white and color photographs underwater (and in rain, mud, snow, and other difficult situations). It costs about $160 and is worth it.

Waterproof cases can be purchased, or made, for just about any camera. Cases are of metal or plastic. Plastic is cheaper but has to be handled very carefully to prevent scratching. I recommend Underwater Photographic Service, Inc., Box 884, Marathon, Florida 33050. They manufacture inexpensive cases for Instamatic cameras. Also they can make a case for your own camera.

## SPEARFISHING

Spearfishing is the traditional sport of skin divers. In many areas popular with spearfishermen, the fish are spooky and difficult to approach. This means that you will have to seek a seldom visited stretch of coastline for your hunting.

A number of laws have been passed by various countries regulating spearfishing. Usually these laws are rigidly enforced. They are listed in this book.

## WRECKS

I doubt that the first film director to make a motion picture involving wrecks was a skin diver. Contrary to his impression, and the impressions of his successors who follow in his inaccurate footsteps, old Spanish galleons do not sit upright on the sea bottom, intact, with sails set and grinning skeletons for crew. Within a short time after sinking, the worms eat away all the wood and, after a few years, all that remains are cannon, ballast stones, pottery, and an anchor or two.

Only an experienced diver can spot the subtle regularities in an otherwise irregular sea bottom that show the presence of an old wreck. Someone once estimated that over three hundred billion dollars in sunken treasure has accumulated on sea and lake bottoms. New and sophisticated equipment will undoubtedly enable men to locate at least some of this wealth. However, don't expect to stumble onto treasure accidently since the remains of treasure ships are by now well camouflaged.

Modern wrecks are another story. Those of steel construction resist the corrosion of the sea for a few years and can make attractive backgrounds for your photographs. They are also good places to look for fish.

## A FINAL WORD

This chapter is intended only as an outline of basic techniques of shallow-water snorkeling. A separate book would be needed to adequately cover proper diving methods, including scuba. That, of course, is outside the scope of this guidebook.

There are some excellent instruction manuals listed in the bibliography for further reading. However, it is not advisable to attempt to become a qualified diver by reading books. If you are interested in continuing diving, I suggest that you seek qualified instruction and join a diving club. The Underwater Society of America is the nationwide association of diving councils. To obtain the address of the club nearest your home, write to: Underwater Society of America, Room 492, Bourse Building, Independence Square, Philadelphia, Pennsylvania 19106. *Skin Diver* magazine, 5959 Hollywood Boulevard, Los Angeles, California 90028, is published monthly and contains news of current developments in diving.

Have a good vacation, and happy diving!

# PART ONE

# THE ISLANDS

*Chapter 2*

# INTRODUCTION TO THE ISLANDS

Diving conditions in the waters surrounding Bermuda, the Bahamas, and the Caribbean islands are among the best in the world. The water is clear and warm and the submarine scenery is vivid. The reefs are easily reached by swimming from shore or by boat. For novice divers, there are hundreds of shallow, colorful reefs, teeming with brightly decorated tropical fish. Spearfishermen can find plenty of game fish at various depths. Photographers will appreciate the clear water and the impressive variety of gaily colored fish, coral reefs, and other marine life.

The characteristics of the sea bottom in the Mediterranean can be accurately judged by the appearance of the coastline. This is not true in these islands because of the growth of coral reefs. Coral, formed of limestone extracted from sea water by tiny creatures named coral polyps, can be found off rocky shores or sand beaches, on both the windward and leeward shores, and in depths varying from awash to about 150 feet. Reefs are rich with life and are the natural hunting grounds for game fish—and for photographers, spearfishermen, and fish watchers.

While excellent diving conditions exist the year around, the best time for diving is in the summer, between May and September. During this period the water is calmer, therefore clearer, and is at its warmest. Happily, this is the tourist "off season" and hotel rates are at their lowest. The exception to this is Bermuda, where the "off season" is November through March.

Hotels on many of the islands are crowded during the winter, especially from January to April (in Bermuda, summertime is the busy season). During this period, visitors should have confirmed air and hotel reservations.

Underwater visibility in this region is excellent. It rarely is less than fifty feet and sometimes approaches two hundred.

The most commonly seen game fish are mackerel, groupers, crevalles, barracuda, snappers, hogfish, jacks, jewfish, amberjacks, yellowtail, and dolphins. Other species of game fish are occasionally seen. Turtles and spiny lobsters are common in some areas. In addition to these game fish, there is a wide variety of small reef fish, most of which are beautifully colored. These lovely reef dwellers are inoffensive, small, usually inedible, and they should be left alone, especially by spearfishermen.

There are a few creatures in these waters that should be avoided. Sharks are unpredictable, but their behavior depends to some extent on how hungry they are. They are attracted by juices and blood from speared fish. This attraction can be greatly minimized by immediately boating all speared fish. Never string fish around your waist. In the unlikely event of a shark encounter, face the shark at all times and move slowly back to your boat. Shouting into the water sometimes deters them. Most importantly, never dive alone. Stay close to your diving buddy since the chance of an attack will be lessened if there are two of you together.

The probability of seeing a shark is usually not too great in shallow-water reefs which are popular for underwater sightseeing. On such reefs there are usually few fish of any size because they will have been frightened away long ago by inexperienced snorkelers and spearfishermen. Remember that the staple diet of sharks is fish. If there are no large fish in your diving area, the chance of seeing a shark is small.

Sharks have unbelievable vitality, so don't try to kill them with a spear gun. In case of necessity, use the gun to fend them off. If you do shoot them, aim for the gill slits, fire, and drop the gun or cut the line.

Barracuda have a ferocious reputation and a frightening appearance. However, divers have little to fear from them unless speared fish are carried around in the water. Again, boat all speared fish immediately. If a barracuda darts in to take a bite of a wounded fish, he may take a piece of you with him.

There is nothing to fear from moray eels, despite their menacing appearance, if they are not disturbed. They breathe by constantly opening and closing their vicious-looking jaws. If an incautious diver puts his hand into a hole occupied by a moray, the chances are that it will attack. Experienced divers keep their hands out of holes in the reef and never enter caves unless they are sure they can see everything inside.

Some jellyfish, notably the Portuguese man-of-war, can give a painful sting. Divers should avoid them and leave the water if they are seen in any quantity.

Coral is sharp and will inflict skin abrasions if brushed against or handled. These cuts can take some time to heal and can be avoided by swimming with care. Experienced Caribbean divers wear a work glove which permits them to hold onto coral (to remain motionless for spearfishing or photography) without damaging their hands.

Fire coral is about the color of mustard. It should be avoided since it can give a painful "burn" which will hurt for about half an hour. There are no aftereffects.

Sea urchins are bottom dwellers, round in shape, and resemble a pincushion. There are several varieties, but the ones to avoid are the black urchins. Their spines are sharp, barbed, and brittle. They penetrate the skin at the slightest contact, then break off. It is almost impossible to remove the spines, despite various home-grown native remedies, which are largely ineffective. There are usually no aftereffects, except that the puncture hurts for half an hour or so. The spines are not poisonous.

The islands described on the following pages are unique in their diversity of cultures, breathtaking scenery, ideal year-round climate, and marvelous diving conditions. At one time or another these islands have been discovered, colonized, fought over, or owned by England, France, Sweden, Holland, Spain, Denmark, Italy, Portugal, the Knights of Malta, and the United States. One small island was even officially commissioned a ship of the line in the British Navy: H.M.S. Diamond Rock, near Martinique.

This vast region has been the setting of bloody duels between pirates and treasure-laden Spanish galleons and was the scene of uncounted shipwrecks and other disasters. Today, the lure of sunken treasure attracts an increasing number of modern adventurers, armed with sophisticated metal-detecting devices, including submarines and other Jet Age recovery tools.

Altogether, these islands are fascinating from a historical and skin diving point of view and have the added attraction of being but a short jet flight from the United States. Detailed tourist information can be obtained from the Tourist Boards of the various islands and, for some of the Caribbean islands, from the Caribbean Tourist Association, 20 East 46 Street, New York City (Tel: MU 2-0435).

*Chapter 3*

# BERMUDA

**How to Get There:** By Pan Am Jet Clipper from Boston or New York. Flight time is two hours.

**Customs Regulations:** Personal clothing and two hundred cigarettes or one hundred cigars or one pound of tobacco will be admitted duty free. There is a Government departure tax of $2.85. Visitors flying from Bermuda directly to the United States will be cleared through U. S. Customs and Immigration at the Bermuda airport. Further processing in the United States is unnecessary.

**Travel Documents Required:** Passports or visas are not required, but a return or onward ticket is necessary. U. S. Immigration authorities require proof of citizenship.

**Currency:** Bermuda sterling, currently valued at $2.80 per pound, is based on English sterling. American and Canadian currency is accepted everywhere. Bermuda currency may not be taken out of the island.

**Hotels:** There are fifty-nine hotels, guesthouses, and cottages offering accommodations for over five thousand guests at rates ranging upward from $6.00 per day, European plan.

**Transportation:** Taxis, rental bicycles and motorbikes, buses, and ferries provide internal transportation. There are no rental autos in Bermuda. All parts of the island can be reached by 150 miles of paved road. Drive on the left side of the road. Taxis displaying a blue flag are driven by Qualified Tour Guides, who have successfully passed a Government test of their knowledge of Bermuda history, points of interest, etc.

**Medical Facilities:** There are excellent doctors and hospitals.

**Other Information:** Short shorts, bathing suits, or hair curlers are not worn on the streets or in the dining rooms, bars, or lobbies of the larger hotels. Men wear coats and ties to dinner and to night clubs.

An excellent selection of duty-free liquor is available to tourists. Items purchased are delivered to the airport and picked up on departure.

The Flatts Village Aquarium is well worth a visit. In addition to an interesting collection of fish, the Aquarium houses the Teddy Tucker Treasure collection. This display includes several rare and valuable artifacts collected by Mr. Tucker during his years of exploring Bermuda wrecks.

The Pan American Airways office at 61 Front Street in Hamilton (Tel: 1-1051) is a good source of local information and sightseeing tips.

The Bermuda Trade Development Board offers a wealth of information on the island. Especially useful is the Bermuda Hotel and Guest House Rate Sheet. The Bermuda office is at 50 Front Street, Hamilton. Overseas offices are at 610 Fifth Avenue, New York; 6 North Michigan Avenue, Chicago; 111 Richmond Street West, Toronto; and Sackville House, 40 Piccadilly, London, W1.

## SKIN DIVING INFORMATION

Bermuda is surrounded by the most northerly coral reef in the world. The Gulf Stream keeps the sea warm enough for coral to thrive, yet the waters are cool enough for microscopic plankton to flourish in larger quantities than in southern waters. This creates an abundance of food for small fish and supports large quantities of them. Since small fish are eaten by larger fish, all along the food chain, each species is found in large sizes and in great quantities.

Quite a bit of the coastline is private property and a boat is necessary for diving along these shores. However, there are several public access areas and beaches, and they are clearly marked.

Underwater visibility is excellent. A visibility test conducted by the Woods Hole Institute disclosed that Bermuda waters were among the clearest in the Atlantic Ocean. Summer visibility is over seventy feet. In winter, visibility frequently approaches two hundred feet.

Summer water temperatures reach 84°. Neoprene diving suits are useful for winter diving when the water temperature drops to about 60°.

It is estimated that over four hundred ships have been wrecked on the surrounding reefs during the past four hundred years. The first recorded wrecks were Spanish galleons in the 1500s. Wreck hunting is not allowed without a Government permit, which is customarily issued only to local residents.

A recompression chamber is stationed at the U. S. Navy Base. If needed, first phone the Officer of the Day at 4-0444.

**Laws:** At the time this is written, the Government is considering legislation to establish two National Underwater Parks.

Spearfishing is prohibited within a mile of the shore. Pole spears are the only underwater weapons allowed. Visitors arriving with spear guns must turn them over to Customs officers, who will return them to the owner on departure.

The use of scuba gear while spearfishing is prohibited. Only two fish of any one species and no more than three lobsters may be taken in one day. Closed season on lobster is April 16 through August 31.

**Diving Gear for Sale:** By local custom, regulators are sold only to buyers producing proof of training in scuba diving. Wadson's, Front Street; The Sportsman's Shop, Reid Street; and Peniston's, Woodlawn Avenue, have a good selection of diving equipment.

**Diving Gear for Rent:** Snorkeling equipment can be rented from Breck's Diving School, Gibbet Beach, North Shore Road, Smith's Parish (Tel: 1-6325 or 1-3030). The Pompano Beach Club in Southampton also rents equipment.

Scuba tanks can be rented from Breck's Diving School; Wadson's; and Bermuda Industrial Gases, Ltd., in Somerset. Proof of training in scuba diving must be produced in order to rent tanks.

Scuba divers should bring their own regulators, which cannot be rented in Bermuda.

**Instruction:** The oldest diving school in the Atlantic is Breck's Diving School, where instruction in snorkeling and underwater photography is available the year around. Scuba instruction is also available during the summer. Instruction may also be obtained during the summer at the Pompano Beach Club.

**Diving Trips:** Bermuda Divers Co. have the 38-foot diving boat *Shearwater* which is available for diving trips, for qualified scuba divers only, on Thursdays, Sundays, and holidays. Phone Harry Cox at 1-1234. The Pompano Beach Club has daily diving trips during the summer and use 14-foot outboard boats.

**Boat Rentals:** Evans Marine, Salt Kettle, Paget (Tel: 2-1510); Sherwood Manor, Fairylands, Pembroke (Tel: 1-6261); Robinson's Boat Works, Somerset Bridge, Sandys (Tel: 4-0235); and Flatts Marine Center, Flatts Village, Smith's (Tel: 2-2854) all offer a variety of rental boats.

**Compressed Air:** Wadson's; Breck's Diving School; Bermuda Divers Co.; Bermuda Industrial Gases, Ltd.; and Peniston's.

**Helmet Reef Trips:** The personally escorted, shallow-water reef trips offered by Bronson and Harriet Hartley are an excellent introduction to the underwater world. These safe, exciting excursions are suitable for even nonswimmers. They afford a close-up look at tame fish, sponges, coral, and other reef dwellers by using a specially designed helmet which allows their guests to wear spectacles and keep their hair dry. These trips are especially suitable for persons who are interested in reef life but who have never before been underwater. The Hartleys' 53-foot yacht *Carioca* leaves from the Coral Island Club at 10 A.M. and at 2 P.M. daily except Monday from June 1 through October 30. During the winter the Hartleys offer similar tours in Nassau. Highly recommended.

**Currents and Winds:** The general ocean drift is from southwest to northeast, with some local variations. The result of this drift is that most of the west-coast waters are murkier than in other areas. Currents are not ordinarily a problem for divers.

Summer winds are usually from the south or southwest and from the quadrant west to northeast in the winter. Accordingly the best diving is along the north-coast reefs in summer and along the south coast during the winter.

**Fish:** Dr. William Beebe catalogued 602 different types of fish in Bermuda's waters. The most common game fish seen around the reefs are pompano, mackerel, snappers, tuna, wahoos, amberjacks, bonitos, Bermuda chub, barracuda, groupers, and occasional dolphins. Frequently seen reef fish are sergeant majors, butterfly fish, jewel fish, and parrot fish.

Except in summer when southerly winds frequently create rough seas and plankton lowers the visibility, the south coast is best for diving. A paved road parallels the coastline and several public beaches make access to the diving sites easy.

### SOUTH COAST

From Battery Bay, in the east, to Soldiers Point the water is not usually clear, particularly in the region south of Castle Harbour. From Battery Bay west for twelve miles to Church Bay, there is a wonderful variety of underwater formations and plenty of game and reef fish can be seen. Beginning snorkelers will find attractive coral in shallow water close to shore almost everywhere. The following paragraphs describe some of the other highlights of south-coast diving, in geographical order, from east to west.

In Sam Hall's Bay, just off the Mid-Ocean Golf Club, the coral is attractive and diving conditions are good. Access is by boat since the shoreline is private property.

John Smith's Bay and nearby White Hill Park are excellent diving areas and are favorites among local snorkelers. Many reef fish and beautiful underwater formations are found here. John Smith's Beach is public. West of John Smith's Bay is a double reef where sizable quantities of tarpon are seen in winter.

Farther west the waters off Spanish Rock offer excellent diving. Access is by boat since the road trends inland at this point.

The wreck of the S.S. *Pollockshields,* an ammunition ship which sank in 1915, lies in about twenty-five feet of water a third of a mile east of the Elbow Beach Hotel. This part of the coastline is very attractive for diving. Access is through the Tribe Road public beach in Elbow Bay.

West of Elbow Bay are five public beaches providing access to the nearby shallow reefs. They are Warwick Long Bay, Jobson Cove, Stonehole Bay, Chaplin Bay, and Horseshoe Bay. Champagne-glass coral heads are found in this area. These are circular coral formations, narrow at the base, flaring out to a wide rim at the surface. At low tide the rim is out of water and brightly colored small tropical fish can be seen swimming in the "tidal pool" inside the "glass"—which probably makes this the world's only natural fish cocktail(!).

West of Horseshoe Bay a wreck lies very close to shore on the northwest side of Sinky Bay. Access is by boat.

At Christian Bay and Church Bay the barrier reef is quite close to shore and a wide variety of underwater formations can be explored. There is a public beach access at Church Bay.

Beyond Church Bay the coastline trends north, then northeast. The offshore waters here are quite shallow and usually murky. Quite a number of centuries-old wrecks lie in these shallows several miles offshore.

Scuba divers will find the south-coast barrier reef of interest in winter. It runs the entire length of this coast. At some places it is three hundred yards or more offshore, and at the western end, near Church Bay, it comes in quite close to shore. It has a stunning variety of underwater formations such as caves and ravines. Coral heads rise vertically off the bottom for sixty feet or more.

Visibility is usually not good on the east and west ends of the island.

## NORTH COAST

In the summer, when southerly winds prevail, the best diving is on the north coast. Shallow coral reefs, excellent for snorkeling, lie just off the north coast. The north-coast road parallels the shoreline. Scuba divers will need a boat to get to the offshore diving areas, beyond the shallow reefs which extend for ten miles north.

The wreck of the 200-foot four-masted schooner *Constellation* lies in about thirty feet of water four miles northwest of Daniel's Head, Somerset.

The wreck of the *Cristóbal Colón* lies in forty feet of water seven and a quarter miles due north of the Martello Tower (near Whalebone Bay), St. George's. A mile and a quarter due east of this wreck are two more sunken vessels, the yacht *Elda* and, nearby, the ship *Eagle of London*. Water depth is about thirty feet.

About two and a quarter miles southeast of these two wrecks, on a magnetic compass bearing of 115°, is the wreck of the S.S. *Iristo*, with a cargo of autos, trucks, and motorcycles. It is forty feet deep.

Another sunken ship lies about sixty feet deep four miles southwest of *Iristo*. It is a mile and three quarters east-northeast of Kitchen Shoals on a 67° magnetic compass bearing from the St. Catherine Point Light, St. George's.

The above-mentioned wrecks are fairly recent ones and do not, of course, include the hundreds of very old sunken ships scattered along the outer rim of the vast reef lying to the west and north of Bermuda.

*Chapter 4*

# THE BAHAMAS

The Bahamas consist of almost seven hundred islands and over twenty-four hundred small cays (pronounced: keys) in a total of more than 100,000 square miles of the Atlantic Ocean. They extend from sixty miles east of Palm Beach, Florida, to within fifty miles of Haiti and Cuba. Within this vast area is an uncommonly beautiful assortment of coral reefs in one of the best fishing areas of the world.

Conditions for skin diving in the Bahamian archipelago are among the best anywhere. Lateral underwater visibility in most areas is normally in the hundred-foot range. Fish of all kinds are abundant. The water is warm with surface temperatures varying from about 70° in winter to about 85° in summer. Around almost any island there are easily accessible reefs suitable for beginners or advanced divers. Several underwater movies have been filmed in the Bahamas, including the underwater scenes for *Thunderball.*

Treasure is the magic word which lures many underwater explorers to these islands. It has been estimated that over $150 million in sunken treasure remains to be discovered. For many years, pirates made the Bahamas their base and plundered the treasure galleons and rich merchantmen bound for Europe. Most of the treasure sank with the ships and much of it is still on the reefs, awaiting recovery.

From the mid-1600s through the 1800s, Bahamian shipwreckers brought doom to many vessels. Highly organized, even licensed, they placed false lights to lure unsuspecting ships onto the reefs and would remove all they could before the ship sank.

Shortly after the multimillion-dollar treasure discovery at Grand Bahama in 1965, the Bahamas Government passed laws regulating treasure hunting. Treasure hunters must be licensed to recover objects from wrecks. All the treasure must be reported to the Harbour Master in Nassau or to the Crown Lands Office. The Government is entitled to one half of the total value of items recovered. Divers are advised to adhere closely to this law since the penalties for infractions are heavy.

These islands can be most comfortably explored by sail or power boat. Charter yachts can be engaged in several of the islands or in the yachting centers of the United States. Specially equipped diving boats crewed by experienced divers can be chartered from Lee Turcotte, Triton Underwater Tours, P. O. Box 303, Miami Shores, Florida 33153 (Tel: 531-0185). Advance bookings are recommended.

Snorkeling and scuba diving can be enjoyed in the Bahamas the year around. The best time is from April through September. During this period the seas are almost always calm and the hotel rates are lower than during the winter tourist season.

**How to Get There:** Nassau is forty-five minutes from Miami and two and three-quarter hours from New York by Pan Am Jet Clipper. Rock Sound, Eleuthera, is linked to Nassau by a fifteen-minute Pan Am jet flight. Several of the islands can be reached by air from Miami.

**Customs Regulations:** Personal belongings and up to two hundred cigarettes and a quart of liquor will be admitted duty free.

**Travel Documents Required:** Passports and visas are not required of U.S. citizens, but some proof of nationality is necessary. Visitors returning from Nassau directly to the United States will be cleared through U. S. Customs and Immigration at the Nassau airport. Further processing on arrival in the United States is unnecessary. There is a $2.00 Government departure tax; for children from three to twelve years old it is $1.00.

**Currency:** The Bahamian dollar is valued at 98¢ U.S. It is divided into 100 cents. Dollars may be brought in in unrestricted amounts, but not more than £25/- may be imported in Bermudian, Jamaican, or English pounds.

**Hotels:** Reservations are essential in the winter months and are advisable during the summer. There is a wide variety of hotels, residential clubs, guesthouses, apartments, and rooms in private houses. The widest selection of accommodations is in Nassau. Winter rates range upward from $6.00, single.

**Other Information:** An up-to-date list of hotels, with current rates, plus other detailed tourist information is available from the offices of the Bahamas Ministry of Tourism at: P. O. Box 818, Nassau, Bahamas (the head office is in Rawson Square); 307 British Empire Building, 620 Fifth Avenue, New York; 1701 First National Bank Building, Miami; 1230 Palmolive Building, Chicago; Adolphus Hotel Arcade (1406), Dallas; 1015 Locust Building, St. Louis; 510 West 6 Street, Los Angeles; Room 707, Victory Building, 80 Richmond Street West, Toronto.

The Pan American Airways offices are on Matthew Avenue in Nassau (Tel: 2-3394) and at the Passenger Terminal at the South Eleuthera Airport in Rock Sound, Eleuthera (Tel: Ask operator for Pan Am).

## SKIN DIVING INFORMATION

Skin diving information applying to the Bahamas as a whole is given here. Specific information is included with the description of each island.

**Laws:** Spearing fish or capturing any marine product while using scuba equipment is prohibited. Only a Hawaiian sling or a hand (pole) spear may be used for spearfishing and the use of any other type of spear gun is illegal. Spiny lobsters may be speared only for the personal use of the diver and may not be sold.

An underwater nature reserve is established on the eastern,

northern, and western sides of New Providence Island (Nassau). Diving is perfectly legal in the nature reserve, but it is illegal to remove any marine organism of any kind within this area.

The closed season for lobster is from March 15 to October 1.

**Currents, Winds:** The general set of the ocean current is west and northwest. The velocity of the current is affected greatly by tidal currents and by the configuration of the sea bottom. When the tide flows with the ocean current, the combined effect is to increase the tidal velocity. A contrary tidal current will reduce, or eliminate, the flow. Stiff currents can be expected in the waters in a narrow passage (between two nearby islands, for example) and around the extreme points of islands. Currents are usually negligible along the coastlines and behind barrier reefs.

South of Crooked Island (the Lower Islands) the easterly trade winds prevail. Thus, the west coasts are the leeward, and calm, coasts. North of Crooked Island light summer winds of five to twelve knots are ordinarily from the east and southeast. In winter, winds of variable force (up to twenty-five knots) can be expected from the quadrant northeast to southeast.

**Fish:** Reef fish seen in the greatest quantities are the butterfly fish, rock beauties, clown fish, neon gobies, angelfish, demoiselles, royal grammas, squirrelfish, jewel fish, and tangs. The most common game fish are tarpon, tuna, amberjacks, groupers, and barracuda. There are many other deep-water fish in the Bahamas but they ordinarily inhabit deep water and are not frequently seen by divers.

## GRAND BAHAMA

**How to Get There:** By Pan Am Jet Clipper to Nassau with connecting flight to Freeport or West End, Grand Bahama.

**Hotels:** There are eleven hotels on the island with over two thousand rooms. Winter rates range upward from $7.00, single, European plan.

**Transportation:** Taxis and rental autos. Some hotels have bus service into town.

**Medical Facilities:** There are excellent hospitals and doctors.

**Diving Gear for Sale:** The Grand Bahama Underwater Explorers Club (Tel: 6849), Box 233, Freeport (adjacent to the Oceanus Hotel), and the Fishin' Hole, Box 33, Freeport (Tel: 6001), both offer a complete line of snorkeling and scuba equipment for sale.

**Diving Gear for Rent:** The above-mentioned dive shops plus the underwater shop at the King's Inn, Freeport (Tel: 6721), and the Grand Bahama Hotel and Country Club, West End, Grand Bahama, have snorkel and scuba gear for rent. Scuba divers must be prepared to demonstrate ability in the use of the lung before renting it.

**Dive Shops, Instruction:** The Underwater Explorers Club is the most completely equipped dive shop on Grand Bahama. Instruction by NAUI qualified instructors, underwater photography instruction, equipment repairs, and many other services are available here.

**Trips, Guides, Boats:** The Underwater Explorers Club and the King's Inn have daily diving trips, with underwater guides. The Fishin' Hole and the Grand Bahama Hotel at West End rent out scuba gear and can supply a guide.

**Compressed Air:** The Underwater Explorers Club.

**Recompression Chamber:** Dr. Forsyth, Doctors Pavilion, Freeport Hospital (Tel: 6735).

SOUTH COAST

From Settlement Point east to Riding Point the south coast offers excellent diving conditions, with the exception of the region near the Freeport Harbor. There is a shallow reef up to half a mile offshore with a least depth of about four feet. The offshore side of this reef drops off to fifteen to twenty feet, then slopes gradually down. Farther out, a deeper reef can be found about fifty feet deep. The offshore side of this reef drops off into very deep water. Access to this reef is by boat from Freeport or West End. Large quantities of staghorn coral are found in the waters surrounding Petersons Cay, west of Free Town.

From Riding Point east to the eastern tip of the island, the shoreline drops off into deeper water and there are fewer shallow reefs. This region is more suitable for scuba divers than for snorkelers.

### NORTH COAST

The water on this coast is too shallow and muddy for diving. Not recommended.

## ABACO AND THE ABACO CAYS

**How to Get There:** By Pan Am Jet Clipper to Nassau with a connecting flight to Green Turtle Cay or to Marsh Harbour.

**Hotels:** There are twenty small hotels in the Abacos with a total of 159 rooms. Reservations are recommended.

**Transportation:** Taxis. A road extends for the length of the island.

**Medical Facilities:** There are two doctors in Green Turtle Cay, two doctors and a complete medical clinic in Marsh Harbour, and one doctor in Hope Town. A clinic with a resident nurse is located on Man of War Cay.

## SKIN DIVING INFORMATION

This is a region of extensive rocks, reefs, and islands which extends for about one hundred miles, roughly from northwest to southeast. Diving conditions along the northern edge of this archipelago are excellent except when the wind is from the quadrant northwest to northeast, which occurs mostly during the winter. These winds create heavy seas, making diving difficult. Therefore the best time for visiting this area is during the summer.

The reefs vary from awash to more than one hundred feet. Access is mostly by boat except in the areas adjacent to the hotels.

Centuries-old wrecks share the reefs with fish of all kinds, lobsters, and turtles. Shipwreckers were particularly active, and well organized, in Hope Town and Gun Cay. Treasure was recently found near Gorda Cay, west of South Abaco. Many ships, some of them with treasure, were wrecked along the lonely 75-mile shallow bank stretching from Hole-in-the-Wall, South Abaco, to the eastern tip of Grand Bahama. Here, a massive underwater cliff rises almost vertically from hundreds of feet deep to within ten feet, or less, of the surface. Unwieldy treasure galleons were sometimes unable to change course in time to avoid going aground after the sudden appearance of shoal water.

**Diving Gear for Sale and Rent:** Mr. David Gale, Island Marine Co. in Hope Town, maintains a stock of diving equipment for sale. Limited quantities of equipment can be found in the hardware stores and marinas on Green Turtle Cay, Marsh Harbour, and Hope Town. The larger hotels can supply guests with basic equipment.

**Guides, Boats:** Many of the islanders are good divers and their services as guide/companion can be obtained through the hotels. Several hotels and marinas have equipment and boats for hire and can offer assistance and advice to visiting divers. They are: The Elbow Cay Club in Hope Town; Captain Frank Kenyon, Abaco Interests, Ltd., in Hope Town, has a specially outfitted 48-foot boat equipped for diving and treasure hunting; Mr. Marcel Maury of Hope Town Harbour Lodge has a wealth of local information (and an excellent tropical fish collection); The Fin and Tonic on White Sound, near Hope Town, has boats; The Walker Cay Club on Walker Cay welcomes visiting divers; The Guana Harbour Club on Great Guana Cay can arrange for boats; Mr. Richie Albury of Alburys Water Taxi is an excellent guide on Man of War Cay; and Mr. Colin Redfern of the Treasure Cay Inn on Green Turtle Cay can arrange for boats and trips.

Beginners will be able to enjoy shallow-water snorkeling and fish watching near almost any of the hotels. It is recommended that spearfishermen and scuba divers save time by hiring a boat with a local guide.

**Compressed Air:** The Elbow Cay Club in Hope Town has a compressor, and there is one aboard Captain Kenyon's diving boat in Hope Town.

## NORTHWEST AND EAST COASTS

This is the best area in the Abaco area for diving, except in winter when the north winds prevail. From Matanilla Reef, at the northwestern tip of the extensive chain of islets and reefs extending to the northwest of Little Abaco, to Hole-in-the-Wall, at the southern tip of Great Abaco, there extends a wonderful selection of beautiful coral reefs in varying depths.

Many reef and game fish can be found here, making this an ideal area for underwater photography, fish watching, or any other underwater activity. The reef at Sandy Cay, near Hope Town, was featured in the film *Secrets of the Reef.*

Most diving activity is between Green Turtle Cay and Hope Town because all the hotels are in this area except for the three-room Hilltop Estates on Cherokee Sound and the seventeen-room Walker Cay Club on Walker Cay (the northernmost island of the Bahamas). A chartered boat, however, will open up the entire hundred-mile-long reef area to divers.

## WEST COAST

Almost the entire area here is shallow and muddy. Not recommended for diving.

## THE BIMINI ISLANDS

**How to Get There:** By Pan Am Jet Clipper to Nassau and connecting flight to Bimini. Bimini is also served by air from Miami.
**Hotels:** There are eight hotels on Bimini with a total of 227

rooms. Rates range upward from $8.00 per day, single, European plan.

**Transportation:** Taxis—and walking.

## SKIN DIVING INFORMATION

Included in this group are North and South Bimini, numerous small cays to the south, Great Isaac Island to the north, and the shoals and rocks extending southeast of Great Isaac.

This region is full of interesting coral formations and is visited frequently by divers from Florida since it is only about fifty miles from Miami. Many fish of all kinds are found here, and there are a sizable number of wrecks to be discovered, since shipwreckers were especially active in Bimini and nearby Gun Cay.

The Lerner Marine Laboratory is situated on Bimini and is well worth visiting. Specimens of most of the fish found in the Bahamas are on display. The fish are fed at 9 A.M. and the porpoises at 11 A.M. Visitors are welcome.

**Diving Gear for Sale and Rent, Guides, Boats, Compressed Air:** These services are available at the Skin and Scuba Diving Shop at the Sunshine Inn, at the Forty Fathoms Club, and at the Avis Bimini Club as well as at the Ocean Reef Dive and Surf shops in Brown's Hotel in North Bimini and Buccaneers Point in South Bimini.

### GREAT ISAAC ISLAND

This is a small, barren island about seventeen miles north of North Bimini. Accessible only by boat, it is surrounded by numerous rocky shoals and coral reefs. When seas are calm, this region is excellent for diving.

Hundreds of reefs and rocks extend from here for well over twenty miles to the southeast. This entire area is shallow, with depths varying from three to forty feet.

About five and a half miles southwest of Great Isaac, and a mile east of Hen and Chicken Rocks, there is a wreck in about thirty-five feet of water. Another wreck lies in about twenty-five feet of water approximately one and a quarter miles east of Hen and Chicken Rocks. Another wreck can be found about forty feet deep about twelve miles southwest of Great Isaac, and a little over a mile southwest of Eldorado Shoal.

Moselle Bank, a coral reef, lies about two and a quarter miles northwest of North Bimini. Plenty of coral will be found here in minimum depths of about four feet. Fish and lobster are plentiful.

A wreck, in shallow water, lies just west of North Rock, which is about a mile north of North Bimini.

Since all the above-mentioned areas are exposed to winds from any direction, diving is not recommended in windy weather: the seas will be too choppy for safe diving.

### NORTH AND SOUTH BIMINI

Except to the west, the waters surrounding North and South Bimini are shallow and the bottom is mostly sandy. Along the western edge are reefs with shallow depths close to shore. Less than a mile offshore, the bottom drops off into the depths of the Straits of Florida.

For well over twenty miles south of Bimini a broken chain of barely submerged rocks, reefs, and small cays offers some of the best diving conditions to be found anywhere. Access to these excellent diving spots is only by boat, preferably skippered by someone with a thorough knowledge of the area. One of the best spots is the area between Turtle Rocks (one and a quarter miles south of South Bimini) and Triangle Rocks, half a mile south of Turtle Rocks. Halfway between, the surrounding reefs are beautiful, the fish plentiful, and the water very clear. The concrete ship *Sapona* lies stranded in Barnett Harbour. It is usually loaded with fish.

Tidal currents in this area are frequently strong, especially between the rocks and cays. Also, the Gulf Stream current is occasionally felt in the shallower areas close to the reefs.

## THE BERRY ISLANDS

**How to Get There:** By Pan Am Jet Clipper to Nassau and by yacht or fishing boat to the Berry Islands. The M.V. *Four Kids* leaves Nassau every other Friday at 6 A.M. for the Berry Islands.

**Hotels:** Frazer's Cay Club on Frazer's Hog Cay has six rooms. Single rates in winter are $17.00 per person, European plan. The Rhoda Cay Club can accommodate eight guests.

## SKIN DIVING INFORMATION

The Berry Islands are a chain of over a hundred small islands extending from Great Stirrup Cay about forty miles south to within twenty-eight miles of Nassau. Diving conditions are excellent with clear water, strikingly beautiful reefs, and plenty of fish of all kinds.

As yet, there are no facilities for divers so it is best to bring everything necessary. The marina adjacent to the Crown Colony Club on Chub Cay is a good source of local diving information.

Shallow water is found up to a mile offshore along the eastern side of the chain. Farther offshore, the bottom gradually deepens to over a mile in the northwest Providence Channel.

The western side of the chain is all shallow with a sand and mud bottom. Not recommended for diving.

## ELEUTHERA

**How to Get There:** By Pan Am Jet Clipper to Rock Sound via Nassau.

**Hotels:** There are twenty-four hotels on Eleuthera and adjacent islands and a total of 374 rooms with rates ranging upward from $7.00 single, winter rate, European plan.

**Transportation:** Taxis and rental autos. A paved road extends for the full length of the island.

**Medical Facilities:** There are two doctors in Rock Sound, one on Harbour Island, and a dentist on Spanish Wells.

## SKIN DIVING INFORMATION

For convenience, Spanish Wells and other small islands adjacent to Eleuthera are included in this section.

Eleuthera is a narrow hundred-mile-long island with diving conditions suitable for almost every interest and level of ability. Beginners will find plenty of shallow, beautiful reefs and more advanced divers will have their choice of almost any kind of underwater terrain, including the sheer drop-off into the very deep water of the Northeast Providence Channel.

**Diving Gear for Sale:** The Rock Sound Hardware Store, near the airport, has snorkeling equipment for sale.

**Diving Gear for Rent:** Most hotels have diving equipment for the use of their guests. The most complete selection of equipment is at The Lloyds Spearfishing Resort on Spanish Wells. All kinds of underwater equipment, from snorkels to a dry, two-man submarine, is available to guests. Snorkeling and scuba gear can be rented from The Water Sports Centre, a mile northwest of Governor's Harbour at Balara Bay (Tel: Governor's Harbour 001).

**Trips, Guides, Boats:** The Dive Center at Balara Bay has thirteen-foot Boston Whalers for hire. From November to May scuba instruction is available. The Center can also arrange for diving "buddies" the year around.

Both the Hatchet Bay Plantation in Hatchet Bay and the Current Club on Current Island can arrange for boats and snorkeling trips. Boats can be rented at Davis Harbour.

Certified guides, boats, snorkeling and scuba trips, underwater camera rentals, submarine trips, scuba instruction, and just about anything else of possible interest to divers is availabe at The

Lloyds. Only certified divers are permitted to use scuba gear.

**Compressed Air:** The Lloyds and the Dive Center at Balara Bay have air.

There are lovely reefs for almost the entire length of the east coast. Unfortunately this coast is unprotected from winds coming from the quadrant north to east. These winds, if strong, create choppy seas and difficult diving conditions.

Spanish Wells, on St. George's Cay, lies to the east of the north tip of Eleuthera. From there, a chain of reefs and small cays extends in a southwesterly direction to New Providence Island (Nassau). This entire area is an excellent one for diving, with underwater visibility over one hundred feet, and plenty of coral and fish. Depths along this broken reef vary from awash to sixty feet. A boat is essential here.

Another very good diving spot is found off the north tip of Eleuthera from Spanish Wells north and east to Harbour Island. The ten-mile-long Egg Reef is well known for water clarity and beautiful reef formations. It runs roughly east/west and is less than a mile north of Spanish Wells. Diving is not recommended here when winds are from the northeast or northwest.

The remains of a railroad locomotive and tender from the U. S. Civil War days can be found in about thirty feet of water a few hundred yards north of Current Point.

Two shipwrecks are situated a few hundred yards north of Spanish Wells. One is north of Pierre Reef, the other is northwest of Ridley Bluff. The depth of both wrecks is about thirty feet.

Shipwreckers were quite active in Eleuthera waters, especially around Harbour Island. Many sunken ships still lie on the reefs, awaiting discovery.

The southern tip of Eleuthera, near Rock Sound, is another good diving area, with fringing reefs found on both the east and west coasts. Depths vary from two to fifty feet.

Little San Salvador, also called Little Cat Island, lies about nine miles southeast of Eleuthera Point. It is highly recommended for skin diving because of the lovely coral gardens found along the entire length of the north coast. A shallow reef extends north from the western tip of the island. Another shoal extends north from the eastern tip of the island, as far as Goat Cay. Still another reef is found to the north side of Long Rocks, which lie eastward and roughly parallel to Little San Salvador. This last-mentioned reef is exceptionally beautiful. Since these small, un-inhabited cays are not regularly visited, the fish are uncommonly tame. This area is well worth a visit. A boat is, of course, a necessity.

## NEW PROVIDENCE

**How to Get There:** By Pan Am Jet Clipper from New York or Miami.

**Hotels:** There are fifty-three hotels, guesthouses, and private homes offering over 2600 rooms at rates ranging upward from $4.00, single, European plan, winter rate.

**Transportation:** Taxis, rental autos, and rental bicycles and scooters. Most all roads are paved. The large hotels have scheduled bus service into town.

**Medical Facilities:** There are two hospitals, several doctors and dentists.

**Other Information:** The Bahamas Ministry of Tourism is in Rawson Square. The Pan Am office is on Matthew Avenue (Tel: 2-3394).

## SKIN DIVING INFORMATION

Spearfishing, or removing any underwater organism, is prohibited around the eastern, northern, and western coasts of New Providence. This area is a Bahamas Government underwater nature preserve.

**Diving Gear for Sale:** Maura Lumber Co., Shirley Street; The

Ironmongery, Bay Street; Palmdale Shopping Center, in Nassau; and the Nassau Bicycle Co., Bay Street, are sources of diving equipment.

**Diving Gear for Rent, Diving Trips, Guides, Instruction, Boats:** Bahamas Water Sports Co., Ltd., P. O. Box 537, Nassau (Tel: 5120), and MM Underwater Tours, Ltd., Nassau Yacht Haven, P. O. Box 1216 (Tel: 24011), are both well organized and equipped for instructing in scuba diving, daily reef trips, and underwater guide service. They both have rental scuba equipment for qualified divers.

Captain Greg Nico, the Cruising Club Ltd., Box 22, Nassau, offers week-long cruises through the Out Islands aboard yachts equipped for both snorkeling and scuba diving. These diving cruises are suitable for either individuals or for groups.

**Helmet Reef Trips:** Over forty thousand persons have enjoyed the personally escorted, shallow-water reef tours offered by Bronson and Harriet Hartley. These safe, interesting excursions are suitable for even nonswimmers. They afford a close-up look at tame fish, sponges, coral, and other reef dwellers by using specially designed helmets. Their 63-foot yacht *Pied Piper* leaves daily except Sunday from the Nassau Yacht Haven (Tel: 2-8234 or 9-4369) from December 1 through May 15. During the summer they offer similar tours in Bermuda. Highly recommended.

**Compressed Air:** MM Underwater Tours, Ltd., and Bahamas Water Sports Co. have compressors.

NORTH COAST

Goulding Cay, about a mile west of West Bay, is fringed by a lovely coral reef. Depths vary from five to thirty feet. The reef extends southwest to Clifton Point on the mainland.

A fringing reef extends from Simms Point east to Delaport Point. The coral is attractive, and there are plenty of fish to be seen. A sharp watch should be kept for small boats which frequent this area.

The coral reefs lying between North Cay and Hog Island are attractive and among the best in the Bahamas. This area is easily accessible from Nassau and the north-coast hotels by boat.

## EAST COAST

This area includes the extensive shallow reefs from the eastern tip of Hog Island, south to East End Point, then east to Rose Island. The entire area is full of reefs varying in depth from awash to twenty feet. This area is recommended for beginners and shallow-water fish watchers. The wreck of an LST lies just off the eastern tip of Athol Island. East of Rose Island is the group of cays which extend to Eleuthera, described in the Eleuthera section.

## SOUTH COAST

The entire coastal waters are shallow, from awash to six feet, with many coral heads. This area is not as spectacular as the east-coast waters, but some of the reefs are quite beautiful and are excellent for beginners.

## THE EXUMAS

**How to Get There:** By Pan Am Jet Clipper to Nassau. From Nassau by boat to the Exumas or by connecting flight to Great Exuma Island and by boat from there to the surrounding cays.

**Hotels:** There are six hotels in the Exumas offering a total of eighty-four rooms at rates ranging upward from $7.00 per day, single, winter rate, European plan.

**Transportation:** Taxis and rental autos are available in George Town, Great Exuma. On the other islands, transportation is by boat and walking.

**Medical Facilities:** A doctor and a clinic are situated just outside George Town on Great Exuma.

# SKIN DIVING INFORMATION

The Exumas begin about twenty-five miles southeast of New Providence and curve southeast for one hundred miles. Diving conditions are superb in this chain of over three hundred islands. The water is exceptionally clear, fish abound, and the reefs are magnificent.

There is only one full-fledged skin diving business in this region: the Staniel Cay Club. Compressed air, scuba rentals, etc., are not available on the other islands. Scuba diving enthusiasts wishing to visit these other islands can best do so by chartered yacht from Nassau.

**Laws:** The Exuma Cays Land and Sea Park extends south from Wax Cay Cut for twenty-two miles to Conch Cay Cut. Though skin diving is permitted here, spearfishing or taking anything from the sea in this wildlife sanctuary is strictly prohibited.

**Diving Gear for Rent, Trips, Guides, Boats, Instruction, and Compressed Air:** The Staniel Cay Club, a hotel and yacht marina, offers a complete skin diving facility: equipment rentals, guides, boats, scuba instruction, compressed air, even underwater cameras and submarines for rent.

The Compass Cay Club on Compass Cay has some diving equipment and can organize diving trips. Fishing boats are available from the Pieces of Eight Hotel or the Club Peace and Plenty in George Town, Great Exuma. Mr. Basil Minns operates a boat rental business in George Town and knows the surrounding waters intimately.

### DIVING AREAS

West of Sail Rocks (the northernmost rocks of the Exumas) about five miles is Middle Ground, an extensive, shallow reef area. It adjoins Yellow Bank a few miles to the west. This entire reef, over fifteen miles long, is an extraordinarily attractive one for divers. The water is gin clear and the fish abundant. Depths vary from two to fifteen feet, making it a perfect area for beginners, photographers, and fish watchers. This area is most easily reached by boat from Nassau.

To describe each of the islands of the Exumas would be repetitive and unnecessary, since the entire area is excellent for diving. A fringing reef extends to the eastward of these cays for up to two miles, with excellent diving conditions to be found along almost the entire length of the island chain. On the western sides of the islands the water is quite shallow and is seldom deeper than nine feet.

The Staniel Cay Cave is an unusual and very beautiful sight. It can be entered only by swimmers. Inside, the light is subdued, and very blue. Sea life of several kinds is present and can be observed closely. This cave was featured in the film *Thunderball*.

The tidal flow is on and off the reefs. Extreme care should be observed if diving near a "cut," Bahamian for a passage between two cays. The tidal current through the cuts sometimes reaches four knots.

## ANDROS

**How to Get There:** By Pan Am Jet Clipper to Nassau with connecting flight to Andros Town.

**Hotels:** There are six hotels on Andros, offering a total of 168 rooms at rates ranging upward from $7.50, single, winter rate, European plan.

**Transportation:** Taxis and jitneys (small, truck-type buses). Some hotels provide bicycles for their guests. Roads are poor.

**Medical Facilities:** There is a nurse in Andros Town.

## SKIN DIVING INFORMATION

**Laws:** Efforts are being made to establish an underwater park along the east coast from Fresh Creek north to Staniard Creek.

It is advised not to spear fish or remove coral or other marine organisms from this area.

**Diving Gear for Sale and Rent, Trips, Guides, Boats, Compressed Air:** Diving gear is not available for sale on Andros. Dick and Jack Birch of Small Hope Bay Lodge, Fresh Creek, have a well-equipped skin diving resort. Mask, fins, and snorkel are supplied to their guests at no charge. Scuba gear is available for qualified divers. Also offered are boats, guides, compressed air, and reef trips. Scuba instruction is free to guests. Group rates for accommodations and diving are available. The Birches are both qualified instructors and know the Andros reefs well. Their hotel is a short drive from the Andros Town Airport.

Andros, nearly one hundred miles long and up to forty miles wide, lies twenty miles west of New Providence and about seventeen miles southwest of Frazer's Hog Cay in the Berry Islands. The chief attraction for skin divers here is a 120-mile-long barrier reef. It is said to be the second longest barrier reef in the world, after Australia's Great Barrier Reef.

On the inside, or west side, of the reef the water is seldom deeper than ten feet. There are quite a number of coral gardens in this region and they are ideal for beginners. On the outside of the reef the bottom drops off very sharply into the mile-deep Tongue of the Ocean. Visibility "over the wall" is ordinarily in the 200-foot range.

Thus, the Andros Barrier Reef affords excellent diving conditions for all divers, from expert to novice. It is inadvisable to take a boat through the reef except with a guide who has knowledge of the various shoals.

A wreck lies in sixty-five feet of water just off Small Hope Bay Lodge. Farther north, another wreck is located in shallow water on the reef east of Conch Sound.

Blue Hole diving is also available to expert scuba divers. The Blue Holes are found in many places on the island. They are deep inland sinkholes connected to the Tongue of the Ocean by underground caves. Many fish and huge lobsters are found in these unusual caverns. They should be explored only by highly experienced scuba divers accompanied by one of the Birches, since the tides ebb and flow through the narrow underground channels with considerable force.

A recompression chamber can be found at the U. S. Navy Atlantic Undersea Testing and Evaluation Center (AUTEC) at Young Sound, south of Andros Town.

The west coast is impossible for diving. The water is very shallow and the bottom muddy. There are no settlements on this coast.

## SAN SALVADOR

**How to Get There:** By Pan Am Jet Clipper to Nassau with connecting flight to San Salvador.

**Hotels:** The Riding Rock Club has seven apartments and six cottages with rates that start at $14.00 per day, single, winter rate, European plan.

**Transportation:** Taxis and rental autos in Cockburn Town. A good road encircles the island.

## SKIN DIVING INFORMATION

Visitors must bring all necessary equipment since there are no facilities for skin divers on this island, yet. The island is about six by sixteen miles in size and is located about two hundred miles southeast of Nassau.

Reefs almost completely encircle the island. The best reefs are those at the north end, just off the U. S. Coast Guard base. A wreck can be seen about one and a half miles northeast of Green Cay. Due to the easterly trades, the reefs on the east coast are frequently difficult to explore because of choppy seas.

Columbus is said to have landed here in 1492.

## LONG ISLAND

**How to Get There:** By Pan Am Jet Clipper to Nassau, with connecting flight to Long Island.

**Hotels:** There are three hotels on Long Island, offering a total of thirty-one rooms at rates ranging upward from $10.00, single, winter rates, European plan.

**Transportation:** Taxis and rental cars.

**Medical Facilities:** There are two clinics, with resident nurses.

## SKIN DIVING INFORMATION

There are no facilities for visiting divers on this island. Heavy seas frequently make the east coast unsuitable for diving.

The west coast is mostly sandy and shallow with occasional coral patches. There are some scenic reefs west of New Found Harbour.

## GREAT AND LITTLE INAGUA

**How to Get There:** By Pan Am Jet Clipper to Nassau with connecting flight to Great Inagua.

**Hotels:** The Flamingo Lodge and Restaurant on Great Inagua has four rooms at $2.00 single and $3.00 double, with bath, year-round rate, European plan.

**Medical Facilities:** There is a modern hospital in Matthew Town.

## SKIN DIVING INFORMATION

There are no organized facilities for visiting divers. Boats may be rented from fishermen in town. Great Inagua is almost wholly encircled by reefs and offers wonderful opportunities for diving in clear, warm waters of any depth desired. Fish are plentiful.

The south-coast reef extends offshore for over five miles from the southeast point. Off the southwest point there are two reefs: the one fringing the coastline, and Molasses Reef, two miles off-shore.

The best diving area on the northwest (leeward) coast can be found on the reef fringing the coast from Northwest Point to Carmichael Point. Access is by boat. Depths vary from awash to the very deep water found about a quarter mile or more offshore.

Little Inagua is about five miles north of Great Inagua. This small island is fringed with reefs and offers good diving, especially on the leeward (west) coast. It is accessible only by boat, which should be piloted by someone familiar with the reefs.

## THE TURK ISLANDS AND CAICOS ISLANDS

**How to Get There:** By Pan Am Jet Clipper to Nassau with connecting flight to South Caicos or Grand Turk.

**Hotels:** The Admirals Arms Inn on South Caicos has seven rooms at reasonable rates.

**Medical Facilities:** There is a doctor and a small hospital on Grand Turk.

## SKIN DIVING INFORMATION

Diving conditions on this reef-fringed island group are wonderful. A profusion of reefs surrounds the islands, offering visibilities normally well over one hundred feet. There are large numbers of fish of all kinds, an almost unending variety of reef formations, and depths varying from awash to over one hundred feet.

There are no facilities for visiting divers. All visitors should bring their own equipment with them.

Politically, these islands are under the direct control of the

British Colonial Office and are not a part of the Bahamas. However, they are included in this Bahamas section because of their location.

The Caicos Islands consist of six larger islands and several small cays. The most important is South Caicos, which has the only hotel and airstrip in this group. To describe each island in detail would be repetitive and unnecessary: reefs fringe the eastern, northern, and western edge of this island group. The southern coasts of the islands are fronted by shallow water, with a sandy bottom. The Admirals Arms Inn can arrange for boats. Sometimes, boats can be hired from fishermen, who know the surrounding reefs well.

The Turk Islands consist of two larger islands and several smaller islets. There are no hotels here and this island group is best visited by yacht.

Grand Turk is the most important, with an airstrip, a hospital, and the only community of any size—Cockburn Town. A Pan Am missile tracking station and a U. S. Navy station are located here. Around Grand Turk can be found a wide variety of reefs of all depths. Inside the barrier reef on the east coast, the water is shallow, clear, and calm. There are numerous underwater caves to be explored here. The west coast has an almost continuous reef with a sharp drop-off on the offshore side to hundreds of feet. Fish of all kinds, lobsters, and turtles are found around this island in impressive quantities.

Salt Cay is a small islet over five miles southwest of Grand Turk. There is a small community, but no tourist facilities of any kind. The surrounding waters offer some of the best diving conditions to be found anywhere. Reefs extend in almost every direction for several miles and are loaded with fish, lobsters, and other marine life.

# Chapter 5

# COZUMEL

**How to Get There:** By Mexicana Airlines direct from Miami or Mexico City.

**Customs Regulations:** Personal effects and two hundred cigarettes or fifty cigars or fifty grams of tobacco and twelve rolls of film, plus a bottle of liquor are admitted duty free. The exporting of gold coins or jewelry containing gold coins is prohibited.

**Travel Documents Required:** Proof of identity and nationality, a tourist card, and a smallpox vaccination certificate issued within three years are required for entry. Yellow fever and cholera vaccination certificates are required of visitors arriving from infected areas.

Tourist cards valid for thirty days are issued free; those valid for six months cost $3.00; and a multiple entry card, valid for several visits within six months, costs $5.00. Tourist cards are issued at Mexican Consulates, Mexican Tourist Commission offices, Mexicana Airlines offices, and by some Pan Am offices.

**Currency:** The Mexican peso is valued at 8¢ and is exchanged at 12.50 pesos to $1.00 U.S.

**Hotels:** There are seven small hotels with single rates ranging upward from $3.00, single, European plan. Advance reservations are essential since Cozumel is an increasingly popular resort.

**Transportation:** Taxis and rental bicycles.

**Medical Facilities:** There is a doctor and a clinic.

**Other Information:** The Mexican Government Tourist Department main office is on Reforma y Lafragua, Mexico City, U.S. offices are at 630 Fifth Avenue, New York City.

Cozumel was considered sacred to the Mayans and other Indian tribes. Quite a few ruined Mayan monuments are found throughout the island. Visitors are allowed to visit the ruins, but it is forbidden to disturb or remove any of the artifacts.

## SKIN DIVING INFORMATION

Cozumel waters are among the clearest in the world and are so warm that a diving suit is unnecessary even during prolonged dives. Visibility is well over one hundred feet. So far, the area has not been fished out and there are plenty of game fish, lobsters, and turtles. The island is exceptionally well equipped with diving equipment, boats, and guides and is highly recommended for either beginners or expert divers.

Guides make a point of inquiring which particular activity is of interest to the visitor in order to select the reef best suited to their guests: there are reefs for beginners, spearfishing, photography, black coral collecting, lobstering, shell collecting, etc. The best months for diving are July and August. The worst months are from the end of November through February.

**Laws:** Diving on ancient wrecks or in sacrificial wells is prohibited except by written permission from CEDAM, the national diving club of Mexico. To obtain permission, apply to Mr. Pablo Bush Romero, Director of Explorations, CEDAM, 5 de Mayo 131 Sur, Cd. Juárez, Chih., Mexico.

Female lobsters with eggs may not be taken. The closed season on lobster is March 1 to July 15.

**Diving Gear for Sale:** El Clavado, in the Hotel Islena, maintains an ample stock of diving equipment for sale.

**Diving Gear for Rent, Compressed Air:** El Clavado; Aquasafari, near the town pier; and the Hotel de Quintana Roo all rent gear. El Clavado has a compressor.

**Trips, Guides, Boats:** These services are arranged through the hotels. There is no shortage of guides and boats.

**Currents, Winds:** Currents ordinarily flow from south to north at about two knots. The best practice is for divers to drift with the current, accompanied by the diving boat. Winds usually are from the east. In February they frequently shift to the southwest and in November/January are from the north.

The waters off San Miguel, the principal town, are clear, but there is no coral and little of interest can be seen underwater. Farther south a small reef about ten feet deep is situated north of the entrance to Caleta, near the Presidente Hotel. This reef is a good one for beginners and shallow-water divers. It can be reached by swimming out from shore.

South of Caleta Bay is Laguna Chancanab. This shallow, land-locked pool is excellent for beginners since there is no current and the water is always calm. There are caves for exploring and inlet and outlet tunnels that link the lagoon with the sea.

South of the lagoon, the islanders have built palm-thatched shelters where they cook freshly caught fish and lobster for their diving guests, who can enjoy a wonderfully relaxing lunch break from their diving trip. The beach is lovely and the whole setting is everyman's dream of a tropical hideaway. A shallow reef rims the beach.

South of this beach, at the southwestern tip of the island, is Balancar Reef, the best reef on the island for diving. Depths vary from thirty to over a hundred feet. The currents are not usually too strong, and visibility is exceptional—well over one hundred feet. Plenty of game fish are found here plus the usual assortment of coral and brightly colored reef fish. Black coral, used for jewelry, is also found here at deeper levels. The experienced scuba diver should not miss a trip to this reef.

The east coast is frequently too rough for diving, although there are reefs along this shoreline. During calm weather, when diving is possible, access is by boat or by jeep trip across the island from San Miguel to San Gervacio on the east coast. There, an excellent reef is situated a short distance offshore. This jeep trail is, so far, the only trail across the island.

Off the north coast there are large rocks which fringe the

shoreline underwater. There is little coral here except for a horse-shoe-shaped reef, with a least depth of about ten feet, off Punta Molas at the northeastern point. Sizable quantities of lobsters are usually seen on this coast.

*Chapter 6*

# GRAND CAYMAN

**How to Get There:** By LACSA Airlines from Miami, flight time about one hour; or by connection with Pan American flights to San Jose, Costa Rica, or Jamaica (flight time forty-five minutes).

**Customs Regulations:** Visitors may bring in items for personal use without payment of duty.

**Travel Documents Required:** U.S. and Canadian citizens must have proof of identity and a return ticket. Passports are required only for visits exceeding six months.

**Currency:** Jamaican pounds are used. One pound equals $2.80 U.S. There are 20 shillings (14¢ each) in a pound and 12 pence (approximately 1¢ each) in a shilling. U.S. currency is accepted everywhere.

**Hotels:** There are ten hotels and guesthouses on the island with rates ranging upward from $10.00, single, winter rates, modified American plan. Advance bookings are essential during the winter.

**Transportation:** Taxis, rental cars, and rental bicycles are available. There are no telephones on the island, so arrangements for taxis must be made through the hotel.

There are sixty miles of paved road. The unpaved roads are very poor. A temporary driver's permit, issued free, must be obtained from the police.

**Medical Facilities:** There are good doctors and a hospital.

**Other Information:** Grand Cayman lies 475 miles south of Miami and 180 miles west-northwest of Jamaica. English is the native language.

This is an ideal skin diving area. The term "unspoiled island" truly applies to this small British Crown Colony. The islands are friendly, happy, honest, and always willing to make visitors feel at home. There are no telephones, or television, or highly organized vacation resorts.

Duty-free shopping is available to tourists. Items purchased are delivered to the airport to be claimed before departure.

Current information on the island, including a hotel list, with rates, can be obtained from the Cayman Islands Information Center, 17150 N.E. 10th Avenue, North Miami Beach, Florida.

## SKIN DIVING INFORMATION

Skin diving conditions are among the best anywhere. Beginners will find fringing reefs close to shore almost everywhere. Advanced divers will find plenty of wrecks, offshore reefs, and fish to make a trip here worth while.

Reefs almost completely encircle the island. The water is exceptionally clear with underwater visibility of one hundred feet or more. There are 325 known wrecks in the surrounding waters. The island was used by pirates, and coins and cannonballs are frequently discovered. Stories of buried treasure, and sunken treasure, persist. The location of several wrecks is indicated in the booklet "An Adventurers Guide to the Unspoiled Cayman Islands," by George Hudson. It is available for $2.00 from the Cayman Islands Information Center and is well worth it.

Over two hundred species of seashells have been found here.

**Laws:** Closed season on lobster is April 1 to August 1. Do not take female lobsters with eggs.

**Diving Gear for Sale:** Bob Soto's Sportfishing Headquarters, a half mile west of Georgetown, offers basic equipment for sale.

**Diving Gear for Rent:** Bob Soto and Tom Hubbell, at Pedro Castle, rent scuba equipment, except regulators. Visitors must bring their own regulator. The Tortuga Club and Cayman Kai, a

[1] Fins should be put on just before entering the water. First, dip your feet and your fins in the water, then insert your foot into the foot pocket, and pull the fins on as shown here. The fins may become torn if you pull them on by tugging sharply at the back of the foot pocket.

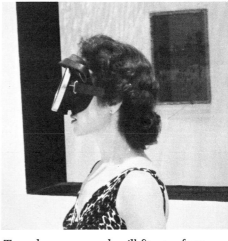

[2] To make sure a mask will fit your face properly and will not leak, place it on your face, as shown above, and inhale through your nose. The suction should keep the mask in place even though the head strap is not used. If the mask leaks air during this test, it will probably leak water when used and should be exchanged for another one.

[3] The snorkel is placed under the mask strap with the mouthpiece resting comfortably in your mouth as shown here. The J-type snorkel is preferred and is more dependable than snorkels with gadgets designed to keep the water out of the snorkel tube.

[4] Two methods of entering the water are commonly used. The giant stride entry is shown here. Be sure to hold your mask firmly against your face.

[5] Another water entry method is the backward roll. First, make sure there are no obstructions, or other divers, in the water. Then, squat on the gunwale of the boat, hold your mask against your face, and roll backward into the water.

[6] The snorkel is used for breathing while swimming facedown on the surface of the water. Look up periodically to make certain that there are no obstructions in your way and that you are swimming in the desired direction. Use just your legs for propulsion. Trail your arms along your sides. Try to avoid splashing the water with your fins: splashing reduces the efficiency of the fins, and it frightens the fish.

[7] Float facedown on the surface. Drop your arms down so they point to the bottom. Take a deep breath and hold it.

[8] Bend at the waist. Your upper torso is now pointed down, toward the bottom.

[9] Thrust your legs straight up. Your body is now pointed straight down. Use both hands to pull yourself under. The weight of your body will help carry you under the surface. Do not kick with your fins until they are under the surface. [10] Once you are completely submerged, begin a steady, rhythmic kick.

[11] Should you become interested in scuba diving, be sure to obtain competent instruction. This student has just successfully completed a scuba training course at a professional diving school. It is important that all equipment is of excellent quality and lovingly cared for, as shown below.

cottage colony, have basic equipment and scuba gear available for their guests; again, guests should bring their own regulators.

**Diving Trips, Guides, Boats:** Bob Soto and Tom Hubbell offer scuba lessons and diving trips. Hubbell specializes in treasure hunting and has an exhibit of artifacts in his Pedro Castle.

The Tortuga Club, a comfortable hotel, has an excellent array of diving equipment and "Woody," a first-class diving guide. Boston whalers are used for trips to the nearby barrier reef and the many wrecks on the east end of the island.

Experienced divers will find the services of Captain Ertis or Crosby Ebanks, both of West Bay, useful. They are excellent diving guides and thoroughly familiar with local waters. Their services can be arranged for through the hotels.

Boats can be rented from Jim Bodden at the Galleon Beach Hotel.

**Compressed Air:** Bob Soto, The Tortuga Club, and Cayman Kai all have compressors.

**Currents, Winds:** Ocean currents are usually negligible and are not a problem for skin divers. Wind currents can reach two to three knots in the southwest corner of the island after a lengthy wind. Winter winds are usually from northeast to north. In summer, winds vary from east-northeast to south-southeast.

An occasional northwester will cause murkiness on the north and west coasts but will not affect the visibility on the opposite coasts.

**Fish:** Large quantities of many different types of fish are seen here. Common game fish include amberjacks, hogfish, tarpon, dolphins, groupers, snappers, tuna, crevalles, pompano, and jewfish. Among the many reef fish seen are royal grammas, rock beauties, trunkfish, triggerfish, grunts, parrot fish, sergeant majors, and squirrelfish. Lobsters, conchs, and turtles are also present in quantity.

Tropical fish collectors will find large numbers of valuable fish at various depths. The most commonly collected tropicals are longnose butterfly fish, small queen triggerfish, jewel fish, yellow butterfly fish, royal grammas, rock beauties, and jackknifes.

## NORTH COAST

A magnificent barrier reef stretches along most of this coastline just a short distance offshore. Snorkeling and scuba diving are very good both in the shallow water inside the reef and in the deeper water outside the reef. Portions of the reef are awash at low tide. Access is from the nine-mile, unpaved, very rough road which parallels the north coast from Rum Point eastward. Other portions of this coast are accessible only by boat.

Hotels can arrange all-day boating/diving trips during which guests can swim, snorkel, and spearfish. The guide, or the guest, catches fish and lobster, which are cooked on the beach for lunch. Door-to-door transportation is included in the low rate. This trip is an excellent and entertaining way to spend a day.

The North Sound is a large, reef-protected bay on the northwest coast. Turtles, fish, and spiny lobsters are found in large quantities. The water is shallow. The "Adventurers Guide" charts nine wrecks and traces of wreckage in the North Sound, and four other wreck locations along the north coast.

## EAST COAST

Once a stronghold of such famous pirates as Blackbeard, Henry Morgan, and Sir Francis Drake, Gun Bay is now one of the richest wreck-hunting areas in the Caribbean. In one spot, near the entrance through the reef, there are five separate wrecks, stacked one atop the other. Two beached freighters, a Liberty ship and a bauxite carrier, mark the channel through the reef. The remains of an old sailing ship lie between them, in the channel. The remains of another wreck can be found between the reef and the Liberty ship.

In 1785, ten British sailing ships, in an unbeatable display of nautical ineptitude, sailed one by one on the east-end barrier reef. For their heroism in saving all hands, the Cayman Islanders were exempt forever from wartime conscription or payment of income taxes by King George. The wrecks are still on the reef. "Woody," the diving guide at the Tortuga Club, knows this area intimately.

## SOUTH COAST

A barrier reef protects Frank Sound and Red Bay, which are at the eastern end of this coast. Fringing reefs are found elsewhere along this coast except at Pedro Point and Half Moon Bay. This entire coastline is excellent for diving, with good visibility and plenty of fish. There are at least seven wrecks on this coast, and they are charted in the "Adventurers Guide." Access to diving sites is by road, which parallels this coast, or by boat.

## WEST COAST

The best diving in this area is from southwest point north to Seven Mile Beach, and from northwest point to Conch Point. Many seashells can be found on Seven Mile Beach, and a few coral heads, ideal for beginners, can also be seen just offshore.

There are two recent wrecks in Georgetown Harbour. They are in shallow water and their locations are known to the townspeople. Unlike most harbors, the water here is clear and clean.

The reefs on this coast fringe the shore. Access is by road, which parallels the coast, or by boat.

# Chapter 7

# JAMAICA

**How to Get There:** By Pan Am Jet Clipper. Montego Bay is one and a quarter hours from Miami and three and three-quarter hours from New York. Kingston is a half hour from Montego Bay, one and a half hours from Miami, and has a direct 3½-hour Jet Clipper flight from New York.

**Customs Regulations:** Visitors may bring in, duty free, personal clothing and a carton of cigarettes, or fifty cigars, or a half pound of tobacco, plus a pint of liquor or a quart of wine. Foreign rums may not be brought in.

**Travel Documents Required:** U.S. citizens will not need passports or visas for visits of up to six months, provided the trip originates and terminates in the United States and the traveler has a return ticket and proof of citizenship.

**Currency:** The Jamaican pound is exchanged everywhere at $2.80 U.S. There are 20 shillings (14¢ each) in a pound. A shilling is divided into 12 pence (approximately 1¢ each).

**Hotels:** Jamaica offers a wide selection of hotels and guesthouses at rates ranging upward from $6.00 per day. Reservations are essential during the busy winter months.

**Transportation:** Taxis and rental autos are available everywhere. A passenger train runs between Kingston and Montego Bay and Port Antonio. Drive on the left. Foreign drivers' licenses are accepted. All main, and most secondary, roads are paved. Buses are quite crowded and are not recommended for visitors.

**Medical Facilities:** There are excellent doctors and hospitals.

**Other Information:** The Pan Am offices, staffed largely by knowledgeable Jamaicans, are excellent sources of general tourist information. They are at 117 Harbour Street, Kingston; Casa Montego Arcade, Montego Bay; and 2 Pineapple Place, Ocho Rios.

The Jamaica Tourist Board can supply tourist information and a list of hotels with current rates. The head office is at 80 Harbour Street in Kingston. Overseas offices are at 200 Park Avenue, New York; 278 Post Street, San Francisco; 403 Joseph Vance Building, Seattle; Room 712, Champlain Building, Chicago; John A. Tetley Co., Inc., 3440 Wilshire Boulevard, Los Angeles; Suite 517, First National Bank of Miami, Miami; 9th Floor, Board of Trade Building, 11 Adelaide Street, Toronto; and 6–10 Brudon Street, London, W1.

## SKIN DIVING INFORMATION

Jamaica is discussed here in two sections: the north coast and the south coast. The north coast is fringed by lovely coral reefs for almost its entire length. The north-shore road, paralleling the coast, provides easy access to the nearby reefs. Diving conditions here are good, except when strong northerly winds, especially in winter, create heavy seas. When this occurs, the south coast is best for diving.

The waters in Kingston Harbour, on the south coast, are murky. However, there are some excellent diving areas farther offshore. A boat is necessary to reach these offshore reefs.

**Laws:** It is a strictly enforced, punishable offense to disturb any artifacts in the area of the sunken city of Port Royal. Preparations are being made for a methodical archaeological survey of this seventeenth-century pirate stronghold.

Do not take female lobsters with eggs.

**Diving Gear for Sale:** The Jamaica Sub-Aqua Club, 71 Lady Musgrave Road, Kingston 10 (Tel: 7-9222), has an excellent selection of American and European equipment at reasonable prices. Most sporting goods stores in the larger cities offer a good selection of equipment. A comprehensive line of gear is offered by Andrew H. B. Aguilar, Ltd., 95 Harbour Street, Kingston.

**Diving Gear for Rent:** In Kingston, the Jamaica Sub-Aqua Club rents equipment to members. Qualified divers may become members upon application. Rates are low.

In Montego Bay, the Sea Crabs Diving School, Hotel Chatham (Tel: 2112), has gear for rent.

**Trips, Guides, Boats:** Kent Eldemire, Trade Winds Underwater Tours, P. O. Box 56, Stony Hill, Kingston (Tel: 2-4810 or 2-4818), is one of the island's champion divers and can arrange for boats, guides, transportation, and hotels. He knows Jamaican waters thoroughly.

The Jamaica Sub-Aqua Club in Kingston will help visiting divers to the fullest extent possible, including helping with arrangements for hotels and diving trips.

In Montego Bay, the Sea Crabs Diving School offers scuba and snorkeling instruction, diving trips, guides, and boats.

In Ocho Rios, the Playboy Club offers instruction, trips, guides, and boats for their hotel guests only.

**Compressed Air:** In Kingston: Kent Eldemire, the Jamaica Sub-Aqua Club, and Jamaica Oxygen, Ltd., Spanishtown Road.

In Montego Bay: Sea Crabs Diving School.

In Ocho Rios: The Playboy Club—for guests only.

Boats may be hired from fishermen in most fishing villages. The cost varies from $5.00 to $10.00 per day, depending on the size of the boat and the ability of the bargainer.

**Currents, Winds:** Ocean currents are to the westward. Except at the eastern and western tips of the island, currents are not strong enough to affect skin divers.

Along the north coast the northeasterly trades prevail. Southeast winds are encountered along the south coast.

**Fish:** The coastal waters, particularly along the north shore, are just about fished out. Sizable quantities of the standard variety of Caribbean game fish are seen on the reefs off the south coast. There are plenty of small, beautiful tropical fish on all reefs.

### SOUTH COAST

The best diving area off the south coast lies in the region from Lime Cay (which is south of Palisadoes Airport) southwest to Portland Point. The nearer cays are a half-hour boat trip from Kingston. The best diving in these nearby islets is around Lime Cay, Gun Cay, Rackhams Cay, Drunkenman's Cay, Maiden Cay, and Southeast Cay. Depths vary from awash to forty feet. Reefs and game fish are plentiful in this area. Visibility is normally seventy-five to over one hundred feet. A wreck is stranded on the southeast side of Drunkenman's Cay.

Wreck Reef lies southeast of the nearby group. An old wreck, cannons, and persistent rumors of treasure make this an interesting diving spot. Underwater visibility is usually around one hundred feet.

Old Harbour Bay, about forty miles by road west of Kingston, is a good spot to hire a boat for some offshore diving. Fishermen will usually hire out boats for from $6.00 to $10.00 per day. A variety of seashells can be found here. The better diving spots near Old Harbour Bay are around the small island and extensive reefs north of Rocky Point and the waters around Pigeon Island, Pelican Reefs, Big Pelican Cay, and, farther out, Bare Bush Cay and Portland Cay.

This entire region offers excellent diving in a variety of depths.

### NORTH COAST

The north-coast reef provides safe, sheltered waters for shallow-water snorkeling on the inside of the reef and deep diving on the outside. Since these waters are pretty well fished out, all that remain are the usual small reef fish and an occasional mackerel, jack, tarpon, or barracuda, and these are usually found outside the reef.

Except in heavy weather or after heavy rains, visibility is usually seventy-five to one hundred feet. The best time of day for diving is early morning, before the onshore wind creates choppy seas.

Good diving spots are found almost anywhere along this coast. The following are some of the north-shore attractions, listed from west to east.

**Negril:** Excellent for a family diving outing since one of Jamaica's best beaches is situated here. Offshore there is a variety of diving opportunities. About two hundred yards offshore there is a shallow reef for snorkeling. Farther out, about a mile, is a deeper reef well worth a visit by experienced scuba divers. This reef is about forty feet deep at its shallowest, and offers caves, ravines, and other lovely coral configurations. Boats can be hired from fishermen or through the Rendezvous de Terrier Guest House or the Sundowner Hotel.

**Negril to Montego Bay:** Good diving conditions are found along this section of the coast, especially around the reefs just off Mosquito Cove and Sandy Bay. There are several beach access areas just off the coast road.

**Montego Bay Area:** A shallow reef is found about two hundred yards off Doctor's Cave Beach and is recommended for snorkelers. Almost half a mile offshore is a deeper reef—quite beautiful—about fifty to sixty feet deep. The bottom drops off sharply on the outside of this reef.

Another excellent snorkeling area for beginners is found just off the airport runway. Depths vary from ten to thirty-five feet. There are many large caves in this reef. Visibility is usually from seventy-five to one hundred feet. Access is by swimming from shore to the shallow reefs or by chartered boat from the Sea Crabs Diving School.

**Silver Sands:** Here, the reef is about half a mile north of the Silver Sands Hotel beach. The reef is lovely but too deep for beginners. Experienced scuba divers will find a wide variety of beautiful coral and brightly decorated reef fish here in depths of seventy-five feet or more. Boats can be hired from fishermen.

**Braco:** A shallow, attractive reef fringes the coastline here, with a deeper reef located about two hundred yards offshore. The shallow reef is excellent for beginners. The deeper reef slopes off steeply to very deep water and is excellent for exploration and photography by experienced scuba divers. A boat, obtainable from fishermen in the area, should be used for offshore diving. A sign, about two miles west of Río Bueno, marks the secondary road leading to Braco.

**Discovery Bay:** A shallow reef is found about four hundred yards offshore in the center of Discovery Bay. The reef slopes off to over one hundred feet. This reef is worth a visit and has conditions and depths for divers of various interests and abilities. The water is usually rather calm.

**Eaton Hall:** For experienced scuba divers, a reef in minimum forty-foot depths is found about a quarter mile off the Eaton Hall pier. The reef drops off sharply to over one hundred feet. This is a spectacular reef and well worth a look. A boat is essential.

**Dunn's River Beach:** This is highly recommended for families since there are picnic tables and showers on this lovely beach, and there is a barrier reef less than two hundred yards offshore. Since the reef is quite shallow, divers who want to visit the outside face should go through the entrance at the eastern end. Outside, the reef drops off gradually to about fifty feet. This reef is quite pretty and exhibits a varied array of small tropical fish. A parking area is not far from the beach, with steps leading down to the beach.

**Sans Souci:** About one hundred yards off the Sans Souci Hotel beach is a reef, awash at low tide, which offers good snorkeling on the inside and good scuba diving on the outside. A channel through the reef is marked by a pipe imbedded in the coral. A variety of crevices and caves is found in the deeper coral. A boat can be rented from the hotel.

**The Blue Hole** is a well-known attraction a few miles east of Port Antonio. Depth is just over 185 feet. The water is brackish due to freshwater springs, and is chilly. Scuba divers will find a dive here interesting and unusual. Diving should not be attempted soon after a rain, as visibility will be poor. The blue light within the hole is unusual and has been compared with the Blue Grotto in Capri.

Snorkelers exploring the nearby reefs must be careful of the offshore current which comes from the Blue Hole.

# Chapter 8

# HAITI

**How to Get There:** By Pan Am Jet Clipper from New York in four and three-quarter hours or from Miami via Jamaica.

**Customs Regulations:** Visitors are allowed to bring in, duty free, personal clothing and a carton of cigarettes or fifty cigars or two pounds of tobacco plus a bottle of liquor.

**Travel Documents Required:** Visitors must have proof of identity and nationality and a smallpox vaccination certificate issued within three years. A Haitian tourist card is issued on arrival, and costs $2.00.

**Currency:** The Haitian gourde, valued at 20¢ U.S., is divided into 100 centimes. U.S. currency is accepted everywhere. There are no exchange restrictions.

**Hotels:** There is a fairly wide selection of hotels and guest-houses in Port-au-Prince and Pétionville with rates ranging upward from $5.00 per day. There are three good hotels and a guesthouse in Cap-Haïtien.

**Transportation:** Taxis and rental cars with or without chauffeur are available. Shared taxis, called Service (as in "rare niece") taxis, cost 50 centimes (10¢ U.S.) from point to point within the city. They have a strip of red cloth tied to the rear-view mirror and sometimes the word SERVICE stenciled on the side of the car.

Public transportation to outlying areas is by taxi, mostly unmetered, or Camiones, which are truck bodies with wooden seats. Check with the Pan Am office for current Camione schedules. Roads in Port-au-Prince are fair. Outside the city they are very poor.

**Medical Facilities:** Hospitals and doctors are situated in Port-au-Prince.

**Other Information:** French is the official language, but English-speaking Haitians are found almost everywhere. Transportation outside Port-au-Prince is difficult, due to the poor roads. Cap-Haïtien is accessible either by sea or by domestic air flights. Roads to Cap-Haïtien are in very poor condition.

The Pan Am office, at Place de la République Argentine (Tel: 3451 or 3200) is an excellent source of local information. The Haitian Government Tourist Bureau is about a block from the Pan Am office. The Tourist Bureau office in New York is at 30 Rockefeller Plaza.

## SKIN DIVING INFORMATION

Due to bad or nonexistent roads most of Haiti's beautiful coastline is inaccessible except by boat. Thus the diving spots available to most visitors are limited to the Port-au-Prince area (in the Gulf of Gonâve) and to a small stretch of coastline near Cap-Haïtien, on the north coast. Also, at the time of this writing, a number of police checkpoints in rural coastal areas inhibit free travel. The checkpoints were originally installed to guard against Cuban invasion. Visitors interested in traveling to the more isolated areas are advised to check with the Pan Am office or with the American Embassy to obtain current information about checkpoints.

**Laws:** Do not take female lobsters with eggs.

**Diving Gear for Sale:** A. de Metteis and Co., Place Geffard, and "Stecher," L'Abeille Building, Place Geffard, both in Port-au-Prince, offer a selection of basic equipment, including spear guns, at reasonable prices. Scuba gear is not available.

**Rental Gear:** None.

**Trips, Guides, Boats:** There are no diving specialty shops. However, Messrs. Gaston Baussan and Jean Coicou offer three-hour glass bottom/snorkeling trips daily. Their excursions leave at 10 A.M. from the Casino Pier, in Port-au-Prince. These trips are highly rec-

ommended for beginners. Guests are provided with a mask and a
float and are towed over Sand Cay—a lovely, shallow reef—by a
crewman. The trip provides an exciting, safe look at a coral reef
and is an excellent introduction to the busy life of the coral reef.
Baussan can also arrange for diving trips for experienced divers.

**Compressed Air:** Powell Industrial Works, Rue des Casernes,
Port-au-Prince, has a compressor. It is suggested that scuba divers
planning to bring tanks to Haiti contact this firm in advance to
make sure their compressor is operating.

**Currents, Winds:** The set of the current is to the west, but currents are seldom strong enough to be a problem to divers except
at the northwest and southwest tips of the island, and in narrow
passages between islands, or between shallow reefs.

In the Gulf of Gonâve, the winds usually blow offshore (from
the east) in the morning and onshore (from the west) in the afternoon. Consequently, morning is the best time for diving in this
Gulf, as the onshore winds are frequently strong enough to kick
up quite a surface chop. Northeast winds are usually found on the
north coast. Southeast winds are common on the south coast.

### GULF OF GONÂVE—NORTH SHORE

The shoreline trends northwest from Port-au-Prince to Montruis.
Within this area there are a number of close-in reefs which have
attractive coral but few fish. At the east end of Caicque Island
there is a shallow, attractive reef with plenty of pretty, small
tropical fish. It is a good area for beginners.

The best spot for diving in this region is "Les Arcadins," three
small islands about four miles southwest of Trou Forban Point.
The water is unusually clear (visibility over one hundred feet)
and the reef formations are exceptionally pretty. Plenty of game
fish, including schools of tarpon, are found here. Boats are available from the Kyona Beach Hotel, near Trou Forban, or from
fishermen at Saintard, a nearby village.

About three miles east of Les Arcadins (approximately two
miles offshore) is another excellent diving spot—Arcadins Reefs.

Depths vary from two to sixty feet. The coral is beautiful and the fish are plentiful. Highly recommended.

Many conchs are found in the waters west of the Kyona Hotel. Boats can be hired in the village of Carries.

Since the roads are very poor, the coastline north and west of Montruis is almost inaccessible except by boat. Visitors planning to explore this area are strongly urged to obtain the latest information about travel regulations and police checkpoints.

## GULF OF GONÂVE—SOUTH SHORE

There are two beautiful offshore reefs in the Gulf: Sand Cay and Pelican Cays. Sand Cay is about three miles offshore (west) of Port-au-Prince. Pelican Cays are about four and a half miles northwest of Port-au-Prince. Both are very attractive for exploration and fish watching. Few, if any, large fish are found here.

From Port-au-Prince west to Pointe Lamentin there are few reefs and little of interest to a diver.

From Pointe Lamentin to Pointe Gressier, a fringing reef offers very good snorkeling conditions in varying depths. Access is by car. This is a good area for beginners.

Divers wishing to explore reefs west of Pointe Gressier are urged to check with Pan Am or the Embassy in Port-au-Prince regarding current regulations on auto travel in this area. In any event, the roads here are not good and it is best to plan on visiting this region by boat.

From Grand Goâve Island west to Petit Goâve Bay, the coast is fringed by attractive reefs of varying depths. This stretch of coast offers good diving for beginners and, farther offshore, for deeper divers. Visibility is good and fish are seen in fairly large quantities.

From Petit Trou de Nippes to Pointe de Patte Large, several miles to the west, there is truly fantastic skin diving. Water visibility is excellent. The coral is beautiful and there are fish of all kinds, plus lobster. This is perhaps the best diving area in the Gulf of Gonâve, particularly for spearfishing. Baradères Bay, just west of Petit Trou de Nippes, is well protected and almost always calm and offers an excellent selection of reefs.

## GULF OF GONÂVE—GONÂVE ISLAND

There are no hotels or accommodations of any kind on this island. Visitors will have to sleep aboard their boat. Be sure to check on current Government regulations on visiting this island.

At the East Point there are lovely reefs and several wrecks, in varying depths. One wreck is found on Frigate de Croissant Island, which is one of the better spearfishing and lobstering areas in the Gulf. Reef depths vary from awash to about fifty feet.

Reefs can be found along the north and south coasts, but they are less extensive than along the eastern end.

## NORTH COAST

Cap-Haïtien is the only community of any importance on this coast. Roads are very poor, so divers are advised to hire fishing boats to get to the diving areas. Diving gear should be brought from home or purchased in Port-au-Prince. Compressed air is not available in Cap-Haïtien.

**North Coast, from Cap-Haïtien to the west:** From Cap-Haïtien to Port-de-Paix there are a great many offshore reefs and small islands. The water, except in heavy or rainy weather, is very clear (seventy-five feet visibility or more) and there are many fish. The reefs extend from Limbé Point to Palmiste Point and vary in depth from awash to over one hundred feet. They are extremely attractive and highly recommended for beginner and advanced diver alike.

Île de la Tortue, or Tortuga Island, formerly the stronghold of Pirate Henry Morgan and currently the scene of occasional treasure hunts, lies about four miles north of the mainland. The northern coast plunges vertically into a sea bottom six hundred to twelve hundred feet deep. During the rare periods of calm water, large grouper can be found in the underwater caves here.

The south coast of Tortuga Island shelves off less abruptly with reefs situated at the east and the west ends. There are plenty of fish. Tortuga is not recommended for the beginner but only for experienced divers in calm weather.

**North Coast, from Cap-Haïtien to the Dominican border:** In 1955 the famed undersea explorer Edwin Link recovered an anchor believed to have been from Columbus's flagship, *Santa Maria*. This anchor was found on Grand Mouton reef in Cap-Haïtien harbor and is now in the National Museum in Port-au-Prince. A wreck is stranded on this same reef, on the eastern side. During the course of his explorations, Link found a great number of anchors, cannon, fittings, etc., from old sailing vessles.

The Great Northern Reef extends from Limonade Pass, which is about five miles east of Cap-Haïtien, fourteen miles east to Fort Liberté Bay. This is a superb diving area. Shallow water is found inside the reef and a steep drop-off on the outside of the reef. Fish abound. Remnants of many very old wrecks are found here. A diver could spend weeks exploring this reef.

The best place for north-coast spearfishing is at the mouth of Fort Liberté Bay. Literally hundreds of large game fish of all kinds patrol the area. A fairly recent practice of dumping sugar-mill waste into the bay has clouded the water inside the bay to some extent.

### SOUTH COAST

Access to this coast is by yacht or by domestic airline flights to Les Cayes and by car or boat from there to the diving site. Due to the very poor condition of the roads here, overland travel is difficult.

Some of the missionaries at the West Indies Mission Headquarters, "Cité Lumière," near Les Cayes, are divers and are willing to assist visiting divers. Boats can be rented at Les Cayes.

The best diving area on the south coast is from Pointe Abacou east to Pointe Morne Rouge. There is an abundance of reefs in clear water, and there are plenty of fish and lobsters. This area is suitable for either beginners or advanced divers. Depths vary from awash to fifty feet.

Île-à-Vache—Cow Island—was a pirate headquarters. Many wrecks are located in these waters, especially on the eastern side of East Reef. The whole coastline of this offshore island is excellent for diving and is accessible by boat from Les Cayes. A freshwater lake, thought to have been caused by a meteorite, is located on the northwestern end of Vache. Fish are found in the lake.

*Chapter* 9

## PUERTO RICO

**How to Get There:** By Pan Am Jet Clipper from New York nonstop in three and a half hours or from Miami nonstop in two and a quarter hours. Service is also provided from Boston, Philadelphia, and Baltimore–Washington, and there are direct flights from Europe, Central and South America, and from the West Indies.

**Customs Regulations:** There are no customs formalities for visitors arriving direct from the United States. Visitors arriving from foreign islands or countries are allowed three hundred cigarettes, or fifty cigars, or three pounds of tobacco and a quart of wine or liquor duty free.

**Travel Documents Required:** Proof of identity and nationality is required of U.S. citizens.

**Currency:** Since Puerto Rico is a Commonwealth of the United States, U.S. currency and postage are used.

**Hotels:** There is a wide variety of hotels and guesthouses at rates ranging upward from $5.00 per day. Reservations are essential during the busy winter months.

**Transportation:** Taxis, buses, and rented cars are available. The roads are good, especially around San Juan. Intercity travel is by rented car or by bus.

**Medical Facilities:** There are excellent doctors and hospitals.

**Other Information:** The official language is Spanish. English is spoken in most places, but visitors might have language difficulties in remote villages.

The Pan Am ticket offices are located in San Juan at 665 Ponce de León Avenue; 307 Recinto Sur; at the Caribe Hilton Hotel; and at 1022 Ashford Avenue in Condado.

Offices of the Commonwealth of Puerto Rico Department of Tourism are at: Stop 22, Ponce de León Avenue, San Juan; at the International Airport; and at the Tourism Pier, Pier No. 3, Old San Juan. The New York office is at 322 West 45 Street.

## SKIN DIVING INFORMATION

Puerto Rico is a good place to learn diving since there are several well-qualified diving instructors and a variety of reefs suitable for divers of all levels of ability. This island is becoming increasingly popular with American divers because of its nearness to the United States and because of the close political associations which exist.

**Laws:** At the time of this writing, the Government is considering various conservation measures which would regulate some aspects of diving. Check with one of the professional dive shops, the Pan Am office, or the Government Tourist Office for current regulations.

**Diving Gear for Sale:** Don's Aquatic Shop, Highway No. 2, Km. 3, in San Juan (Tel: 782-0072) has a complete selection of diving equipment. Also, most sporting goods shops in the larger towns have a good stock of diving gear.

**Diving Gear for Rent:** Snorkeling gear is rented by Chuck Bangert, Holiday Watersports, Inc., Holiday Inn, San Juan (Tel: 791-2300, ext. 2484).

Snorkeling and (to qualified scuba divers) scuba equipment is rented by Don's Aquatic Shop; Jim Wilson, Caribe Divers, Hotel El Ponce Intercontinental, Ponce (Tel: 842-1140 or, at home, 842-5780); and by Walt Hendricks, El Conquistador Hotel, Fajardo (for hotel guests only, accompanied by instructor/guide) (Tel: Fajardo 560).

**Dive Shops, Trips, Guides, Boats, and Compressed Air:** Don's Aquatic Shop is a well-stocked dive shop, managed by a NAUI instructor. Regulators can be repaired here. Instruction in snorkeling and scuba diving and a variety of snorkeling and scuba trips is offered by Holiday Watersports in San Juan, by Walt Hendricks in Fajardo, and by Jim Wilson in Ponce. These diving excursions are planned and operated by professional divers and are highly recommended.

Compressed air is available from each of these diving specialists.

Bill Brown operates all-day trips to the Icacos Islands on a sailboat. Auto and boat transportation, diving equipment, and, if required, instruction in snorkeling are included in the rate for these all-day trips. This is an excellent way for a beginner to be introduced to diving. Tel: 724-3013, ext. 300, or 791-0726.

Fishing boats can be rented in the small coastal villages at varying rates, depending on the ability of the diver as a bargainer and his knowledge of Spanish.

Instruction in scuba diving is available at the San Jerónimo Hilton (Tel: 724-4000) and the Caribe Hilton (Tel: 725-0303) hotels. The instructors are Charles McCarthy and Jerry Crossman. Lessons are given in a swimming pool. Reef trips can be arranged.

At the La Concha Hotel (Tel: 723-6090), instructor Greg Kworek offers scuba lessons and reef trips, plus surfing and water skiing.

**Currents, Winds:** Currents are usually slight and not a problem for diving except that a stiff current, setting to the south, usually prevails off the eastern shores of the small islands off the eastern tip of the mainland.

North and northeasterly winds prevail during the winter months, creating heavy seas along the north coast. The north coast experiences easterly winds during the day for most of the summer months. The prevailing winds on the south coast are southeasterly.

Following is a description of the major diving spots, listed clockwise around the island beginning with the northwestern tip of the island.

NORTH COAST

The better diving areas here are those protected by offshore barrier reefs. Depending on the weather, visibility varies between thirty-five and seventy-five feet. The north coast is described below from west to east, beginning with Punta Borinquén on the northwestern tip of the island.

**Punta Borinquén to Punta Sardina:** Reefs and rocks extend up to a quarter mile offshore here. Snorkelers and scuba divers will find this area interesting. Access to the diving areas is by boat, available in the town of Aguadilla. Personnel at nearby Ramey Air Force Base have organized a large diving club, the Ramey Sea Lancers, whose members know the area thoroughly.

**Punta Puerto Nueva:** This point is fronted by reefs and small rocky islands which extend offshore about a mile to the west and a quarter mile to the east. This area is accessible by road. There is a good beach nearby for nondivers. Isletas de Garzas are a group of small islets lying about one and a quarter miles east of the point.

**From Punta Boca Juana east to Punta Salinas:** A reef parallels this shoreline about a mile offshore. This is a good diving area for experienced divers. East and west of Punta Salinas are small islands where spearfishing is usually good.

**The San Juan area:** An offshore reef lying from a half to one mile offshore is positioned along the coast opposite San Juan. The reef varies in depth from awash to forty feet. The outside of the reef drops off sharply to deep water. It can be reached by boat from the city and is used quite a lot by the professional diving instructors in the San Juan area. The "Submarine Gardens" are located near Boca de Cangrejos, east of San Juan.

EAST COAST

The east coast extends from Cabeza de San Juan, the northeast tip of the island, southwest to Punta Tuna. Except during heavy northeast winds, this coast offers excellent diving spots, principally around the several islands off the northern part of the coast. Culebra and Vieques islands are within this area. While diving conditions are quite good around these two islands, check first with local professional divers or with the U. S. Navy regarding the military control of this area. Large military installations are stationed on both islands, and the nearby waters are part of a naval firing range.

Varied conditions are experienced around the small islands off the northeast coast. Reefs here are suitable for most any underwater activity.

Diablo, a small islet off Cayo Lobos, offers spectacular underwater scenery, with many reefs and plenty of tropical fish, and is excellent for underwater photography. The east end of Isla Palominos contains many deep caverns, ravines, and spectacular coral formations. This area is excellent for sightseeing and photography. The western end of Isla Palominos is almost always calm, with reefs in varying depths. This is an excellent area for beginners.

The southern end of Icacos Island, north of Palominos, is another exceptionally good area for sightseeing, photographers, and snorkelers. There is a variety of coral here in depths of a foot or two down to forty feet. The northwestern tip of Icacos is a good area for shell collectors and spearfishermen. Quite a number of large yellowtail can be found here.

The areas just described are highly recommended and are easily accessible from the El Conquistador Hotel where Walt Hendricks makes his headquarters. He offers scuba and snorkeling lessons and specializes in trips for beginners. In this region, visibility varies between forty and, on rare occasions, one hundred and fifty feet.

**Punta Lima:** This point is just south of Fajardo. It is another area with offshore reefs of varying depths. Lima reef is about a half mile offshore of the point and, in calm weather, is a good spearfishing area.

**Cayo Santiago:** Cayo Santiago is surrounded by reefs, some of them less than two feet deep. Access is by boat, rented from fishermen at Punta Santiago. After a rain, this area is sometimes murky due to the discharge of nearby rivers. A wreck is in about twenty feet of water, one and a quarter miles southeast of this island. Another wreck in the same depth is about one and a quarter miles south of the island.

**Morro de Humacao south to Puerto Yabucoa:** In this region, there are numerous reefs extending offshore about a half mile. Boats can be hired from local fishermen.

## SOUTH COAST

The south coast extends west from Punta Tuna to Punta Jagüey (also called Cabo Rojo). Headquarters for south-coast diving is in Ponce, where Caribe Divers offer full facilities for visiting divers at the El Ponce Intercontinental Hotel.

**Punta Tuna west to Punta Pozuelo:** Reefs lie from a quarter mile to one mile offshore, in varying depths. This area is usually rather rough and diving can be done only on calm days. For this reason, however, spearfishing can be good—few divers have fished here.

**Punta Pozuelo west to Santa Isabel:** There are a number of small islets and rocks lying up to a mile offshore. The fringing reefs create good diving conditions. Access is by rented fishing boat.

**Isla Bebería, Isla Morrillito, and Isla Caja de Muertos:** Diving conditions around these islands are excellent. They are fringed by reefs and, usually, good spearfishing can be found in the area. Reefs vary in depth from less than two feet to forty feet. Spearfishing and sightseeing are the two main attractions here.

**Cayo Gata:** This is a small island about one third mile west of Punta Carenero (near Ponce). The entire area here is shallow and is good for spearfishing. Depths vary. The area is marked by light buoys. The island can be reached by boat. Amberjacks, lobsters, snappers, tarpon, and hogfish are found here.

**Ponce west to Punta Huyanilla:** Along this shoreline a reef is situated offshore in depths of thirty-five to 175 feet. For experienced divers, this area is good for spearfishing; however, it is a little deep for beginners. Silt from the Río Tallaboa can cloud the water after a rainfall. There are a number of small, reef-fringed offshore islands in this area which are good for diving.

**Punta Peñones west to Punta Tacón:** A reef, with various depths, extends across the western part of this area.

### WEST COAST

This coast extends northward from Punta Jagüey to Punta Borinquén. Since the prevailing winds are from the northeast and the southeast, the west coast, protected by the landmass of the island, is ordinarily calm. Unfortunately there are no professional diving guides or instructors here and the visiting diver will have to make arrangements with fishermen for boats to reach offshore diving sites.

Diving equipment is sold in sporting goods stores in Mayagüez, the largest city on this coast. Most of this shoreline can be reached by road. The entire coast, except in the vicinity of larger communities and rivers, has good diving conditions.

**Punta Jagüey north to Punta Guanajibo:** In this region there is a broken reef situated from a quarter mile to four miles offshore. Depths on the reef vary from awash to thirty feet. This area is good for spearfishing and, in some spots, photography. It is strongly urged that a local boat, manned by a crew with local knowledge, be used. Except for an occasional shallow reef near shore, this offshore reef is the only part of this region of interest to divers. Beginners are advised to stay close to the shallow reefs near shore, as the offshore reef is too deep.

**Mayagüez north to Punta Cadena:** Several rivers empty into this area and create cloudy water after a rain. There is a shallow reef, marked with a buoy, about a quarter mile southwest of Punta Algarrobo (north of Mayagüez). The water between the point and the reef is less than twenty feet deep and is rocky. Other reefs lie west and northwest of Punta Algarrobo, from one and a quarter to two and a half miles offshore.

# Chapter 10

# THE U. S. VIRGIN ISLANDS

**How to Get There:** (1) St. Croix: By Pan Am Jet Clipper nonstop from New York in three and a half hours, or three and a half hours from Miami via San Juan. (2) St. Thomas: Pan Am Jet Clipper nonstop from New York in three and a half hours, twenty minutes from San Juan by connection from Miami or New York. (3) St. John: By Antilles Air Boats (scheduled amphibian airplane service) from either St. Croix or St. Thomas, or by scheduled ferry boat from Red Hook, St. Thomas.

**Customs Regulations:** These islands are owned by the United States, so there is no customs inspection for arrivals from the U.S. Visitors arriving from non-U.S. points will be cleared through U. S. Customs as in any other U. S. Port of Entry

**Travel Documents Required:** Passports are not required of U.S. citizens, but some proof of identity and nationality should be brought along.

**Currency:** U.S. money is used.

**Hotels:** Both St. Croix and St. Thomas offer a wide variety of hotel and guesthouse accommodations at rates ranging upward from $6.00 per day. Reservations are essential in winter.

Accommodations on St. John are limited to the luxurious 108-room Caneel Bay Plantation and four cottage colonies, offering a total of thirty cottages. Reservations must be made well in advance.

Camping facilities are provided at the Virgin Islands National Park on St. John by the National Park Service. Complete camping equipment may be rented at the Park's Cinnamon Bay Campground, which is five miles by paved road from Cruz Bay. Completely furnished tents are $25.00 per week per couple, plus $7.00 per week for each additional person. Small, screened beach cottages can also be rented for $10.00 per day per couple, plus $2.00 per day for each additional person. Reservations are essential. Write, airmail, to The Concessioner, Cinnamon Bay Camp, St. John, Virgin Islands 00830. An Information Sheet on the Virgin Islands National Park is available from the National Park Service, Box 1707, St. Thomas.

The U. S. Virgin Islands Government Information Center publishes a summer and a winter hotel rate schedule and guide, "Where to Stay in the U. S. Virgin Islands."

**Transportation:** Taxis and rental autos are available. Drive on the left side. Interisland transportation is by air or scheduled ferry boats.

**Medical Facilities:** There is a hospital on each island.

**Other Information:** The Pan Am offices are excellent sources of local information. They are on the main streets of St. Croix and St. Thomas. Also, the Chambers of Commerce and the Department of Commerce Visitors Bureau in St. Thomas and Christiansted, St. Croix, can provide general tourist information. The Virgin Island Government Tourist Information office is at 16 West 49 Street in New York.

Specific information on skin diving, and fishing, is available from the Commissioner of Water Sports, Department of Commerce, St. Thomas.

U. S. Customs regulations provide that American visitors to the Virgin Islands may bring back purchases having a retail value of $200.00, including one gallon of liquor. Americans visiting other countries are limited to a $100.00 exemption, including one quart of liquor.

## ST. CROIX

The eastern end of this island is ringed by barrier reefs from Christiansted Harbor on the north shore around the east point to Manchenil Bay on the south shore. Diving conditions in this region are excellent, with plenty of shallow, colorful reefs for beginners and deeper reefs for experienced divers. Little diving is done at the western end due to lack of reefs.

Buck Island National Park is a priceless asset to St. Croix and is an area that should not be missed by any visitor. It is described below.

**Laws:** It is forbidden to spearfish, remove coral, or in any way disturb anything under the water at Buck Island, which is a National Park. This law is rigidly enforced.

Do not take female lobsters with eggs.

**Diving Gear for Sale:** Equipment is available at Water Sports Club International, Beach Hotel of St. Croix (Tel: 773-0576); C & M Caron, King's Alley, Christiansted; Bill Miller's Dive Shop, King's Wharf, Christiansted (Tel: 773-1355); and at Sea Rovers, Inc., King's Wharf, Christiansted (Tel: 773-0232).

**Diving Gear for Rent:** Snorkeling and scuba gear can be rented from Water Sports Club International and C & M Caron.

**Instruction, Guides, Boats:** Water Sports Club International offers instruction in snorkeling and scuba diving as well as boat rentals, reef trips, and other water sports. Trips to Buck Island are listed separately, below.

**Compressed Air:** Water Sports Club International and C & M Caron have compressors.

**Currents, Winds:** Currents are generally not strong enough to affect divers. At the east point, currents are usually one knot.

Winds are from the east and east-southeast most of the year. North and northeast winds occur at times during the winter.

**Fish:** Most commonly seen game fish are yellowtail, snappers, groupers, pompano, mackerel, and barracuda.

NORTH COAST

A reef of variable depth extends across the western half of Christiansted Harbor. The outside of the reef has yielded good catches of game fish.

About a quarter to one-half mile offshore, opposite Beauregard

Bay, is a coral area in water fifty feet deep or deeper. This coral garden extends east to Green Cay. This area is recommended for advanced divers but is too deep for beginners. Many game fish can be found here.

Green Cay, about a quarter mile offshore, is fringed with reefs, particularly on the eastern side. Good snorkeling and scuba diving conditions are found here.

From Coakley Bay east to Cottongarden Point, a reef extends almost continuously from one hundred to three hundred yards offshore. The reef is thirty to forty feet deep and is suitable for advanced divers. Large groupers are found here.

### BUCK ISLAND

A trip to Buck Island is strongly recommended. The coral formations are exceptionally beautiful and there are many shallow reefs on the eastern side of the island. Underwater signs help beginners identify the underwater growth. Three specialists offer boat trips daily from Christiansted:

1 – The Buck Island Ferry leaves at 10:30 A.M. from the Comanche dock and returns at 4 P.M. Tel: 773-1745 or 773-1049.

2 – Sea Rovers, Inc., King's Wharf, offers a choice of sailboats or diesel-powered boats. Trips leave at 10 A.M. from King Christian Wharf and return at 4. Sea Rovers can also arrange special snorkeling or scuba diving charter parties to Buck Island. Tel: 773-0232.

3 – Bill Miller's Shop offers trips on West Indian sailing sloops which leave King's Wharf at 10:15 and return at 4:30. Lunch is included with the trip. Diving trips can also be arranged. Tel: 773-1355.

Each of these organizations supply snorkeling equipment (and instruction, if needed) to their guests plus safety floats for beginning swimmers. Nonswimmers can view the reef through glass-bottomed boxes. These trips provide an excellent introduction to skin diving in an ideal setting.

SOUTH COAST OF ST. CROIX

Beautiful reefs lie about one hundred yards off Isaac Bay and Jack Bay and are ideal for beginning snorkeling enthusiasts. Experienced divers will find deeper water outside the reefs. Fish, conchs, and turtles are found here.

A barrier reef extends across Grapetree Bay and adjacent Turner Hole. The reef dries at low tide. Inside the reef the water is ten to fifteen feet deep, with lovely coral formations. It is an ideal, calm, safe spot for beginners. Outside the reef the bottom drops off to about forty feet. About one hundred yards farther offshore is the outer reef, which drops off steeply into very deep water.

This is an excellent area for divers of all interests and levels of ability. Instruction, boats, and guides are available from Water Sports Club International at Turner Hole.

A barrier reef, named the Seven Mile Reef, stretches almost unbroken from Grass Point west to Halfpenny Bay. It varies from fifty to two hundred yards offshore. Reef depths vary. This is another extremely interesting area for divers of all interests.

From Manchenil Bay west to Canegarden Bay, there are broken patches of coral at varying depths. This stretch of coast is similar, underwater, to Seven Mile Reef, except that the reef is not continuous.

Access to these reefs is by car or boat. A good road leads as far west as Grass Point. From there on, the road is not very good and, in many places, does not afford access to the coastline. For exploration west of Grass Point, it is suggested that boats be hired from Water Sports International at Turner Hole.

## ST. THOMAS

There are many good diving spots around this island, and the many nearby islands, suitable for everyone from novice to expert. Equipment and qualified instruction is readily available. Visibility is normally in the fifty- to hundred-foot range, and sometimes reaches 150 feet. The sea is calmest and clearest in summer.

**Laws:** None, at the time of this writing. However, the Government is considering the enactment of various regulations. Visiting divers are urged to consult with the Virgin Islands Diving Council, P. O. Box 2091, St. Thomas, or the Commissioner of Water Sports, Department of Commerce, St. Thomas, before planning spearfishing trips.

**Diving Gear for Sale:** Equipment is available from C & M Caron, Main Street (Tel: 774-2220); John Hamber, Sapphire Beach (Tel: 774-2375), and at Pineapple Beach and Bluebeard's Beach Club; and from Sea Saga Enterprises, Inc., on the waterfront, near the Antilles Air Boats office.

**Diving Gear for Rent:** Snorkeling and scuba gear can be rented from John Hamber and C & M Caron. Hamber rents tanks only; visitors must bring their own regulator.

**Scuba Instruction, Boats:** Joe Vogel at C & M Caron and John Hamber are instructors. Boats and diving trips can be arranged by John Hamber and by Virgin Islands Cruises (Tel: 774-2421). Current information on the availability of charter boats can be obtained from the Director of Water Sports, Department of Commerce, Box 1692, St. Thomas (Tel: 774-1331).

Joe Vogel is also president of the Virgin Islands Diving Council, P. O. Box 2091, St. Thomas, V.I. 00802.

**Compressed Air:** C & M Caron and John Hamber have compressors.

**Currents, Winds:** Currents are negligible in protected bays. They can reach four knots in some portions of Pillsbury Sound. Tidal currents reach three knots in Current Hole, which separates Great St. James Island from St. Thomas. It is recommended that the services of a professional diving guide, who will be familiar with the local currents, be used for diving trips to the offshore islands.

The easterly trade winds prevail.

NORTH COAST

This coast is described in geographical order, from west to east. From Mermaids Chair east to Target Point the water is accessible only by very poor dirt road to Botany Bay. This Bay is good for snorkeling among the many shallow reefs. Occasional large fish are seen.

From Target Point east to Neltjberg Bay, the shoreline is inaccessible except by boat with the exception of Stumpy Bay, where there is a road, of sorts. It is very poor and impassable in rainy weather. In Stumpy Bay the bottom drops off rather sharply to about eighty feet. There are game fish here and attractive reefs as well as several large caves. Since the current is sometimes strong, this area is recommended for advanced divers only.

Dorothea Bay is frequently lashed by heavy surf. During calm weather, this is a very good diving area, with lovely reefs and some game fish. Access is by road or boat.

There are plenty of shallow coral reefs on both sides of Hull Bay. The water is clear and calm since it is protected by a peninsula from the heavy surf. This area is recommended for beginners. Access is by road.

A spectacular beach and good swimming will be found at Magen's Bay, though there is little coral for snorkeling. The lifeguards on the beach prevent swimmers from going beyond the swimming area. This Bay is accessible by road but is not recommended for diving.

The coast from Picara Point east to Spring Bay is accessible by boat. The water is usually rough here and diving is not recommended, except when the water is calm.

Coki Bay is an excellent area for snorkeling and scuba diving. The water is quite clear, and there are beautiful reefs beginning about twenty feet offshore. The reef slopes off from shallow depths to about sixty feet maximum. This is highly recommended and is accessible by road.

Sapphire Beach is another excellent area for snorkeling and scuba diving. The reefs are close to shore, especially at the eastern end, and are twenty to twenty-five feet deep. There are no currents in this protected bay. Highly recommended. Accessible by road.

Cabrita Point is a good spearfishing area for experienced divers. The current is sometimes strong around the point. Frequently a heavy surf makes water entry and exit difficult. This area is accessible by boat or unimproved road.

### SOUTH COAST

Good snorkeling reefs are situated on the north and south sides of Bluebeard's Beach. The water is shallow and usually clear. Some game fish can be seen here. Access is by road.

Nazareth Bay is good for beginning snorkelers because of the shallow, calm water and attractive reefs. Reefs are located on either side of the bay. Access is by road, in poor condition.

Shallow reefs edge the eastern and western sides of Morningstar Beach. A few game fish are found here. This area is easily accessible from Charlotte Amalie by good road.

Water Island is not far from Charlotte Amalie and can be reached by the Water Island Ferry. Honeymoon Bay is an excellent snorkeling area with a good beach for nonswimmers. Visibility and spearfishing are good. A wreck is located just off Shipwreck Point in about twenty-five feet of water. Scuba diving is good in Flamingo Bay, on the southwest side of Water Island. Reefs, in clear water, are found just offshore with least depths of about forty feet. Access is by boat. Limestone Bay, on the northern part of Water Island, offers outstanding coral for photography and sightseeing.

Lindberg Bay is on the south coast of St. Thomas. On the eastern side of the bay are shallow reefs which are good for snorkeling. Quantities of conchs are seen here. Access is by road.

Brewers Bay features lovely reefs, which are excellent for snorkeling. The water is shallow and clear. Access is by road and swimming off the shore. Exercise care in entering the water, because of sharp coral and stones on the shore.

### SMALL ISLANDS OFF THE NORTH COAST OF ST. THOMAS

Inner and Outer Brass islands are easily reached by boat. These waters should be explored only by experienced divers.

Around most of the shoreline the bottom drops off sharply into deep water. Spearfishing is very good here and the visibility is seventy-five to one hundred feet.

Thatch Cay, off Coki Point, has a shallow reef along the south coast and an extensive reefy area off the southeastern end. The bottom drops off sharply to about one hundred feet along the northeastern end of the island, which is recommended only for experienced scuba divers.

Grass Cay is just east of Thatch Cay. The best diving spot around this small island is around the western point. This is a deep reef which should only be explored by experienced scuba divers.

Shark Island is a small islet about two hundred yards off Sapphire Beach. It can be reached by boat or by swimming. Snorkeling is very good here with lovely reefs in clear, shallow water.

## ST. JOHN

About seventy percent of St. John has been declared a National Park and is administered by the U. S. Department of the Interior. Spearfishing is prohibited in waters adjacent to the National Park shoreline. It is strongly recommended, therefore, that visiting divers not attempt to use spear guns along the St. John coastline at all. Should a spearfisherman inadvertently stray into the Park-controlled waters, he may be heavily fined.

**Compressed Air, Instruction, Gear for Sale and Rent, Trips:** All the services listed here are provided by Beth-Cruz Enterprises, Inc. (Tel: 774-1605). They specialize in pool lessons for novices. Snorkeling equipment can also be rented at the Cinnamon Bay Camp, Cinnamon Bay, and at Trunk Bay.

Snorkeling conditions are good around almost the entire coastline. Some of these diving areas are worthy of special mention.

Trunk Bay is the site of the National Parks Underwater Trail which features underwater signs identifying the various formations. The coral is lovely and in shallow water. Many species of tropical fish can be seen here. The beach is magnificent. Access is by road.

Johnson Reef, about three quarters of a mile off Hawksnest Point, and opposite Trunk Bay, is excellent for sightseeing and photography. Many fish are seen here. Depths vary from awash to over one hundred feet on the north side. Access is by boat.

Cinnamon Bay is another exceptionally good snorkeling area. The extensive reefs are in shallow water. Caves, lobsters, and fish are seen here. The beach is lovely. Access is by road.

Stevens Cay is the site of a reef and the wreck of a World War II gunboat. The surrounding waters are excellent for photographers. Access is by boat.

Chocolate Hole is another excellent diving spot for beginners. The reef is from awash to thirty feet deep. The water is very clear and many lovely tropical fish are found here. Access is by boat.

Lovengo Cay and the adjacent sea gardens are worth exploring. Coral heads are found in various depths. Access is by boat.

*Chapter 11*

# THE BRITISH VIRGIN ISLANDS

**How to Get There:** By Pan Am Jet Clipper to St. Thomas or St. Croix, with Antilles Air Boats flight from there to Tortola, or by scheduled ferry boat from St. Thomas.

**Customs and Travel Documents:** Personal clothing and equipment may be brought in duty free. Visitors must have proof of identity and nationality.

**Currency:** Although these are British islands, U.S. currency is used everywhere.

**Hotels:** Accommodations in the fourteen hotels are extremely limited and reservations are essential, especially during the winter. Rates start at $10.00 per day.

**Transportation:** On Virgin Gorda and Tortola there are taxis.

**Medical Facilities:** There is a doctor and a small hospital on Tortola.

**Other Information:** Tourist information is available from the British Virgin Islands Tourist Board, Road Town, Tortola, British Virgin Islands.

## SKIN DIVING INFORMATION

The thirty-six islands and the reefs of the British Virgin Islands offer skin diving conditions the equal of those anywhere. Since relatively few tourists visit these islands, there are plenty of fish in most areas. Interisland transportation is by boat and should be arranged for in advance, except for the daily ferry boats from St. Thomas. Several charter yachts in St. Thomas specialize in trips to the British V.I. Write to Island Yachts, Inc., Yacht Haven, St. Thomas, U. S. Virgin Islands (Tel: 774-2200), or to Blue Water Cruises, Box 748, St. Thomas, U. S. Virgin Islands (Tel: 774-0650).

**Diving Trips, Guides, Boats, Compressed Air:** Paul West, Long Bay Estate, West End, Tortola (Telephone or cable Virgin Isles communications, St. Thomas 774-1504), specializes in wreck diving (principally on Anegada Reef) and spearfishing. Diving trips of all types can be arranged, using his Bertram cabin cruisers. He has a compressor and rents equipment.

Bert Kilbride, Mosquito Island, Tortola (Telephone St. Thomas 774-1503), offers trips of all kinds to the numerous reefs. Equipment rentals and compressed air are available.

Air is available, at $2.50 per tank, from the Mariana Cay Hotel on Marina Cay, Tortola. Diving facilities are maintained for guests only. Equipment rentals and scuba instruction is not offered. Air is sold Monday to Friday during normal working hours. This small hotel is a relaxing and informal hideaway and is highly recommended, especially for experienced divers.

**Currents, Winds:** Currents are negligible, except through narrow passages between islands or reefs.

The easterly trade winds prevail.

It is reported that Robert Louis Stevenson's *Treasure Island* was based on pirate activities on Norman Island. Stories of sunken and buried treasure in these parts recur periodically.

The following islands are all very good diving sites. They are mostly reef fringed, have clear water, and are not yet fished out. To describe each separately would be repetitive and unnecessary. They are Peter Island, Cooper Island, Ginger Island, Round Rock, Fallen Jerusalem, Great Dog, West Dog, George Dog, Scrub Island, Guana Island, and Dead Man's Chest (where the pirate Blackbeard marooned fifteen of his pirates and started the Yo-ho-ho jingle).

The wreck of the S.S. *Roan* lies in from twenty feet of water at the stern to ninety feet at the bow, off the southwest tip of Salt Island. The remains of this old steam sailing vessel are suitable for photography and are the home of quantities of game fish.

Around Tortola, there are excellent areas for snorkelers on the reef off the northeast portion of Fat Hog Bay, on the east coast. Another excellent reef trends southwest from Hodges Fort over a mile to Nora Hazel Point. Access is by boat from Road Town.

Around Beef Island the best places for snorkeling are the reefs along the south coast in Well Bay and in the bay west of Well Bay. The depths vary from awash to thirty feet. The water is almost always calm. Access is by boat.

Visitors to Virgin Gorda will find excellent diving conditions around the southern portion, near Spanish Town. Perhaps the most interesting section of the island is The Baths, where there are strikingly beautiful granite formations, lovely coral, and fish in variable depths. The huge granite boulders here are unique in the Caribbean and are thought to have been brought to the island by glaciers during the Ice Age.

Gorda Sound, on the north shore, contains many rocks, reefs, and small islands, and is an excellent diving area. Mosquito Island and Prickly Pear Island are fringed with reefs. Since these outlying reefs are exposed to the trade winds, the water is sometimes a bit rough.

The barrier reef extending from Pajaros Point (at the eastern tip of Virgin Gorda) west to Prickly Pear Island affords good snorkeling when seas are calm. Inside the reef, depths vary from awash to thirty-five feet. Outside the reef, the bottom shelves off gradually to about sixty feet. Access is by boat.

About ten miles north of Virgin Gorda is the island of Anegada. The surrounding reefs here provide some of the best diving conditions in the Caribbean, but for experienced divers only. Experienced spearfishermen, photographers, and wreck hunters will find a wide variety of lovely reefs, many large fish, and over one hundred known wrecks, all in water having visibility consistently over one hundred feet. This reef can be reached only by boat, which must be skippered by a man thoroughly familiar with the reef. Over the centuries this reef has doomed many ships, some of which no doubt contained treasure. Most of the wrecks are on the northeastern edge of the reef.

# Chapter 12

## ST. MAARTEN

**How to Get There:** By Pan Am Jet Clipper, five and a half hours from New York via St. Croix and St. Thomas.

**Customs Regulations:** None. This is a free port. Baggage is not inspected.

**Travel Documents Required:** Proof of citizenship and identity, a smallpox vaccination certificate issued within three years, and a return or onward ticket are required.

**Currency:** Dutch guilders, also called florins (written: Fl.), are exchanged at Fl. 1.85 to $1.00 U.S. On the French side of the island, French Francs (written: N.F.) are exchanged at N.F. 5 to $1.00 U.S. U.S. currency is accepted everywhere and changing U.S. currency into local currency isn't absolutely necessary.

**Hotels:** There are thirteen hotels with accommodations at rates ranging upward from $8.00 per day, single, winter races, European plan. Reservations during the winter months are advised.

**Transportation:** Taxis and rental autos are available. Most roads are paved.

**Medical Facilities:** There is a small hospital.

**Other Information:** The island is half Dutch (St. Maarten) and half French (St. Martin). There are no restrictions on travel between the two halves. The island is a completely free port with extremely low prices on cameras, liquor, jewelry, etc. Philipsburg is the Dutch capital; Marigot, the French capital. Complete tourist information and a current hotel list can be obtained from Pan American agents, S. E. L. Maduro and Sons in Philipsburg

(Tel: 2202); the St. Maarten Tourist Commission in Philipsburg; or from the Netherlands Windward Islands Information Center, 1270 Avenue of the Americas, New York City.


## SKIN DIVING INFORMATION

Conditions are good for beginning snorkelers, with many shallow, attractive reefs. Spearfishermen will find more fish at nearby Anguilla, which can be reached by diving boat from St. Maarten.

Because of copper deposits on some parts of the sea floor, the fish in some areas are not edible. If these fish are eaten, copper poisoning is likely to occur. Be sure to consult with locals before eating fish taken from these waters.

**Diving Gear for Sale and Rent, Trips, Guides, Boats, Compressed Air:** Jeff Adams operates a well-equipped dive shop, Water World, Inc., in Philipsburg. Snorkeling and scuba instruction and trips are available, plus equipment sales and rentals (scuba gear is not rented). Adams has the island's only air compressor.

Equipment can also be purchased in Marigot from Jules Petit, Vere Richardson, or Emilio de Polo et Fils.

Boats can be hired from Jeff Adams; Claude Lake of the Lido Guest House (Tel: 2371), which is right on the beach in Philipsburg; Charles Oberle, Simpson's Bay; or Fritz Halley, Simpson's Bay. All these men are good divers and guides. Boats can also be obtained from fishermen on the dock at Marigot.

**Currents, Winds:** Currents around the island are normally not too stiff. A strong east-to-west current is frequently felt on Man o' War Reef, about two miles offshore from Philipsburg.

The easterly trade winds prevail.


### NORTH COAST

Along the entire coast are shallow reefs which are excellent for beginners. Few game fish are seen here, but the lovely coral and small tropical fish make this area a good one for sightseeing.

Visibility is usually between fifty and seventy-five feet. When the sea is calm, the North Point is good for spearfishing.

Also, in calm weather, the Anguilla Channel (between St. Maarten and Anguilla) offers good spearfishing for experienced divers. The bottom here shelves off from the shore to depths of ten to fifteen feet, then drops off again to about forty to sixty feet about 250 yards offshore. Hire a boat in Marigot.

### EAST COAST

This is the windward side and is frequently too rough for diving. In calm seas this area is fine for all diving activities. The best diving area on this coast is Green Cay, in Oriental Bay. Access is by boat. Clear water, big fish, and beautiful coral in variable depths are found here.

The waters around Pinels Island and Château Cay are also attractive.

Tintamarre Island (also called Flat Island) waters are excellent for diving, especially around the south coast. The reefs are photogenic and the fish are plentiful.

### SOUTH COAST

This coast is not especially good for experienced divers, except for Man o' War Reef. Beginners will find some coral along the coastline from Gray Point (the northwest end of Simpsons Bay) north to the north point. However, this coast is not as interesting for divers as the north coast.

Man o' War Reef (also called Proselyte Reef) is the site of the wreck of the 32-gun English frigate *Proselyte*, which ran aground here in 1801. Several cannon, anchors, and various fragments of copper sheathing and spikes are found here. There is plenty of coral and there are some game fish to be seen. Depths vary from eighteen to fifty feet. The reef is slightly over two miles south-southwest of Philipsburg. Access is by boat. This reef should be explored only by experienced scuba divers because of the sometimes stiff current.

# Chapter 13

## SABA

**How to Get There:** By Pan Am Jet Clipper to St. Maarten with a connecting flight by Windward Islands Airways or by boat to Saba.

**Customs Regulations:** Saba is a free port. No customs examination.

**Travel Documents Required:** Proof of identity and nationality and a return ticket off the island are required.

**Currency:** Dutch guilders are used here—see the chapter on St. Maarten. U.S. currency is accepted everywhere.

**Hotels:** The Captain's Quarters is the only "tourist" hotel on the island. There are three guesthouses: Caribe Guest House, the Windwardside Guest House, and the Bottom Guest House. Rates are modest. Advance reservations are suggested in winter.

**Transportation:** One or two jeep taxis meet incoming flights. Roads are very steep and narrow—visitors are advised to use a taxi.

**Other Information:** Nights can be chilly, so bring a sweater. Tourist information and current hotel rates can be obtained from the Netherlands Windward Islands Information Center, 1270 Avenue of the Americas, New York, or from The Administrator, Saba Tourist Commission, Saba, Netherlands Antilles. Although the island is Dutch, English is spoken everywhere.

## SKIN DIVING INFORMATION

Saba is ruggedly beautiful, unspoiled, and unique in appearance. The island is the mountainous tip of a long dead volcano and rises vertically out of the sea. There are two communities (where women greatly outnumber the men), Windwardside and Bottom (which is eight hundred feet above sea level). Due to the depths of the surrounding waters, this is not a good area for beginners. For experienced divers who can snorkel down to thirty to fifty feet, Saba is ideal.

Underwater visibility is usually one hundred feet or more. There are extensive forests of large staghorn coral "trees" as well as plenty of large game fish and Hawksbill and Green turtles.

Visitors must bring all necessary equipment since neither equipment nor compressed air is available here. A boat is necessary for diving anywhere around the island.

Calvin Holm is an expert diver who will guide visiting divers around the island. He can also arrange for boats. Address is: Calvin R. Holm, Windwardside, Saba, N.A. During the weekdays, he can be found at the Bottom Government Garage, in Bottom.

A ledge, mostly coral, encircles Saba at a depth of thirty to fifty feet. This ledge extends to seaward for one hundred to three hundred feet, where the sea bottom drops off into very deep water. Diving is good around the entire island, except that the east (windward) coast is frequently too rough.

To describe each portion of the coastal waters would be repetitive due to the similarity of all portions of the coast. Exceptionally lovely coral gardens and large fish are found on the northwest coast between Torrens Point and North Point. Generally, more big fish are found along the north coast than elsewhere.

The Saba Bank is an excellent place for the truly expert spearfisherman to explore. It commences about three miles southwest of Saba and is several miles wide and over thirty miles long.

Depths vary from twenty-five to over one hundred feet. The
bottom is mixed: coral, sand, and rock. It has not been completely
explored, although many large game fish have been taken here.
It can be reached by boat from Saba and can be considered
virgin territory for skin diving.

*Chapter 14*

# ANGUILLA

**How to Get There:** By Pan Am Jet Clipper to St. Maarten and from there by Windward Islands Airways, Leeward Islands Air Transport, or boat to Anguilla.

**Customs Regulations:** Personal belongings and a maximum of one hundred cigarettes are allowed duty free.

**Travel Documents Required:** Proof of identity and nationality and an onward or return ticket are required.

**Hotels:** The Rendezvous Hotel has ten double rooms at winter rates of $15.00 single and $20.00 double. Summer rates are $10.00, American plan. There are three other small guesthouses with a total of twenty rooms. Rates are modest.

**Transportation:** Taxis.

**Other Information:** The island is English, so language is no problem. For tourist information and the current hotel list write to the St. Kitts, Nevis, Anguilla Tourist Board, P. O. Box 132, St. Kitts, W.I. Accommodations are quite limited, so advance reservations are advised, especially in winter.

## SKIN DIVING INFORMATION

Anguilla is a flat, low island surrounded by some of the most beautiful beaches in the West Indies. The reefs are exceptionally beautiful and the water is gin clear. These features make Anguilla one of the best diving spots in the Caribbean. There are plenty of fish of all kinds, plus turtles and lobsters. If accommodations

on the island are not available, the diving sites can be reached
in day trips by boat from St. Maarten.

There are no dive shops or any facilities for visiting divers.
Visitors must bring all their own equipment. Boats can be hired
from fishermen on the beach or through the hotels. Currents are
negligible. The easterly trade winds prevail.

### NORTH COAST

Beginners as well as expert divers will find wonderful diving
conditions along this coast. Extensive coral reefs fringe the coastline at depths varying from awash to sixty feet, depending on the
distance from shore. Roads lead to West End Bay, Road Bay,
Crows Bay, and Island Harbour. Elsewhere, access is by boat.

Sandy Island is a small, palm-studded island surrounded by
unbelievably beautiful reefs in very clear water. The island lies
north of Road Bay. These reefs form one of the prettiest coral
gardens in the Caribbean.

Scrub Island, off the northeast tip of Anguilla, is a very good
area for spearfishing except along the northeast end, where heavy
seas are usually encountered.

About two miles north of Flat Cap Point on Anguilla will be
found Seal Islands Reefs. This six-mile-long reef extends westward
to Prickly Pear Cays and is another exceptionally good diving
area. Depths vary from awash to fifty to sixty feet.

Dog Island, about eighteen miles north-northwest of the western
tip of Anguilla, is one of the few remaining spearfishing paradises.
Large amberjacks, mackerel, tuna, dolphins, barracuda, and other
game fish are seen here in schools. Highly recommended for
experienced divers.

### SOUTH COAST

There is plenty of lovely coral along this coastline, but seas
are too heavy for diving when the trades are from the southeast.
However, in Sandyhill Bay, Little Harbour, and Rendezvous Bay,

peninsulas protect the water on the eastern sides of the bays and wonderful snorkeling conditions are found. The reef off Rendezvous Bay is especially lovely and the beach itself is remarkably beautiful. The comfortable Rendezvous Hotel is situated here.

Along this coast, roads lead to Sandy Hill Bay, Forest Bay, Blowing Point Harbour, and Shoal Bay. Elsewhere, access to the reefs is by boat.

*Chapter 15*

# ST. BARTHÉLEMY

**How to Get There:** By Pan Am Jet Clipper to St. Maarten with a connecting flight by Windward Islands Airways to St. Barts.

**Customs Regulations:** This is a free port. There is no customs examination of luggage.

**Travel Documents Required:** Proof of identity and nationality and a return or onward ticket.

**Currency:** The island is French, so francs are the official currency. However, U.S. dollars are accepted freely and there is no real necessity for changing money.

**Hotels:** There are only three small hotels on the island. Reservations are essential in winter.

**Transportation:** Taxis, auto rentals, and motor scooters (from the St. Barts Yacht Club).

**Other Information:** The island's shortened name, St. Barts, is commonly used. Perfumes, cameras, and other items can be purchased here at low, duty-free prices. The landlocked harbor is one of the best, and most picturesque, in the West Indies. Further tourist information can be obtained from The Mayor, Gustavia, St. Barthélemy, French West Indies.

## SKIN DIVING INFORMATION

The coastlines can be described as follows: the north coast runs roughly from east to west, and has many deep indentations, the largest of which is St. Jean Bay; the south coast runs from northeast to southwest; the west coast runs roughly from northwest to southeast. Gustavia, the capital, is on the west coast.

**Diving Gear for Sale:** Limited quantities of snorkeling equipment can be found at Establishment Magras, Berry et Fils, and at the Yacht Club, all of which are in Gustavia.

**Diving Gear for Rent:** The only equipment available is that which is used on diving trips arranged through the Yacht Club.

**Boats and Guides:** Boats can be rented through Mr. De-Haenen, Eden Rock Hotel, the Yacht Club, or direct from fishermen. The Yacht Club supplies guides for trips arranged through the Club.

**Compressed Air:** The Yacht Club has a compressor.

**Currents, Winds:** Currents are weak except between the offshore rocks and the mainland. The easterly trade winds prevail.

Good quantities of game fish can be found around the entire island. However, not all of the coastline has attractive underwater scenery.

### NORTH COAST

It is frequently rough here and diving should be attempted only by experienced divers used to choppy seas. Good diving conditions are found around the offshore islands of Chevereau, Fregate, and Tortue. Many fish and lobster as well as coral reefs and underwater caves are located in this region. Beginners can snorkel here on the leeward sides of the islands. Access is by boat. The depths of the reef vary.

A fringing reef in varying depths is situated in St. Jean Bay. However, this bay is exposed to northeasterly winds which create choppy waters unsuitable for diving.

### SOUTH COAST

From the southeast point, southwest to the point just off Coco Island, the seas are frequently heavy, there is little coral, and access is difficult. Not recommended. Saline Bay has a little coral, but the bottom is mostly sandy.

## EAST COAST

The rocks just off Gustavia are worth exploring. The coral is attractive and access is no problem. This is the best place for beginners to snorkel. North and south of Gustavia the coastline is steep and suitable for spearfishing. Access is by boat.

## OFFSHORE ISLETS

North of St. Barts is a group of widely separated rocks. The surrounding waters are excellent for spearfishing. It is strongly urged that only experienced divers attempt diving here since strong currents and heavy seas are common.

Great Grouper Rocks and the nearby Little Groupers are exceptionally good areas. Northeast, about one and a half miles, is Roche Table, another good spearfishing area. East of the Groupers is Fourche Island and east of Fourche, about a mile, is Boulanger and, nearby, Navire Island. Beef Barrel Island is south of Fourche. Excellent spearfishing is found around all of these small islets.

*Chapter 16*

# ST. EUSTATIUS

**How to Get There:** By Pan Am Jet Clipper to St. Maarten with connecting flight on Windward Islands Airways to St. Eustatius.

**Customs Regulations:** Personal equipment and clothing may be brought in duty free.

**Travel Documents Required:** U.S. citizens must have proof of identity and nationality and a return or onward ticket.

**Currency:** Dutch guilders, or florins, are used here. See the chapter on St. Maarten.

**Hotels:** There are two small guesthouses.

**Transportation:** Taxis.

**Other Information:** Although the island is Dutch, English is spoken everywhere. Tourist information can be obtained from the Administrator, Oranjestad, St. Eustatius, N.A., or from the Netherlands Windward Islands Information Center, 1270 Avenue of the Americas, New York.

St. Eustatius is usually referred to as Statia.

## SKIN DIVING INFORMATION

The island shoreline is rather steep. Shallow water is found for about two hundred yards or so offshore, then the bottom shelves off to fifty feet or more. The best diving is on the west (leeward) coast from Interlopers Point north to the south end of Jenkins Bay.

Visitors should bring all their own equipment since none is available for purchase or rent, and compressed air is not available. Currents are usually weak and do not present a problem for divers. Easterly trades prevail. Boats can be hired from fishermen.

### WEST COAST

Much of this coastline has a sandy bottom, but some coral is found north of Oranjestad, beginning at Interlopers Point and continuing north to Jenkins Bay. Depths are variable. Access is by boat.

North of Jenkins Bay the coast is fringed by coral and rock up to the North Point, where heavy seas are usually the rule. A similar-type bottom extends about a mile southward from the old fort near Oranjestad.

### EAST COAST

Most of the time, the sea breaks heavily here. However, on the rare calm days, diving conditions are suitable along this coast from the southern end of Concordia Bay to White Wall. This coast should be explored only by experienced divers.

Generally speaking, the reefs and underwater terrain around Statia are not attractive enough to attract divers and the island, although charming and peaceful, is hardly worth visiting for diving. However, since very little diving is done here, visitors will find good quantities of game fish.

*Chapter 17*

## ST. KITTS

**How to Get There:** By Pan Am Jet Clipper to St. Maarten or Antigua with a connecting flight to St. Kitts.

**Customs Regulations:** Personal belongings and one hundred cigarettes will be admitted duty free.

**Travel Documents Required:** Proof of identity and nationality and an onward or return ticket are required of U.S. citizens for stays of up to six months.

**Currency:** B.W.I. (pronounced: Bee Wee) dollars are exchanged at $1.68 B.W.I. to $1.00 U.S. Bills and coins are issued in the same denominations as U.S. currency.

**Hotels:** There are ten hotels, guesthouses, and cottages offering a total of thirty-seven rooms at rates ranging upward from $9.00 per day.

**Transportation:** Taxis and rental autos are available. A paved road encircles the island, except the southeastern tip.

**Medical Facilities:** There are two small hospitals.

**Other Information:** Most beaches have black sand except those around the southeast peninsula, which has white coral sand. Tourist information and a current hotel list, with rates, is obtainable from the St. Kitts, Nevis, Anguilla Tourist Board, Basseterre, St. Kitts, W.I.

### SKIN DIVING INFORMATION

St. Kitts is not one of the better islands for skin diving. Snorkeling can be enjoyable in the areas indicated below, where there are small areas of coral. Experienced divers will find good spear-fishing on the east coast, but only during periods of calm weather, mostly in September and October.

**Diving Gear:** Limited amounts of basic equipment are sold by A. M. Losada, Ltd., and by S. L. Hosford and Co., Basseterre.

**Boats, Guides, Compressed Air:** Boats can be obtained through the hotels or by negotiating directly with fishermen. Compressed air is not available. There are no dive shops or guides, but Captain J. L. Wigley of Delisle, Walwyn and Co., Ltd., Pan Am agents, is an experienced diver and will assist visiting divers wherever possible.

**Currents, Winds:** Currents are not strong, except at times around the southeastern tip of the island. In the Narrows, a shallow passage between St. Kitts and Nevis, east/west currents are sometimes stiff.

The easterly trade winds prevail.

### WEST COAST

The sea bottom along this coast is mostly sandy and uninteresting, except at the southern end. A wreck is situated a few yards south of the pier off Fort Smith, in Basseterre Bay. The depth is about ten feet.

The southeast portion of Frigate Bay is the best area near town for snorkelers. Depths vary from a couple of feet to deeper water. The coral is pretty with sea fans and other marine growth. Access is by boat.

From Salt Point south to Horseshoe Point, the bottom is mixed: rock, sand, and coral. Snorkeling conditions are fair. Access is by boat.

### EAST COAST

This is the windward side and usually is too rough for diving. The following areas should be explored only when seas are calm, and by experienced divers only.

Dieppe Bay Point, on the northeast corner of the island, has extensive reefs where good quantities of game fish can be found. Access is by road. Depths vary from awash to forty feet.

Off Barker's Point is an extensive shoal extending almost due north. Depths are awash to forty feet. Game fish are found here. Access is by road.

From Barker's Point south to Muddy Point, reefs fringe the shoreline. Spearfishing is good. Access is by boat, since there is no road here. Not especially recommended unless a boat can be hired nearby because it is hardly worth the long boat trip around the island from Basseterre.

*Chapter 18*

# NEVIS

**How to Get There:** By Pan Am Jet Clipper to St. Maarten or Antigua with connecting flight to Nevis. A Government boat ferries between St. Kitts and Nevis daily except Sunday and Thursday.

**Customs and Travel Documents:** See St. Kitts.

**Currency:** B.W.I. dollars. See St. Kitts.

**Hotels:** There are nine hotels and guesthouses offering a total of eighty rooms as well as a few private cottages for rent. Rates start at $6.00 per day.

**Transportation:** Taxis. A limited number of rental autos are available. Arrange for these through the hotel. A paved road encircles the northern two-thirds of the island. Secondary roads, in poor condition, give access to the south end of the island.

**Medical Facilities:** There is a small hospital.

**Other Information:** Mrs. Mary Pomeroy at the Nisbet Plantation Inn is extremely well informed on the island, its history, and its people. She is always willing to help visitors wherever possible.

A hotel list with current rates is available from the St. Kitts, Nevis, Anguilla Tourist Board, Basseterre, St. Kitts.

## SKIN DIVING INFORMATION

Diving conditions here are not the best in the West Indies, but, in the spots listed below, are rather good. The island itself is attractive and peaceful, and is an ideal spot for a quiet rest. The waters here have not yet been fished out, so plenty of good-sized game fish, lobsters, and turtles are seen.

**Diving Gear for Sale:** Limited quantities of snorkeling gear can be purchased from Evelyn's and by Trade and Travel, Ltd., in Charlestown. Rental gear is not available.

**Boats, Guides:** Boats and diving trips can be arranged by Mr. Desmond Sargent through Messrs. Trade and Travel, Ltd. Sargent is the most experienced diver on the island. He has an air compressor. Scuba divers planning to bring their own tanks are advised to write to him in advance to make sure that his compressor is available.

**Currents, Winds:** Currents are weak except in the Narrows, between Nevis and St. Kitts. In this narrow, shallow passage the east to west currents can be very stiff.

## NORTH COAST

The best diving on the island is along this coast. A barrier reef, from two hundred to five hundred yards offshore, protects the shallow waters near the shoreline. Inside the reef, depths vary from four to ten feet with good sightseeing for beginners. There are many coral heads, sea fans, and small tropical fish here. The barrier reef is awash at low tide.

Only strong, experienced divers, accompanied by a boat, should explore the waters north of the reef because of the strong current. The depths here vary from ten to forty feet. The nearest road access is through Newcastle Village.

When the sea is calm, Booby Island and Cow Rocks, three quarters of a mile and one and a quarter miles north of Nevis, are fair for spearfishing. Game fish, turtles, and lobsters are found here.

## WEST COAST

The bottom along this shoreline is mostly sandy with little, if any, coral.

In Cade's Bay, about three hundred yards offshore, are the

sunken remains of Jamestown, after which Jamestown, Virginia, was named. An earthquake in 1680 caused the village to sink. Little can be seen now since almost everything lies buried beneath the sand, awaiting proper archaeological excavation. Jamestown lies about a quarter mile north of the ruins of Fort Ashby in twenty to thirty feet of water. Local fishermen know the area well.

A little over three miles due west of Cade's Point is Monkey Shoals. The bottom here is mixed: sand, rock, and coral. Spearfishing here is good in depths varying from twenty-five to fifty feet. For experienced divers, this is one of the best areas near Nevis. Access is only by boat.

### EAST COAST

This coast is usually too rough for diving. It is fringed by a reef. Outside the reef, the depth is about ten feet. The bottom shelves off within a mile to very deep water. Only experienced divers should explore this coast, and only during periods of calm seas.

### SOUTH COAST

This coastline is rocky, with little coral. The seas here are usually pretty choppy. Spearfishing is fair, especially around Indian Castle on the southeast end. Access is by poor road or by a long boat trip from Charlestown. It is hardly worth the long trip to get here.

# Chapter 19

# ANTIGUA

**How to Get There:** By Pan Am Jet Clipper in less than four hours nonstop from New York.

**Customs Regulations:** Personal clothing and equipment are admitted duty free.

**Travel Documents Required:** U.S. citizens must have proof of citizenship and nationality and a return or onward ticket. Yellow fever and cholera vaccination certificates are required if coming from an infected area.

**Currency:** B.W.I. (pronounced: Bee Wee) dollars are exchanged at $1.68 B.W.I. to $1.00 U.S.

**Hotels:** There are twenty-seven hotels and guesthouses offering a total of 818 rooms at rates ranging upward from $6.00, single, winter rates, American plan. Reservations are essential in winter.

**Transportation:** Taxis or rental autos. Divers staying for any length of time are advised to rent a car. Taxis are expensive.

**Medical Facilities:** There is a general hospital in St. John's.

**Other Information:** Antigua and its dependency Barbuda are newly independent members of the British Commonwealth. The Pan Am office is at 37 High Street, St. John's (Tel: 241), and is a good source of general tourist information. Tourist information and a current hotel list is available from the Antigua Tourist Board, P. O. Box 363, St. John's, Antigua, West Indies.

## SKIN DIVING INFORMATION

Antigua is an excellent place to learn diving. Conditions are excellent for both novice and expert. Reefs are situated around the entire island, and the coastline is deeply indented with many protected bays.

**Diving Gear for Sale:** Snorkeling equipment is sold at Stephen R. Mendes, Ltd., and from Messrs. Alexander Parrish, both in St. John's. Rental gear is not available.

**Scuba Instructions:** Antigua Water Sports, Kensington Court, St. John's (Tel: 806), have offices in most of the hotels. As this is written, it seems likely that there will be a change in the management of this diving facility. Therefore, visitors to Antigua are advised to write in advance to learn of the services currently being offered, rates, and the name of the manager.

**Boats, Trips, Guides:** Lee Westcott, P. O. Box 5, Crosbie's, Antigua (Tel: 739), has several boats for diving expeditions. All equipment and instruction are included in his charter rates.

Antigua Water Sports have daily scuba lessons, and reef and wreck trips.

V. E. B. Nicholson and Sons, English Harbour, Antigua, are agents for a great number of yachts. Several of them are fully equipped with diving gear, air compressors, and other necessary equipment. Extended diving trips through the islands can be arranged and are especially recommended for small groups of divers.

**Compressed Air:** Antigua Water Sports and Antigua Gases, Ltd., corner of Factory and Palm roads, can fill aqualung tanks.

**Currents, Winds:** Currents are generally weak and do not present a problem to divers. The easterly trade winds prevail.

NORTH COAST

Skin diving conditions are excellent along this coast. There are numerous offshore islands and reefs in clear water. Beginners will find shallow, fish-filled reefs close to shore. Experts can use the deeper offshore areas. Photographers will find plenty of interesting subjects. Visibility averages fifty to seventy feet, depending on sea conditions.

A more or less continuous reef stretches across the north coast about a mile offshore. Beginning in the west, with Diamond Bank and Salt Fish Tail, it continues east, becoming Kettle Bottom Shoals. At Bird Island Reef, the shoal area trends south through Great Bird Island and continues into Belfast Bay, on the mainland.

The area just described is exceptionally interesting and pretty. Depths vary from awash to forty feet, with much of it less than seven feet deep. Access to this reef is by boat.

The northeast section of the coast is especially attractive, around Maid Island, Long Island, Bird Island Reef (northeast of Long Island), and Great Bird Island (on the eastern end of North Sound).

### EAST COAST

Due to the trade winds, this coast is usually rather rough. There are some good diving areas here, though, which should be explored only by experienced divers.

A reef extends north from Green Island for a mile or so. This reef, and the waters around Green Island, are attractive for diving with numerous coral heads in depths to twenty feet. Access is only by boat.

### SOUTH COAST

Horseshoe Reef is situated on the northeastern end of Willoughby Bay, and Mamora Reef is on the southwest side. Both reefs offer plenty of diving spots, and are especially good for beginners. Depths vary to fifteen feet around the reefs. To seaward, the bottom gradually slopes off into deep water. Visibility in Willoughby Bay is sometimes poor, but the waters outside the reef are ordinarily very clear.

To the west, Middle Reef and, farther out, Cade Reef lie a few hundred yards southwest of Cade Bay. These are really very good

diving areas for any underwater activity. The channel separating
the two reefs is twenty to thirty-five feet deep. Quantities of
conchs are found around Cade Reef. Access is by boat.

## WEST COAST

Irish Bank, over a mile offshore, west of Morris Bay, is an
excellent spearfishing area. Depths vary from seven to thirty feet.
Pelagic fish are found here.

A wreck lies about forty feet deep in Deep Bay between
Shipstern Point and Deep Bay Point.

Sandy Island and Weymouth Reef lie about two miles offshore,
west of Shipstern Point. Spearfishing is good here. Depths vary
from awash to twenty feet. Beyond the reef, the bottom slopes off
to over fifty feet deep.

*Chapter 20*

# BARBUDA

**How to Get There:** By Pan Am Jet Clipper to Antigua with connecting flight to Barbuda. A Government mail boat also makes regular trips from Antigua to Barbuda.

**Customs, Travel Documents, Currency:** The port of entry is Antigua. See that chapter.

**Transportation:** Taxis and walking.

**Hotels:** The luxurious and exclusive Coco Point Lodge is a selective, beautiful resort. It is beautifully landscaped and situated on a dazzling beach of white sand the consistency of talcum powder. The year-round rate is $120.00 per couple per day. This rate includes everything: drinks, meals, accommodations, all sports activities, yachting, water skiing, and scuba diving. Their scuba equipment may be used only by guests having a NAUI or YMCA diving certificate. They have the only air compressor on the island and use it for their guests only. Air is not for sale. They have their own airstrip. Apply to: Coco Point Lodge, P. O. Box 90, St. John's, Antigua, W.I.

At the other end of the hotel scale is the simple, very inexpensive Government Rest House in Codrington. It is the only other hotel on the island. Write to The Warden, Government Rest House, Codrington, Barbuda, West Indies. Reservations are essential.

**Other Information:** Tourist information is available from the Antigua Tourist Board, P. O. Box 363, St. John's, Antigua.

## SKIN DIVING INFORMATION

Barbuda is a skin diver's paradise. The island is encircled with reefs, clear water, plenty of game and reef fish, and seventy-three known wrecks which date from 1773. The beaches, one of them over fourteen miles long, are of blinding white, talcum-fine coral sand.

Except for the equipment maintained by the Coco Point Lodge for use of guests, diving gear is not available for either rent or purchase. Boats can be rented from Mr. Eric Burton in Codrington. Currents run southward but are not normally stiff enough to affect diving. Because there are few roads, access to the diving areas is by boat from Codrington.

### EAST COAST

An offshore reef protects this coast from heavy seas. During calm periods, diving outside the reef is possible. When heavy seas occur, which is most of the time, the coral inside the reef can be explored. However, from Hog Point (toward the north end of the island) south to Amasport Reef (north of Welch Point), the reef is deep and diving is difficult during heavy seas. Many game fish are found along the entire coast. The best spearfishing on the island is along this coast and on the offshore banks.

### NORTH COAST

From Hog Point west to Billy Point there are numerous reefs, some of them a mile or more offshore. The entire region is a superb diving area. Depths vary from awash to forty feet or more.

WEST COAST

From Billy Point south to Oyster Pond Landing there are scattered coral heads fringing the coast in depths of about fifteen feet. This is an excellent area for snorkeling.

From Oyster Pond Landing south around Palmetto Point to the Martello Tower, there is little coral, and the bottom is mostly sandy.

From the Martello Tower (the ruins of a fortified lookout point, painted white on its seaward face) south to Spanish Well Point there is a lovely, shallow reef close to shore which is excellent for snorkeling.

There are numerous reefs off Coco Point and Spanish Point. The bay between the two points is excellent for all diving activities. Offshore, about a mile, is Palaster Reef, a superb spearfishing area.

Dodington Bank, about two miles southwest of Coco Point, and Codrington Shoals, over a mile southwest of Dodington, are excellent spearfishing areas for experienced divers. Depths vary from seven to about sixty feet. Pelagic and reef fish of all kinds are seen here.

*Chapter 21*

# MONTSERRAT

**How to Get There:** By Pan Am Jet Clipper to Antigua with a connecting flight to Montserrat.

**Customs Regulations:** Personal clothing and one hundred cigarettes are admitted duty free.

**Travel Documents Required:** U.S. citizens must have proof of identity and nationality and a return or onward ticket.

**Currency:** B.W.I. (pronounced: Bee Wee) dollars are exchanged at $1.68 B.W.I. to $1.00 U.S.

**Hotels:** There are four hotels with rates ranging upward from $15.00 single, winter rates, American plan. There are also several small guesthouses with even lower rates. A large, American-financed, homesite project is located on the west coast, north of Plymouth, the capital.

**Transportation:** Taxis and rental autos are available.

**Medical Facilities:** There is a small hospital.

**Other Information:** This is a lovely, simple, nontouristy, escapist's island. The scenery is magnificent and the inhabitants are friendly. This is a British island. Advance reservations are recommended for air and hotel accommodations in winter. Tourist information and a hotel list is available from the Montserrat Tourist Board, Plymouth, Montserrat, West Indies.


## SKIN DIVING INFORMATION

The beaches are mostly of black volcanic sand on this volcanic island. The coastline rises abruptly from the sea and most of the coast is steep-to with little coral. It is not especially worth making a trip just for the diving, but, for those who do visit this lovely island, there are a few interesting diving areas.

The water is clear, with visibility seventy-five to over one hundred feet. Game fish are not particularly plentiful since the islanders have dynamited the waters.

**Diving Gear for Sale:** It is advisable to bring all necessary gear. A limited line of cheap masks is offered for sale by Lindy A. Eid General Store in Plymouth. No other gear is available.

**Rentals, Compressed Air:** None available. There are no facilities, at the time this is written, for visiting divers.

**Boats, Guides:** Pan Am agents Messrs. W. Lewellyn Wall and Co. can contact Mr. John Bernard of George Street, Plymouth. Bernard has a small open boat with outboard engine and can arrange for larger boats, if needed. He is a diver and can guide visitors to various diving spots.

**Currents, Wind:** Ocean currents are negligible. Tidal currents are weak except off the north and south ends of the island, where the westbound currents reach up to four knots. The eastbound currents are weak. Tidal currents set in both directions, parallel to the coast. The easterly trade winds prevail.

### WEST COAST

The best diving along this coast is toward the north end in Rendezvous Bay. The depth of this reef varies from fifteen to twenty feet and drops off to deep water a few hundred yards offshore. Visibility is about seventy feet or more. Access is by boat, which can be hired in Carr's Bay, about a mile south of the reef.

About two miles north of Plymouth, there is a small amount of coral to be found south of Bransby Point. This is not an outstanding reef, though. Depth varies between fifteen and twenty-five feet. Access is by boat from Plymouth.

South of Plymouth, off the O'Garra Estate, one can usually find quantities of conchs and an occasional fish. The bottom slopes off to thirty feet, then drops off to deep water. Access is by boat or road.

## EAST COAST

This side is usually too rough for diving. Visibility here ranges between forty and sixty feet. On calm days the fairly shallow reefs (to thirty feet deep) from the south end of Yellow Hole south to Statue Rock are rather pretty, and fish are usually seen here. Access is by boat only.

The unnamed point south of Farm Bay also is fringed by pretty coral in depths to thirty feet. Access is by boat.

Farther south, around Roche Bluff, is a good spearfishing area. Not much coral can be seen here. There are some groupers in the holes here, and some pelagic fish such as mackerel, barracuda, and dolphins.

*Chapter 22*

# GUADELOUPE

**How to Get There:** By Pan Am Jet Clipper, four and a half hours from New York or about four and three-quarter hours island-hopping from Miami.

**Customs Regulations:** Personal clothing and up to one thousand cigarettes and a bottle of liquor are allowed duty free. The air departure tax is $3.00.

**Travel Documents Required:** Proof of nationality and identity is required for stays of seven days or less. Passports are required for stays of up to three months. A smallpox vaccination certificate, issued within three years, is required. Visitors arriving from South America must also have a certificate of vaccination for yellow fever.

**Currency:** Francs (written: N.F.) are exchanged at N.F. 5 to $1.00 U.S.

**Hotels:** There are fourteen hotels offering a total of 428 rooms at winter rates ranging upward from $8.00 per day, single, European plan.

**Transportation:** Taxis and rental autos are available. Major roads are paved.

**Medical Facilities:** There are good doctors and hospitals.

**Other Information:** Guadeloupe is a department of metropolitan France and is represented by the French Government Tourist Offices at 610 Fifth Avenue in New York and at 1170 rue Drummond in Montreal. Current hotel lists, with rates, are obtainable at these offices or at the Office of Tourism in Pointe-à-Pitre, Guadeloupe. The Pan Am Office at 34 rue Achille René (Tel: 1280) is an excellent source of tourist information.

## SKIN DIVING INFORMATION

Guadeloupe consists of two islands, Grande-Terre and Basse-Terre, which are separated by a canal. For convenience here, the two islands will be considered as one unit. The nearby islets, Îles des Saintes, Marie-Galante, Petite-Terre, and La Désirade will be discussed separately. Instruction in scuba diving is not available.

**Laws:** None, at present.

**Diving Gear for Sale:** A complete selection of scuba and snorkeling equipment is available at Martin Pêcheur, 9 rue Sadi Carnot, Pointe-à-Pitre (Tel: 1648). Phillipe Martin, the owner/ operator, is captain of the Guadeloupe Spearfishing Team, three-time champions in the Inter-American annual spearfishing tournaments.

Equipment rentals are not available.

**Boats:** Motorboats can be chartered from Mr. Pierre Flamand, Nauti-Flamme, Route du Ojasier, Pointe-à-Pitre. Fishermen in the various coastal villages will sometimes rent their fishing boats. When negotiating with these fishermen, a knowledge of French is essential. The best places to hire these boats are at Port Louis, Anse Bertrand, and Deshayes.

**Compressed Air:** Air is available at SOGIC, Zone Artisanale, Pointe-à-Pitre (Tel: 1335). Ask for Mr. DeMoustier, Manager.

**Currents, Winds:** Currents are from east to west. Around the extremities of the islands the flow can be quite stiff. In other areas the currents are usually weak.

The easterly trade winds prevail.

### GRAND CUL-DE-SAC

This area, extending from Pointe Allègre on the north coast of Basse-Terre east to Port Louis on the west coast of Grande-Terre, is the best area on the island for diving, especially for novices.

The water is clear, with normal visibility of over sixty feet. The area is full of reefs, varying in depth from awash to fifty feet. The waters surrounding Îlet-à-Fajou (in the center of the bay) are particularly good for snorkeling. Depths here are from three to ten feet.

A barrier reef extends across most of the bay, running from east to west, and protects the inner bay from heavy seas. Accordingly, the inner bay is usually quite calm.

Northwest of Pointe Allègre, about a mile offshore, is Îlet-à-Kahouanne. The area around this small island is a good one for spearfishing by experienced divers. Depths vary down to sixty feet. Groupers, snappers, and other game fish are found here. Access is by fishing boat, hired in Port Louis or Sainte Rose.

## NORTHEAST COAST

This coast extends from Pointe de la Grande Vigie (the northernmost point of Grande-Terre) southeast to Pointe des Châteaux. Since the trade winds are from the east, this coast is usually too rough for diving. A wreck lies about thirty feet deep about a mile northeast of the village of Moule. Local fishermen can locate it.

## SOUTH COAST

This coast extends from Pointe des Châteaux on Grande-Terre, west to Pointe-à-Pitre, then south and west to Pointe du Vieux-Fort, on Basse-Terre. The south coast of Grand-Terre is fringed with reefs, extending up to a mile offshore in places. Boats can be rented in Saint François, Sainte Anne, and Gosier. A wreck, which is over two hundred years old, lies in about eighteen feet of water just outside (south) of the reef in Petit Havre. Petit Havre is about two and a half miles west of Sainte Anne. The Petit Havre reef is an attractive diving site in varying depths, with many reef fish and some game fish.

Petit Cul-de-Sac Marin is the bay between Grande-Terre and

Basse-Terre. Pointe-à-Pitre is situated at the head of this bay. The northern portion of the bay is unsuitable for diving because of poor visibility. The best area is in the vicinity of the cays near the village of Goyave, on Basse-Terre. This includes Caye-à-Dupont, Îlet Fortune, and Caye Martinique. South of this area, the Basse-Terre coastline is frequently too rough for diving. A wreck lies in shallow water on the north side of Caye-à-Dupont. Access to this region is by boat from Pointe-à-Pitre or Goyave.

### WEST COAST

This includes the coastline of Basse-Terre from Pointe du Vieux-Fort north to Pointe Allègre. There are few reefs along this coast. The best diving spot is around Îlets-à-Goyaves, about midway along the coast. Some fish can be found here. It is hardly worth a special trip to dive here, since there are so many other much better diving spots around Guadeloupe.

## ÎLES DES SAINTES

This group of small islands lies about seven miles south of Basse-Terre and can be reached by scheduled ferry from either the city of Basse-Terre or the village of Trois Rivières. Conditions are usually good for diving in the area, especially for spearfishing. The best areas are: (1) The northern portion of Terre-de-Haut, especially around Pointe-à-l'Eau. Four wrecks lie in twelve to twenty feet of water off the northeast tip of Pointe-à-l'Eau. (2) The west and south coasts of Grand Îlet (which is south of Terre-de-Haut). (3) The southwest coast of La Coche, a small island west of Grand Îlet. This area is also good for spearfishing.

The most convenient and comfortable way to enjoy diving around the Saintes is by chartering a cabin cruiser from Nauti-Flamme in Pointe-à-Pitre. However, there are plenty of small boats in the Saintes which can be hired.

## MARIE-GALANTE

This island is over fourteen miles off the south coast of Grande-Terre. It is served by ferry from Pointe-à-Pitre. The east coast is usually too rough for diving. The north portion of the west coast is shallow for two hundred to three hundred yards offshore and is a fair spearfishing area. The reef here is intermittent. Access is by boat rented in Saint Louis or Grand-Bourg, the principal town.

The best diving in the area is from Grand-Bourg south and east to Pointe-des-Basses. Extensive reefs are situated near the coastline in depths varying from awash to thirty feet. Access is by boat hired in Grand-Bourg.

## BANC DES VAISSEAUX

This shallow bank is for experienced spearfishermen only. It is located seven miles south-southwest of the village of Saint François on the south coast of Grande-Terre. The best access is by cabin cruiser chartered in Pointe-à-Pitre. The least depth of this bank is twenty-three feet. Surrounding this underwater peak are coral reefs about fifty feet deep. Many game fish such as groupers, mackerel, barracuda, and varieties of jacks are found here.

## PETITE-TERRE

Petite-Terre consists of two small islands, Terre-de-Haut and Terre-de-Bas which lie about five miles south-southwest of Pointe-des-Châteaux, the eastern tip of Grande-Terre. It is suggested that these islands be visited by experienced spearfishermen only, since the underwater scenery is not particularly outstanding. However, there are plenty of game fish of various kinds, particularly on the western side of Petite-Terre. Access to Petite-Terre is by chartered boat from Pointe-à-Pitre.

## LA DÉSIRADE

This island is about five miles east-northeast of Pointe-des-Châteaux on Grand-Terre. Extensive reefs fringe the south shore from Pointe-à-Colibris east to Pointe du Désert. When the wind is from the northeast, this coast is fairly calm and diving is possible; otherwise, it is usually too rough for diving. The north coast is not especially good for diving because of a lack of reefs. However, experienced spearfishermen will find a trip worth while since there are plenty of game fish here. Access is by chartered boat from Pointe-à-Pitre.

[12] Skin diving is rapidly gaining in popularity as a family vacation sport, perhaps because it can be enjoyed equally by parents and their children.

[13] *Above*. One of the most thrilling aspects of diving is wreck hunting. The bow of a coral-encrusted wreck can be seen here. The young diver pictured wears a glove to prevent cuts or abrasions when holding on to objects underwater.   [14] *Below*. This snorkeler is exploring the main deck of an old wreck, now inhabited by small fish. In a few years the steel portions of this wreck will disintegrate and the sea growth will erase any trace of the vessel.

[15] *Above.* A sandy bottom normally resembles a desert, while a coral reef such as this one is usually teeming with marine life. [16] *Below.* The underwater photographer's life is a busy one and he must catch up on outside events wherever he happens to have a few spare moments.

[17] This fish watcher is observing a school of French grunts inside a sunken ship. A bluehead is swimming past his snorkel.

[18] *Above.* Like the big game hunter, the successful fish watcher or spear-fisherman must stalk his prey. Movements should be slow and deliberate or the fish will become frightened and leave. [19] *Below.* This scuba diver is exploring the remains of an old tugboat which sank in 1916 in Carlisle Bay, Barbados.

[20] *Above*. Bronson Hartley is escorting a guest on a tour of a coral garden in Nassau. These trips are especially recommended for persons having an interest in underwater exploration who prefer individual attention during their first experience underwater. [21] *Below*. Bronson Hartley has trained Harry, his pet grouper, to do a number of tricks. Guests may hold the trained fish in their hands.

[22] The author's seven-year-old son adds another specimen to his tropical fish collection.

[23] Scuba instructor Jeff Adams of St. Maarten is surfacing with a fragment of H.M.S. *Proselyte*, which ran aground on Man o' War Reef in 1802.

[24] Clues to the location of wrecked wooden ships are ballast stones, anchors, and cannons. This cannon is from H.M.S. *Proselyte*.

*Chapter 23*

# DOMINICA

**How to Get There:** By Pan Am Jet Clipper to Guadeloupe with a connecting flight to Dominica.

**Customs Regulations:** Personal belongings are admitted duty free.

**Travel Documents Required:** U.S. citizens must have proof of identity and nationality and a return or onward ticket.

**Currency:** B.W.I. (pronounced: Bee Wee) dollars are exchanged at $1.68 B.W.I. to $1.00 U.S.

**Hotels:** There are six small hotels offering a total of fifty-three rooms at winter rates ranging upward from $6.00 per day, single, American plan. Reservations are suggested in winter.

**Transportation:** Taxis and rental autos are available.

**Medical Facilities:** There is a small hospital in Roseau with English-trained doctors.

**Other Information:** The scenery on Dominica is the most beautiful in the West Indies. It is quite a mountainous island, so the road system is not extensive.

Further tourist information and the pamphlet "Come to Dominica" is available from the Dominica Tourist Board, Roseau, Dominica, West Indies. Information is also available from the Caribbean Tourist Association, 20 East 46 Street, New York.

## SKIN DIVING INFORMATION

Since the shoreline of Dominica rises almost vertically from the sea, there are few offshore reefs and shallow areas for snorkelers.

Therefore, it is not particularly recommended that a special trip be made to this island just for diving. Other islands have more to offer the diver. However, there are a few areas which are suitable for visitors who might like to snorkel around a bit.

While spearfishing can be enjoyed in a few areas, only experienced divers will find many fish since they usually stay in depths out of the reach of novices.

There are 365 rivers on the island. During the rainy season, in the fall, silt is carried out to sea which dirties the coastal waters. The rest of the year, the rivers are clear and do not affect underwater visibility.

**Laws:** None, at present.

**Diving Gear for Sale:** A limited selection of French equipment is for sale at P. H. Williams, Great George Street, in Roseau. Rental equipment is not available.

**Boats:** Boats can be hired from fishermen.

**Compressed Air:** Not available.

**Currents, Winds:** Tidal currents on the east coast are strong northbound with a maximum velocity of two knots. Southbound tidal currents are weak. Currents on the west coast are influenced by winds and are usually not strong, except when the winds blow steadily in one direction for several days.

### WEST COAST

This section covers the west coast from Cape Melville south to Scotts Head. The best area in the northern part of this coast is south of Portsmouth, off Point Ronde. A reef about forty feet deep, minimum, lies from one hundred to two hundred yards offshore of Point Ronde. The visibility, except in the rainy season, is over one hundred feet. Many snappers, large parrot fish, and pelagic fish are seen here. Recommended for experienced divers only because of the depth. Access: drive south from Portsmouth and swim out or hire a fishing boat in Portsmouth.

From Point Ronde south to Grand Savanna (which is about at

midpoint on the west coast) the spearfishing is pretty good, but for experienced divers only, because the reef is deep. There is not much coral in this area. Access is by boat, since this section of the coast road is not yet completed.

A reef lies in thirty to forty feet of water about a quarter mile off Grand Savanna. Game fish are found here. Boats can be hired at the nearby village of Salisbury, which can be reached by road.

An extension of the above reef is found off Mero, about two miles south.

From St. Joseph (about a mile south of Mero) south to Check Hall, the bottom is mostly sandy and uninteresting for divers.

From Check Hall south to Morne Daniel there are a number of reefs a short distance offshore. Average depths are awash to forty feet. This is one of the few places where snook may be seen, usually in about thirty-foot depths. A road leads to Morne Daniel from Roseau. Access to the reef is by swimming out, or hiring a boat.

Woodbridge Bay, just south of Morne Daniel, is of little interest to divers since it has a sand bottom.

Roseau Bay has almost no coral, but spearfishermen might want to check out the waters between the Post Office and the jetty. Barracuda and mackerel frequently cruise by here. The sandy bottom slopes off rather steeply here.

The reef closest to Roseau is in the area between Wallhouse (about a mile south of Roseau) and Union River. The reef follows the coastline and is rather pretty. It is in shallow water. Access is by road and swimming off the shore, or by boat from Roseau.

Snorkelers will find another diving area at the southern end of Soufrière Bay, which is about seven miles south of Roseau. A hook-shaped peninsula, terminating at Scotts Head, angles out westward from the mainland. On the northern side of this peninsula, that is, the southern end of Soufrière Bay, there are shallow reefs which are suitable for snorkeling. A road leads to Scotts Head Village. At the tip of Scotts Head a stiff current flows north/south.

## SOUTH COAST

There is a stiff east/west current along this coast. Novices should not attempt diving here. Only experienced divers should explore these waters, while accompanied by a small boat.

The area from the tip of Scotts Head east to Point des Fous is a good spearfishing area, with a reef close to shore, and snappers and other game fish present. Depths on the reef vary. At Point des Fous the current is especially strong.

From Point des Fous east to Petite Savane, spearfishing conditions are good, but for advanced divers only. The coastline is cliffy and depths of twenty feet or more are found close-to, with the bottom angling steeply into deep water offshore. It is advised that divers drift with the current, accompanied by someone in a boat.

## EAST COAST

The water along this coastline is almost always very rough. Only experienced divers, who are strong swimmers, should attempt diving here. However, there are more fish here than elsewhere around the island and competent spearfishermen will find a visit to this coast worth while. The best time of the year for visiting this coast is August/September.

The majority of the coastline is steep and rocky and access from shore is impossible except in a few places. To describe each section of the coast would be repetitive and unnecessary. Therefore, some of the best spots will be described, from south to north.

The area from Rosalie Point north to Pagoua Point is especially good for spearfishing. Huge groupers are found in caves and holes in the rocks here. Large pelagic fish of all kinds are also seen here. A road provides access to this area. Divers can swim out through the surf here, provided it isn't too high.

From North End north and west to Marigot Point, there are

plenty of reefs, rocks, and game fish. Sharks are seen here, although no attacks have been recorded.

Just off Pointe Augustine a few yards is a submerged rock named Captain Scott's Rock, or La Baleine. This is one of the best spearfishing spots on this coast. Large groupers and all types of large pelagic fish are found here. The sea breaks heavily over this rock, so extreme care must be observed.

Londonderry River is about a mile north of Marigot. The offshore rocks nearby are good diving spots, with plenty of game fish in the area.

### NORTH COAST

This includes the area from Crompton Point east and north to Cape Melville. The coastline is identical to the east coast and the same comments apply. The best spearfishing on this coast is between Crompton Point and Hempstead. There is coral in shallow water close to shore. When the wind is out of the southeast, this section is fairly calm. There are plenty of fish of all kinds. The Woodford Hill beach is the best on the island and is the only white sand beach.

*Chapter 24*

# MARTINIQUE

**How to Get There:** By Pan Am Jet Clipper from Miami in four and a half hours, or from New York in five and a half hours' elapsed time.

**Customs Regulations:** Personal clothing and one thousand cigarettes and a bottle of liquor are allowed duty free.

**Travel Documents Required:** U.S. citizens must have proof of nationality and identity and a smallpox vaccination certificate issued within three years. Visitors arriving from South America must also have a certificate of vaccination for yellow fever.

**Currency:** Francs (written: N.F.) are exchanged at N.F. 5 to $1.00 U.S.

**Hotels:** There are a number of hotels and guesthouses, of varying quality, with rates ranging upward from $6.00 daily.

**Transportation:** Taxis and rental autos are available. Main roads are paved.

**Medical Facilities:** There is a hospital on the island.

**Other Information:** Martinique is a Department of Metropolitan France. French is spoken everywhere except in the tourist shops, some hotels, and by some of the cab drivers in Fort-de-France, the capital. A knowledge of French, or at least a bilingual dictionary, will be useful.

A wide variety of merchandise is for sale in Fort-de-France at duty-free prices.

The Pan Am office is at 62 Avenue Duparquet in Fort-de-France (Tel: 6552). Tourist information and a current hotel list can be obtained from the Tourist Office, Avenue Duparquet in Fort-de-

France (Tel: 3960) or from the French Government Tourist Office at 610 Fifth Avenue in New York or at 1170 rue Drummond in Montreal.

## SKIN DIVING INFORMATION

This is not an especially good island for beginners since much of the shoreline rises sharply upward from very deep water. The leeward, or west, coast of the island is pretty well fished out and offers interesting diving only in a few places. Spearfishing is good on the windward, or east, coast when the seas are calm, which happens rarely.

**Laws:** A spearfishing license is required. It may be obtained from the Chef des Services de l'Inscription Maritime in Fort-de-France. Bring two passport-type photos and one franc.

Lobsters smaller than four inches from head to tail may not be taken.

Do not take female lobsters with eggs.

**Diving Gear for Sale:** Equipment is sold, at very low prices, in a number of stores in Fort-de-France. An excellent selection is offered by Société Commerciale et Industrielle Martinique, corner rue Garnier Pages and rue François Arago. Another good source of diving gear is Maison Reynier, 39 rue Schoelcher.

Rental gear is not available.

**Trips, Guides, Boats:** The best place for meeting diving partners is the Martinique Yacht Club, where a knowledge of French is almost essential. A number of local divers keep boats there. Otherwise, there are no facilities for visiting divers on the island. Boats may be rented from the S.HO.T.T.A. rental agency in the Savane, Fort-de-France (Tel: 2179), or they may be rented directly from fishermen.

**Compressed Air:** The only source on the island so far is Hervé et Cie., Habitation Ménard, Sainte Thérèse.

**Currents, Winds:** Except as noted in the following text, currents are weak and not a factor in diving.

The easterly trade winds prevail.

## WEST COAST

In the north, good quantities of game fish are usually found around La Perle Island, which lies about five hundred yards off Anse Céron. Access is by boat. Depths vary from ten feet to very deep water.

In 1902 Mont Pelée exploded and destroyed the town of Saint-Pierre, at that time the principal city on Martinique. Two of the many ships sunk in the holocaust are within aqualung range. The shallowest wreck is 120 feet deep. The other one is somewhat deeper. The best way to locate these wrecks is with the help of a diver from the Martinique Yacht Club. If this is not possible, hire a fisherman in Saint-Pierre, making sure he has exact bearings on the wrecks.

Banc Mitan is a shallow bank in Fort-de-France Harbor. The water is not always clear, but good spearfishing is usually found here when the seas are running heavily on the east coast. It is marked by the last black channel buoy southwest of the city.

West and south of Fort-de-France is a wreck about fifty feet deep. It is about a quarter mile north of Cap Salomon, about one hundred yards offshore. It is well known to the fishermen in nearby Anse Mitan, where a boat may be hired. Currents are sometimes strong here.

The southwestern peninsula from Anse Mitan to Diamond Rock can be attractive for diving; however, the current is sometimes stiff here so it is best to have a boat accompany divers. Some coral is found here in shallow water.

### SOUTH COAST

Diamond Rock was officially designated a British warship in 1804 by Admiral Hood. He fortified and manned this small rock to block the inside channel to the French. The small British garrison on H.M.S. Diamond Rock held out against the numerically superior French for seventeen months. Many old cannon, anchors, and other relics of battle lie on the sea bottom next to this rock. The water is usually clear, but the current is usually stiff here and the seas are frequently heavy. This is a spot for experienced scuba divers only.

Diamond Bank is a reef about three quarters of a mile southwest of Diamond Rock. Depths vary from twenty-five to fifty feet. There are plenty of game fish here, but the current is strong.

From Diamond Rock east to Marin the underwater scenery is fair but not especially interesting. Watch out for natives using dynamite in the water. Visibility is seventy-five to one hundred feet.

The entire south point from Marin around to Cap Chevalier is a good spearfishing area with plenty of game fish, shoals in varying depths, and clear water, although the underwater scenery is not too attractive.

Salines Island, off the southeast tip of the island, is another good spearfishing spot, with large groupers and barracuda in the area.

### EAST COAST

The seas are usually too heavy for diving on this coast. Therefore the following comments apply only on the few days when the water is calm. The description of the coastline is from south to north.

One of the best spots is off Cap Chevalier. The water is usually fairly clear and there is a variety of good-sized game fish. Depths vary from awash to very deep water. Access is by boat, which can be hired locally.

For the expert diver, with plenty of experience in rough, deep water and stiff currents, La Brigo Reef, about an hour by boat from the village of Le Vauclin, is an excellent spot. The least depth of the reef is seventy feet. Huge grouper, huge barracuda, and huge everything else is found here. To get there, hire a fishing boat in Le Vauclin, making certain in advance that the skipper can locate the reef by bearings on land. The reef is marked by buoys, but they are pulled under the surface when a stiff current runs, which is frequently. Consequently, unless the boatman can locate the reef by shore bearings, a lot of time will be lost looking for it.

A much more accessible, shallow reef is north of La Brigo. Pinsonelle Reef is about half an hour by boat off Pointe Cerisiers. Depths vary from fifteen feet to very deep water. There are truly fantastic coral formations here with underwater tunnels through the reef and great quantities of fish.

From Pointe Cerisiers north to Îlet Madame, diving conditions are very good—in calm weather. There are plenty of reefs in varying depths with good quantities of fish. A locally hired boat is almost a necessity.

To the north of Îlet Madame, muddy water is found in Havre du Robert, a bay, and, farther north, in Baie du Galion.

The peninsula of Presqu'île de la Caravelle offers good spearfishing. A boat is necessary. Depths vary, from fifteen feet to deep water. The current is usually very stiff here. This area is for experienced divers only.

Northeast of Caravelle is Roche Caravelle, one of the better spearfishing spots around the island. Experienced divers will find really big fish around this small offshore islet: barracuda six feet and longer, mackerel, large groupers, and plenty of lobsters. This is a full day's trip, so take along food and water.

Saint Aubin Island, about two hundred yards offshore from La Trinité, is an excellent spearfishing area. Depths vary from shallow to quite deep. The usual assortment of game and reef fish are seen. Rent a boat in La Trinité.

From Presqu'île de la Caravelle north and west to Grand' Rivière, diving can be quite good—on calm days. This portion of the coastline rises steeply from the bottom. Close-to, the bottom is about twenty-five feet deep and shelves off steeply.

*Chapter 25*

## ST. LUCIA

**How to Get There:** By Pan Am Jet Clipper in six hours from New York, via Puerto Rico and Antigua.

**Customs Regulations:** Personal possessions, a carton of cigarettes, and a bottle of liquor, for personal use, are admitted duty free.

**Travel Documents Required:** Proof of identity and nationality, a return or onward ticket, and a smallpox vaccination certificate issued within three years are required of U.S. citizens. Persons arriving from yellow fever areas must have a valid yellow fever vaccination certificate.

**Currency:** B.W.I. (pronounced: Bee Wee) dollars are exchanged at $1.68 B.W.I. to $1.00 U.S.

**Hotels:** A total of twelve hotels and guesthouses offer just over two hundred rooms at winter rates ranging upward from $6.00, single, American plan.

**Transportation:** Taxis and rental autos are available. Drive on the left. A scheduled motor launch service plies between Castries, the capital, and Anse-la-Raye, Canaries, Soufrière, Laborie, and Vieux Fort. The boat departs from Castries daily except Wednesday and Sunday at 2 P.M. and begins the return trip from Vieux Fort the following morning around 11 A.M. Make arrangements for this ferry trip through the hotel.

**Medical Facilities:** There is a 200-bed hospital in Castries.

**Other Information:** This volcanic island lies between Martinique and St. Vincent. In 1948 a fire destroyed most of Castries. The rebuilt city is one of the best-planned communities in the West Indies.

Pan Am agents are Peter and Co., Ltd., in Castries (Tel: 96). Their office is an excellent source of local tourist information.

The St. Lucia Tourist Board, Box 221, Castries, St. Lucia, West Indies, can supply general tourist information and the helpful pamphlet, "Where to Stay in St. Lucia."

In New York the island is represented by the Caribbean Tourist Association, 20 East 46 Street.

## SKIN DIVING INFORMATION

Diving is excellent around the steep, rocky shoreline for both novices and experts. There are many rocky headlands, separated by sandy bays, with coral reefs almost everywhere. For nondiving hours (and nondivers) there are beaches, impressive scenery, friendly islanders, and night life.

**Diving Gear for Sale:** A limited selection of equipment is available at Frank H. Johnson and Son, Ltd., Micoud Street, Castries. This is a hardware store.

Rental gear is not available.

**Guides, Boats:** Michael Hackshaw, P. O. Box 52, Castries (Tel: 106), is the only professional guide available. Write in advance to insure a booking. Hackshaw has three boats and can accommodate up to ten divers at a time.

Sportfishing boats can be hired from Robert A. Eliot, The Reef, Castries; Richard J. Egerer, c/o The Seven Seas Restaurant, Bridge Street, Castries; or by inquiring at the Calabash or Seven Seas restaurants, both on Bridge Street.

**Compressed Air:** Not available.

**Currents, Winds:** The ocean current flows north to north-northwest. During the flood tide, which is to the north, velocities reach two and a half knots. The current is weak during a falling tide because of the southerly ebb. There are local variations around rocky promontories and reef areas.

Around the northern end of the island there is an area of slack water which is caused by an eddy resulting from the rejoining of the ocean current which splits at the southern end of the island.

The easterly trade winds prevail.

## WEST COAST

Most diving is done on this leeward coast because the sea is calm. St. Lucians do little diving, so the fish aren't yet spooky. Most diving areas are accessible only by boat.

From Pointe du Cap, the north point, south to Gros Islet Bay, the water shelves off steeply from the shore to about forty feet some two hundred yards offshore. When seas are calm, this is a very good area for spearfishing.

Farther south, in Gros Islet Bay, the area around Burgot Rocks (also called Bird Rocks) is a good one for spearfishing. The water is frequently rough and strong currents are usually present. Depth is forty feet. This should be explored only by experienced divers.

Just south of Burgot Rocks is Pigeon Island, an excellent diving area for beginners or experts. The water is clear, there are plenty of reefs, and fish and lobster abound. Depths vary from six feet on the east side to about sixty feet on the west side. Currents are sometimes stiff here.

At the southern end of Gros Islet Bay there is a small jetty where lobster can be found in about fifteen to twenty feet of water. However, the visibility is not always good.

Lobster, game fish, and numerous coral heads are found around Rat Island, which is northeast of Vigie Airport in Anse du Choc. Visibility is usually seventy-five feet or more. Depths vary from awash to twenty-five feet.

Spearfishing and conditions for underwater photography are good around Vigie Point, just north of Castries Harbour. About two hundred yards offshore, lobster can be found in the coral and rocks. Depths vary from twelve feet near the shore to sixty feet or more a few hundred yards offshore. A wreck about thirty feet deep lies just off the western face of Vigie Point. Grouper and other game fish frequent this area. The area described in this paragraph is the closest one for divers staying in Castries.

From Castries Harbour (Tapion Rock) south to Cul de Sac Bay, the bottom is mostly sand, with little coral and few fish. This part of the coast is not recommended for diving.

From Cul de Sac Bay to Marigot Harbour, there are a number of attractive reefs with good quantities of game fish. Larger fish and lobster are especially plentiful north of the entrance to Marigot Bay.

An attractive, shallow reef lies on the north side of Marigot Harbour, near the entrance. The water is clear and plenty of attractive tropical fish live here. This is an excellent snorkeling area, especially for novices. The rest of Marigot Harbour has little to offer divers, underwater. However, Marigot Harbour is one of the most beautiful in St. Lucia and there are two hotels with dockside restaurants and bars—handy for an after-dive drink.

The entire coastline from Marigot Harbour south to Vieux Fort is an excellent one, especially for experienced divers. The current in the narrow reef channels can be strong. The bottom drops off sharply with over hundred-foot depths close-to in many places. Game fish of all kinds are found here. Belembouche Rocks are where lobsters are found, in depths of ten feet or more. Southeast of these rocks is Laborie, where the most extensive reef formation on the coast is situated. The water is shallow and clear with the usual assortment of tropical fish and occasional game fish. This is one of the best reefs in this region for beginners and it can be reached by boat from Vieux Fort.

The waters off Vieux Fort are also excellent for diving. The area is ideal for beachcombing, loafing, or diving. The clean, white-sand beach, tall palms, and picturesque fishing boats create a lovely tropical scene.

Vieux Fort can be reached by auto from Castries in an hour or by scheduled ferryboat. Local fishing boats can be hired. Spearfishermen will find plenty of groupers, tarpon, kingfish, and barracuda around the small islands in Vieux Fort Bay.

The entire south point, extending from Vieux Fort around the southern tip and north to Pointe Sable is excellent for diving, for novices or experts.

### EAST COAST

Most of the time it is impossible to dive on this coast because of the heavy seas caused by the easterly trade winds. Currents are strong here and the surge is usually strong. The following comments, then, apply only during the few days when the trades reverse themselves. This occurs mostly during July and August.

There are extensive reefs along the entire coastline. Fish are found in very large quantities. Practically no diving has been done here, so the fish aren't yet spooky. The bottom shelves off more gradually than along the west coast, so it is possible to dive a good distance offshore.

A boat is essential. Either charter one of the boats mentioned in "Guides, Boats," or hire a fishing boat in one of the fishing villages on this coast. The best places to find such a boat are Dennery, Micoud, Anse Micoud, or Vieux Fort. The cost will vary from $6.00 a day up—depending on the skill of the bargainers.

# Chapter 26

# ST. VINCENT

**How to Get There:** By Pan Am Jet Clipper to Antigua, Barbados, Martinique, or Trinidad with connecting flight to St. Vincent.

**Customs Regulations:** Personal effects are admitted duty free.

**Travel Documents Required:** U.S. citizens must have proof of identity and nationality plus a ticket to a return or onward destination. Yellow fever vaccination certificates are required if visitors arrive from an infected area.

**Currency:** B.W.I. (pronounced: Bee Wee) dollars are exchanged at $1.68 B.W.I. to $1.00 U.S.

**Hotels:** Accommodations are limited and advance reservations are suggested in winter. Rates range upward from $6.00 per day, single, American plan.

**Transportation:** Taxis and rental autos are available. Drive on the left. The main roads are paved.

**Medical Facilities:** There is a hospital in Kingstown.

**Other Information:** Hotel and tourist information is available from the St. Vincent Tourist Board, Kingstown, St. Vincent, W.I.

## SKIN DIVING INFORMATION

Underwater visibility in most areas is seventy-five to one hundred feet, except after a heavy rain. Spearfishing and underwater photography conditions are good here, and there are shallow reefs, excellent for snorkeling, around Young Island.

**Diving Gear for Sale:** A selection of French snorkeling equipment, including spear guns and spare parts, is available at John H. Hazell and Sons on the main street of Kingstown.

Guests of the Young Island Hotel are provided with snorkeling equipment.

There are no equipment rentals on the island.

**Guides, Boats:** Boats can be rented from the Aquatic Club and from fishermen. Rates vary, depending on bargaining ability. There are no facilities for visiting divers such as compressed air or scuba equipment, or professional guides.

**Current, Winds:** Currents are not usually strong except through narrow passages, such as around Calliaqua Bay in the south and around the north point. The main ocean current is to the north, but surface currents are affected considerably by winds and tidal currents. The tide flows to the north and ebbs to the south.

The easterly trade winds prevail.

## WEST COAST

South of Kingstown is Young Island and Duvernette Island. An attractive reef in from three to thirty feet of water is situated on the south side of Young Island. The underwater terrain is attractive around the entire islet, which is two hundred yards off the Aquatic Club. Conditions are good here for beginning snorkelers.

North of Kingstown, from Old Woman's Point to the North Point, the entire west coast offers excellent conditions for spearfishing, lobstering, photography, or any other underwater activity. The shore is rocky and indented with many coral reefs and some caves. Beginners should remain close to shore, since the bottom drops off steeply to thirty feet or more close to shore, then gradually slopes off to deep water. Access is by boat from Kingstown or one of the many fishing villages near the coast.

About a mile west of Buccament Bay is the extensive Questells Shallows. Depths here vary from thirty feet to very deep water. For experienced spearfishermen this is a good diving area, with mackerel, barracuda, amberjacks, groupers, and other game fish in abundance. Access is by boat from Kingstown. This is not a good area for novices.

For several miles north of Buccament Bay, the bottom close to shore varies from thirty to forty feet. Farther north, many game fish can be seen around Château Belair Island in depths of forty to seventy feet. Access is by swimming offshore or by boat from the village of Château Belair. Currents can be strong on the offshore (west) coast of this small island.

Farther north, above Wallibou, good diving conditions are found around Morne Ronde Point. Here, the depths vary from twenty to thirty feet, with shallows extending to seaward for about one and a half miles. A number of game fish can be seen here. Access is by boat from Wallibou.

### EAST COAST

Except during a few days of the year, mostly in July and August, this windward coast is unsuitable for diving because of heavy seas. In any case, beginners should not attempt diving on this coast. During fine weather the best diving region is the northern quarter of the coast from Espagnol Point south to Georgetown. Boats can be rented at fishing villages here. Since practically no diving has been done here, there are plenty of fish in these waters.

*Chapter 27*

# BARBADOS

**How to Get There:** By Pan Am Jet Clipper from New York in four and a quarter hours.

**Customs Regulations:** Personal effects, half a pound of tobacco, or two hundred cigarettes, or fifty cigars, and a bottle of liquor are admitted duty free.

**Travel Documents Required:** While passports are officially required, authorities usually accept other proof of identity and nationality such as a voter's certificate. A return or onward ticket may be required. Visitors from Central and South American countries must have a valid smallpox and yellow fever vaccination certificate.

**Currency:** B.W.I. (pronounced: Bee Wee) dollars are exchanged at $1.68 B.W.I. to $1.00 U.S.

**Hotels:** There is a wide variety of hotels and guesthouses with winter rates ranging upward from $10.00, single, American plan. Reservations are essential in winter.

**Transportation:** Taxis, buses, rental autos, and rental scooters and bicycles are available. A free local license is issued by Immigration authorities at the airport upon presentation of a valid U.S. driver's license. Drive on the left. There are over six hundred miles of paved road.

**Medical Facilities:** There is an excellent, new, general hospital. There are also private clinics and doctors.

**Other Information:** The Pan Am office (Tel: 6006), on the Careenage in Bridgetown, is an excellent source of general tourist information.

The Barbados Tourist Board has an information booth at Sea-
well Airport. Their main office is on Lower Broad Street in
Bridgetown. Overseas offices are at 355 Lexington Avenue in New
York; 150 Eglinton Avenue East, Toronto; and 229/31 Kensington
High Street, London.

## SKIN DIVING INFORMATION

Compared to other West Indian islands, skin diving opportunities
around Barbados are limited. There are a few good areas on the
west coast for snorkeling, but few game fish are found there
because of the dynamiting of the waters by local fishermen and
because of extensive fishing in this area. The best spearfishing is
on the east coast, which is too rough most of the year for diving.

**Diving Gear for Sale:** South Coast Watersports at the Aquatic
Club (Tel: 70270 days, 5410 evenings) and Harrison's, DaCosta's,
and Cave Shepherd department stores on Broad Street in Bridgetown offer snorkeling equipment for sale. A complete line of French
diving equipment is sold through the textile department of S. P.
Musson Son and Co., Ltd., (on the second floor) on Broad Street.
Snorkeling equipment is also sold at The Fishing Corner, on the
Careenage, near the Pan Am office. Snorkeling equipment is also
available at the water sports shop of the Coral Reef Club hotel.

**Diving Gear for Rent:** The South Coast Watersports shop and
the Coral Reef Club shop rent equipment.

**Boats, Guides, Instructors:** Pat Fletcher of South Coast Watersports can arrange for diving trips with guides and snorkeling or
scuba equipment. Small rowboats can be rented from the head
boatman at the Yacht Club, next door to the Aquatic Club. Scuba
instruction is available at the Coral Reef Club.

**Compressed Air:** Gas Products, Ltd., Clapham, St. Michael,
fills tanks. The entrance is across the street from Banks Brewery.

**Currents, Winds:** Currents along the west coast are negligible.
Along the south coast, the currents flow east and west and can be

stiff. Along the east coast, the currents are from north to south, and are frequently strong. Telephone Barbados Rediffusion, 0811, for information on sea conditions.

### WEST COAST

Along this coast, there are numerous shallow indentations, or bays. At the north and the south end of each bay there is usually a small coral reef extending to seaward. Some of these reefs are attractive and ideal for beginners. Depths vary from awash to thirty feet or more.

Diving is not recommended from North Point to Harrison Point. Ordinarily, seas are heavy here and the underwater scenery is not exceptional enough to justify the long trip to this area. Sharks have been seen here.

From Harrison Point south to Six Men's Bay the visibility and sea conditions are somewhat better but are not always ideal. Close to shore, the bottom is shale and dead coral. About a quarter mile offshore are coral heads in fifty to eighty feet of water. Red and yellow snappers, parrot fish, barracuda, mackerel, and crevalles are seen here.

With one exception, the coastline from Six Men's Bay south to the town of Speightstown is not especially good for diving. The water is calm and clear and there are a few shallow water coral formations, but the reefs are not particularly beautiful.

The exception to this, and the best spearfishing reef on the west coast, consists of a reef about three quarters of a mile offshore in a direct line with the Challenor jetty. This reef is from fifty to one hundred feet deep and is from fifty to one hundred feet wide. It trends from northeast to southwest for about three quarters of a mile. The water visibility is usually seventy-five to one hundred feet, the coral formations are lovely, and there are plenty of game fish: barracuda, snappers, crevalles, and mackerel.

With some exceptions, the underwater terrain from Speightstown south to Freshwater Bay is sandy with occasional coral heads rising six to eight feet from the bottom. There are not many game fish in this area, but conchs are sometimes plentiful, especially on the northern edge of Gibbs Beach—opposite Sunset Lodge. A rather attractive reef lies off the southern end of Gibbs Beach in depths of ten feet and deeper. To find this reef, walk down the beach, south of a hotel beach bar, to a white cottage and swim out from there over shallow water for about two hundred yards. There are very few game fish here.

The best shallow reef for snorkeling on the west coast is directly in front of the Coral Reef Club. Conditions for beginners are ideal: the water is calm and clear, the reef is shallow (from awash at low tide to forty feet), and plenty of small, pretty reef fish inhabit the reef. Game fish are seldom seen, except for an occasional school of barracuda or mackerel.

In Freshwater Bay the underwater scenery is fair. The reef depth varies from awash to twenty feet or more. Underground freshwater springs discharge into this bay and in the vicinity of these springs the water is cold. Occasional mackerel are seen here.

Kettle Bottom Shoal lies just south of Freshwater Bay. Inside this reef, near Brighton, is a shallow, attractive reef, suitable for snorkeling. Unfortunately the water is sometimes murky due to the discharge of waste material from a nearby rum refinery.

Long Shoal is about half a mile southwest of Kettle Bottom and is marked with a bell buoy. The reef is from thirty to over 120 feet deep. This is a good area for experienced scuba divers. The water is clear and there are usually a few snappers, crevalles, and barracuda. Green turtles have been taken here. The current can be stiff, especially during the northward flood tide.

In Carlisle Bay, adjacent to Bridgetown, the only spot of interest is the wreck of a tugboat. It lies in twenty-five feet of water, southwest of the Government buildings and northwest of the Aquatic Club. It is marked with a green buoy. It is about seven feet to the top of the wreck. It is coral-encrusted and the home of a lot of lovely tropical fish. It can be reached by rowboat or even by swimming from the shore. This is a particularly good area for snorkelers. Large fish are very seldom seen here. The rest of Carlisle Bay is uninteresting.

### SOUTH COAST

It is usually rather choppy along this coast, particularly toward the eastern end. When the trade winds are from the southeast, the surface is quite rough. Therefore, this coast is not recommended except when the winds are from the northeast. The tidal current floods to the westward at up to two knots. It is suggested that a boat follow the divers quite closely. Visibility varies widely, from fifty to over one hundred feet, depending on the weather. Underwater scenery is good in some places, but in most areas is dead coral, rock, sand, or weed.

White sea urchins, or sea eggs, are considered a delicacy on Barbados. They are found in quantity on this coast, in various depths. The open season is during the months with "R's." Divers collecting sea eggs out of season can be fined. Local divers collect the eggs, break their shells open, and scoop out the yellowish ovaries. Some Barbadians eat the ovaries raw. Others steam them and mix the result with local seasoning, rice, and avocadoes. Most hotels serve sea eggs in season.

The best spot for diving along the western part of the south coast is about half a mile offshore from St. Lawrence. There is an attractive coral reef in about forty feet of water with sea fans, tropical fish, and the usual mackerel, barracuda, crevalles, and snappers. Large stingrays are sometimes seen here. The offshore (south) side of the reef slopes off to well over one hundred feet.

From St. Lawrence to Long Bay there is little to interest divers. The bottom is mostly dead coral, sand, and shale.

Fathom Bank is about a quarter mile offshore between Long Bay and Salt Cave Point. For experienced divers, in calm weather, this is a good diving area. Barracuda and wahoos are seen here. The current is usually strong, so be sure to have a diving boat nearby. The usual practice is to start "upstream" and drift with the current. Depths vary from fifty to sixty feet.

From Salt Cave Point west to Ragged Point the seas are usually heavy. Diving should be attempted here only by experienced divers in calm weather. Some lobster and game fish are found here. Close to shore, the bottom is uninteresting so diving is on the off-shore reefs, one of which is Cobbler Reef.

Local legend has it that Sam Lord, one of the early English planters, lured many ships onto Cobbler Reef by placing false lights in the trees and on donkeys. When an unsuspecting ship struck the reef, his crew would remove all the valuables they could before the ship sank. His home, now the luxurious Sam Lord's Castle Hotel, looks out directly on this sailing ship grave-yard. Wreckage can be found on the reef and the management of Sam Lord's Castle can arrange for local boats for trips to the reef in calm weather. Depths vary from awash to fifty feet and deeper offshore.

## EAST COAST

Atlantic rollers, constantly crashing on this ragged coastline create surge, bad visibility, and difficult surface conditions for most of the year. Strong currents are to be expected here. Calm water is found on rare days throughout the year but most frequently during September and October. There are plenty of fish and lobster on this coast. An accompanying diving boat is a must here. Boat all speared fish immediately. So far, there have been no shark attacks. Don't start a trend.

The area from Ragged Point north to Conger Point provides some of the best diving conditions on this coast. The easiest spot to enter the water is at Bath. Starting from the beach, the water is shallow and remains chest-deep for a few hundred yards, where there are a number of spectacular underwater canyons dropping off abruptly to fifty feet or more. Some of these canyons are four or five feet wide, others are several yards in width. On calm days the visibility here is excellent—up to one hundred feet. The coral growth is luxuriant, the fish plentiful, and the canyons unique and photogenic. While sharks have been seen here, if speared fish are boated immediately, they shouldn't present much of a problem.

Other fish normally seen here are barracuda, groupers, snappers, mackerel, and crevalles.

From Conger Point north to Pico Tenerife, the water is usually too dirty for diving. A few drainage streams empty out in this region.

If weather and sea conditions are right, spearfishing is good in Gay's Cove. Depths are awash to ten feet inside the cove, dropping off to about thirty-five feet outside. Due to the distance from the hotels, though, it is hardly worth a trip.

From Gay's Cove north to North Point the sea is almost always too rough and dirty for diving.

*Chapter 28*

# THE GRENADINES

**How to Get There:** These islands can be reached by private yacht or by scheduled sailings on the mail boats from either Grenada or St. Vincent. The St. Vincent mail boat leaves from the pier in front of the Kingstown Police Station and makes stops at Bequia, Cannouan, Mayero, and Union islands. The Grenada mail boat makes scheduled departures from the Careenage in St. George's, for Carriacou. Travel between Union and Carriacou is by schooner or fishing boat.

**Customs, Travel Documents, and Currency:** See Grenada and St. Vincent.

**Hotels:** There are two hotels on Bequia, the thirteen-room Friendship Bay Hotel and the nine-room Bequia Beach Hotel. Two guesthouses, the Admiralty Guest House and Mitchell's Guest House, are usually open during the winter season.

The only hotel now open on Union Island is the ten-room Sunny Grenadines Hotel.

On Carriacou, the ten-room Mermaid Tavern is the only hotel.

A new hotel is under construction on Palm (formerly Prune) Island, near Union.

**Transportation:** Bequia has a few Land-Rover taxis which can be hired through the hotels.

Mr. Mitchell of the Sunny Grenadines Hotel on Union transports his guests in the hotel Land-Rover.

Mr. Linton Rigg of the Mermaid Tavern in Carriacou can arrange for taxis or a rental auto.

**Medical Facilities:** There is a hospital on Carriacou with English-trained doctors.

**Other Information:** The Grenadines are a chain of about one hundred islands, rocks, and numerous reefs, lying between Grenada and St. Vincent. Carriacou, Petite Martinique, and the islands to the south are administered by Grenada. St. Vincent exercises jurisdiction over the other islands.

This region is perhaps the finest cruising area for yachts in the West Indies. The inhabitants are primarily seafarers and boatbuilders and are unfailingly courteous and helpful. These islands are among the few remaining places in the Caribbean that are truly unspoiled.

Interisland schooner travel is inexpensive but recommended for men only, except for trips on the scheduled mail schooners.

## SKIN DIVING INFORMATION

Diving is superb in the Grenadines. There are countless reefs with clear water and a rich marine life second to no other area. Beginners will find shallow reefs ideal for snorkeling and fish watching. Photographers will have ample opportunity to take pictures of underwater scenes of all descriptions. Bring along all needed film and camera equipment—it is difficult to get here.

Fish of many kinds abound. In addition to a wide variety of small tropical fish, the most commonly seen game fish are groupers, barracuda, mackerel, jacks, and crevalles, as well as spiny lobsters, conchs, and turtles.

The underwater visibility in most areas is seventy-five to one hundred feet, and it frequently exceeds 150 feet.

Fishing boats can be hired on most islands. The best plan is to stay on one of the islands with a hotel, hire a boat recommended by the hotel owner, and make day trips to nearby islands.

**Laws:** From Petite Martinique and Carriacou south to and including Grenada, the following laws regarding lobsters are enforced: Female lobsters with eggs may not be taken. Lobsters weighing less than one pound or measuring less than nine inches in total body length may not be taken. Lobsters may not be taken at all during the closed season, which is from May 1 to September 13.

**Diving Gear for Sale:** An excellent selection of French and Italian snorkeling equipment is sold at the Bequia Marine Store, Lulley Hill, Friendship, Bequia. Prices are quite low for diving gear as well as a complete line of fishing and yachting equipment. The owner, Ross Lulley, is a diver. His is the only store in the Grenadines with diving gear.

Rental gear is not available in the Grenadines.

**Compressed Air:** Not available.

**Currents, Winds:** Tidal currents can be quite stiff in the restricted passages. The ebb is eastward and the flow, to westward, can combine with the general northwest ocean current to a velocity of four knots in some areas. Always check the direction of currents when first entering the water and make sure that the diving boat accompanies anyone in the water. These comments apply when diving out of the lee of an island or reef.

## BEQUIA

Boats can be hired from Mr. Geoff Wallace through the hotels. The most experienced divers here are the King brothers, who make their living spearfishing. Ask for them in town, at the hotels, or aboard their 45-foot auxiliary sloop, *Eood K.* This boat can be chartered inexpensively.

### NORTHWEST COAST

From Lower Bight east to Low Bay, spearfishing conditions are good. The best snorkeling, especially for beginners, is in Upper and Lower Bight bays where attractive coral reefs are found up to fifty yards offshore.

Princess Margaret Beach (named after her honeymoon visit here) and Admiralty Bay are east of Low Bay. They are scenically lovely but are not especially suitable for diving. The town of Port Elizabeth is situated in Admiralty Bay.

From Rocky Bay (at the northern end of the Admiralty Bay

channel) to Northwest Point, the water is no deeper than about twenty up to one hundred feet offshore, where the bottom gradually drops off into greater depths. This area has plenty of coral and small fish and is a good area for beginning snorkelers. It is easy to reach by boat from town.

From Northwest Point northeast to Bequia Head (the northwest tip of the island), spearfishing is good. Groupers, crevalles, barracuda, and snappers are found here. The bottom is mixed coral and rock and gradually deepens from about five feet near shore to very deep water a few hundred yards offshore. L'Anse Chemin is a lovely bay near Bequia Head with numerous beautiful coral formations in shallow water. This is an especially good snorkeling area.

### NORTHEAST COAST

Seas are frequently heavy along this shoreline and diving is difficult. The exception is in Friendship Bay, which is linked by road to Port Elizabeth. There, protected from the trade winds by a long peninsula, conditions for snorkeling are excellent. There are numerous reefs, clear water, and plenty of fish of various kinds. Boats can be hired directly from fishermen or through the Friendship Bay Hotel.

A shallow, pretty reef is right in front of the hotel and other extensive reef formations are situated to the south, near Anthony Eden's house. At the southern end of the bay can be seen the last remaining West Indian whaling station. This is manned during the January/April whaling season. Bequia whalers use twenty-foot dories and the traditional hand-thrown spears.

The islets south of Friendship Bay are worth a visit by spearfishermen. They are St. Hilaires Cay, Semples Cay, Petite Nevis, Île de Quatre (named after its four hills), and Ramiere. Seas are usually rough on the windward (eastern) sides of these small islands, and the currents between them are frequently rough, especially during the west-going tidal flow. Only experienced divers should explore these waters.

## BALICEAUX AND BATTOWIA ISLANDS

These two small islands are linked by a shoal five to ten feet deep. They are situated a few miles southeast of Bequia. Diving should be confined to the west coast. The islands are best approached from Bequia during day trips, since there are no hotels or tourist facilities here.

An extensive reef extends along the west coast of Baliceaux for up to half a mile offshore in depths varying from five to over one hundred feet. Since this is almost virgin territory, spearfishing here is excellent and most varieties of game fish are seen.

## MUSTIQUE ISLAND

This small, privately owned, island has little to offer visitors at present, since there are no tourist facilities at all. It has been noted for its swarms of mosquitoes. The owners plan to build a resort here, complete with airstrip.

The best diving is along the west coast and on Montezuma Shoal, about half a mile west of Grand Bay. Least depths on the Shoal are five feet. An excellent diving reef fringes the east coast of Mustique from Rabbit Islet north for about a mile. Usually, though, the seas in this area are much too rough for diving.

Several islands lie to the north and south of Mustique. They should be explored only by highly experienced divers, since the currents are strong. To the north are The Pillories, Pillory Rocks, and All Awash Island, while Petit Cay, Petite Mustique, and the Savan Islands are to the south.

## CANNOUAN ISLAND

There is a small community here but no hotel. However, a small hotel is in the planning stages. Charlestown Bay is fairly shallow with a reef extending southward. The northwestern and southwestern ends of the island rise steeply from the bottom.

An extensive reef runs along the south coast and along most of the east coast. Diving is excellent here when the seas are calm. The offshore side of the east-coast reef drops off steeply into deep water.

Petit Cannouan is about four miles north of Cannouan. This small islet rises almost vertically from the bottom and is not recommended except for experienced spearfishermen. Seas usually break heavily here.

## MAYERO

This small island has a good diving reef, in about the center of the west coast, which extends to the west for about three hundred yards. The reef is interesting for snorkeling. Another shallow reef fringes the southern tip of the island.

Catholic Rocks and Catholic Island are about a mile northwest of the island. Seas break heavily here most of the time, making diving impossible.

The east coast of Mayero is fringed with an attractive coral reef. Diving is possible here much of the time, since Mayero is in the lee of the Tobago cays and the extensive reef formations to the east, which protect the east coast from the heavy seas.

Since there are no hotels on the island, it is best visited by day trips from Union Island.

### THE TOBAGO CAYS, HORSE SHOE REEF, EGG REEF, AND WORLD'S END REEF

In this area, there are some of the most attractive coral formations in the Grenadines. The uninhabited Tobago Cays are east of Mayero. Surrounding them to the north, east, and south is the fabulous Horse Shoe Reef, which offers wonderful diving for fish watchers, photographers, or spearfishermen. Egg Reef is southeast of the Cays and adjoins World's End Reef, which is an extensive, irregularly shaped coral formation.

This entire area offers deserted, talcum-soft, blinding-white-sand beaches, exceptionally lovely coral reefs, gin-clear water, and a wide variety of fish of all sizes and types. This area can be reached by boat from Union in day trips.

## UNION

The scenery on this island is the most striking in the Grenadines, with tall, rugged peaks similar to those of Moorea. There are several fine white-sand bathing beaches. The main settlement is Ashton, on the south coast. An offshore reef extends from the southern end of nearby Frigate Island northwest to the southern end of Clifton Bay. Inside the reef, the bottom is very shallow and mostly sand. Depths outside the reef vary from twenty to fifty feet. Plenty of conchs are found here.

A reef encircles the north, east, and south sides of nearby Palm Island and good diving in various depths is found along this reef. This island, originally named Prune Island, was renamed recently by the owner of a small hotel now under construction.

## CARRIACOU

Carriacou is a lovely, mountainous island with lovely, white and pink sand beaches as well as superb skin diving conditions. There are seventy-five miles of paved road. The view from the Hospital is one of the most beautiful in the West Indies. Some of the finest schooners in the West Indies were built on Carriacou, which is populated largely by seafaring people: shipwrights, fishermen, and seamen.

The Mermaid Tavern, operated by noted yachtsman/author

J. Linton Rigg, has ten rooms, at low rates, and has a self-service, honor system bar.

The Government of Grenada, which administers the island, is planning to construct an airstrip soon. For general tourist information write to The Secretary, Carriacou Tourist Committee, Carriacou, Grenada, W.I.

One of the principal attractions, for islanders and tourists, is the annual Carriacou Regatta. This event, held in August, is a three-day affair in which there are yacht races, schooner races, and many other events. It was organized by Mr. Rigg, who also organized the now-famous Out Island Regatta in the Bahamas.

### WEST COAST

The best diving areas are around the small offshore islands: Mabouya, Jack Adam, and Sandy Island. The underwater scenery around Sandy Island is especially lovely. Legislation has been introduced to declare the Sandy Island area an underwater park. Therefore, spearfishing is not recommended here. Be sure to check on the status of this legislation before diving here. The extensive coral formations here are exceptionally lovely and photogenic, particularly around the eastern end of this small island. Depths vary from awash to fifty feet.

The reefs around Mabouya and Jack Adam are attractive but are slightly deeper than those at Sandy Island.

A fringing reef is just off the point north of the village of l'Esterre.

### EAST COAST

A magnificent barrier reef parallels most of this coastline and is up to one and a half miles offshore. There are a few detached coral patches inside the reef, but in calm seas the best diving conditions are on the outside of the reef. Many lobsters and fish are found here.

SOUTH COAST

From Kendace Point southwest to Southwest Point, the coastline is steep in most places and is fringed with coral. When seas are calm, this entire coastline is excellent for diving.

Petite St. Vincent, Petite Martinique, and Petite Tobago are small islets east of Watering Bay, Carriacou. The best diving among these sparsely populated islands is over the barrier reef which lies a few hundred yards north of Petite St. Vincent and continues southeast to a position east of Petite Martinique. This reef should be explored by experienced divers only, who should exercise caution because of the strong tidal currents. The ocean current combines with the tide to create currents of over three knots during the northwestward flow.

A number of islands lie between Carriacou and Grenada. The largest ones are Frigate Island, Large Island, Kick 'em Jenny (*Quai Qui Gêne*), Les Tantes, Ronde, and Caille. Since diving conditions are so good around the larger islands of the Grenadines, these smaller ones are hardly worth visiting since there is usually considerable surge and rough seas around their shorelines.

*Chapter* 29

# GRENADA

**How to Get There:** By Pan Am Jet Clipper to Trinidad (five hours) or Barbados (four and a half hours), then less than an hour by connecting flight to Grenada.

**Customs Regulations:** Personal clothing plus one hundred cigarettes or a pound of tobacco plus a roll of film will be admitted duty free.

**Travel Documents Required:** U.S. citizens must have proof of identity and nationality plus a ticket to a return or onward destination.

**Currency:** B.W.I. (pronounced: Bee Wee) dollars are exchanged at $1.68 B.W.I. to $1.00 U.S.

**Hotels:** There are eleven hotels and guesthouses with 436 rooms at winter rates ranging upward from $9.00, single, American plan. There are also a few cottages for rent by the week.

**Transportation:** Taxis and rental autos are available. Drive on the left. The main roads are paved and they reach most parts of the island. Small boats are used for water taxis across St. George's Harbour.

**Medical Facilities:** There is a general hospital in St. George's.

**Other Information:** Scenically Grenada is one of the most beautiful of the West Indian islands. The principal exports are spices, hence its nickname, "The Spice Island." The best way to approach the island is by sea: the jungle- and spice-tree-covered, mountainous coastline drops steeply into the sea, interrupted by an occasional small beach. As the ship enters St. George's Harbour, the aroma of spices and the lovely, pastel-colored houses clinging to the hills surrounding the Mediterranean-like harbor create an unforgettable impression.

Because of a landlocked harbor and a well-equipped yacht marina, many private and charter yachts make Grenada their headquarters.

For further information and the pamphlet "Where to Stay in Grenada," write to The Secretary, The Grenada Tourist Board, St. George's, Grenada, West Indies, or inquire of the Caribbean Tourist Association, 20 East 46 Street, New York.

## SKIN DIVING INFORMATION

**Laws:** Female lobsters with eggs may not be taken. Lobsters weighing less than one pound or measuring less than nine inches in total body length may not be taken. No lobsters at all may be taken during the closed season, which is from May 1 to September 13. These laws are strictly enforced.

**Diving Gear for Sale:** Water World, on the town square in St. George's (Tel: 2145), has a wide selection of diving equipment. The shop is operated by Bill and Barbara Stevens and is the only dive shop on the island.

Everybody's Store, near the town square, and The Cold Store, on the Careenage, offer a complete line of French snorkeling equipment. Stanley Smith at Everybody's Store and Fred Pressey at The Cold Store are in charge of the diving equipment and are divers themselves.

**Diving Gear for Rent:** Scuba and snorkeling gear can be rented from Water World.

**Trips, Boats, Guides, Instruction:** Bill Stevens is agent for several charter yachts, some of which are completely equipped for scuba diving. He can also arrange scuba instruction and day trips in small boats.

A small boat can be rented from Mr. H. Blanco, Tel: 2362.

Boats of all sizes can be hired by the day, or chartered for extended periods, from Grenada Yacht Services, in the Yacht Basin.

Martin and Clair Matthias offer lessons in scuba diving and can organize diving trips. Their headquarters is the Grenada Beach Club.

Divers visiting the town of Grenville can hire boats from Captain Wells, who can usually be found on the waterfront.

One of the best sources of information on boating and diving is Carl Schuster, a yachtsman who owns and manages the Nutmeg Bar and Restaurant, overlooking the Careenage. Schuster keeps a large scale at the Nutmeg for weighing the big fish caught in local waters.

**Compressed Air:** Water World has a compressor.

**Currents, Winds:** The current is weak and not a problem for diving along the west coast. The ocean current, deflecting off the east coast, divides and flows north and southwest. The west-going tidal flow unites with the westbound ocean current to form stiff westbound currents around the extremities of the island during the flood tide. The eastbound ebb partially checks the ocean current.

Easterly trade winds prevail.

### WEST COAST

A road parallels the entire coastline. Access to various diving spots is by swimming from shore or by boat, obtainable in most villages and in St. George's.

The coastline is mostly steep and rocky. Depths near shore vary from five to twenty feet, with depths of thirty feet or more a short distance offshore. After a rain, the water is usually clouded near river mouths. Otherwise, visibility is normally seventy-five to one hundred feet.

Because the shoreline is so steep, opportunities for shallow-water snorkeling along this coast are limited. It is suggested that beginners explore the reef near Grand Anse Beach, at the southern end of this coast, or visit the nearby south-coast diving areas.

The following describes the diving areas on this coast, from north to south.

A reef about ten feet deep fringes the coastline intermittently from David Point (the north point) south to DuQuesne Point.

From Gros Point south to the village of Goyave, coral heads are found along the shore in varying depths.

Closer to St. George's a fairly extensive fringing reef is situated around Dragon Bay and Moliniere Point. Depths vary from awash to twenty feet.

A reef extends to seaward over two hundred yards from St. Eloi Point; however, the water here is not always clear.

Grand Anse Beach is south of St. George's. Coral is found here mostly at the southern end and in the northern portion of adjacent Morne Rouge Bay. Depths are variable, mostly shallow. This is a place for shallow-water snorkeling.

Long Point Shoal lies a few hundred yards offshore from Long Point, south of Grand Anse. Game fish are found here in depths varying from eight to fifty feet. Access is by boat. Currents are stiff here.

Diving around the southern tip, Saline Point, is recommended for experienced spearfishermen only. A number of game fish, with plenty of barracuda, can be seen here. The current is strong and the surface is frequently choppy. Access is by boat, which should stay close to the divers to receive the speared fish.

### SOUTH COAST

This coast is deeply indented and offers many opportunities for beginning snorkelers as well as experienced spearfishermen and photographers. The seas here are rougher than along the west coast, but many estuaries provide calm, currentless diving spots.

Numerous game fish can be found around Glover Island, which is less than a mile south of Hardy Bay. An old whaling station is situated here. Depths around the island vary from ten to twenty-five feet. The bottom is mixed coral and rock.

Spearfishing is also good around Grampus Rocks (also called The Porpoises). These are less than a mile south of Prickly Point.

The bottom here is about twenty-five feet deep. Be careful of the westgoing current.

The wreck of a small steamer lies in about thirty feet of water seventy-five yards offshore from La Sagesse Bay. Inquire at the La Sagesse Rum Refinery for boatmen and guides to the wreck.

### EAST COAST

The sea usually breaks heavily along this coast. During the few days of calm seas, diving here is excellent. There are many reefs in varying depths along the entire coastline. There are several offshore rocks and islets where spearfishing is good. The best plan, when diving here, is to use the village of Grenville as a base. Many reefs are in Grenville Bay and south of it. Contact Captain Wells (ask anyone along the waterfront) for a boat and a reliable crew.

*Chapter* 30

# TOBAGO

**How to Get There:** By Pan Am Jet Clipper to Trinidad with a connecting flight to Tobago. Before departing from Trinidad, reconfirm your return flight from Tobago. Reconfirm again on arrival and again the day before departure.

Two Government-owned ferries connect the two islands. Tickets are available at the Ferry Office at Queen's Wharf in Port of Spain, Trinidad.

**Customs, Travel Documents, and Currency:** See Trinidad.

**Hotels:** There are nine hotels and guesthouses with over two hundred rooms at winter rates ranging upward from $7.00, single, American plan. Advance reservations are suggested in winter.

**Transportation:** Taxis and rental autos are available. Drive on the left. Main roads are paved.

**Medical Facilities:** There is a hospital on the island.

**Other Information:** Some Tobagoans believe that Daniel Defoe had Tobago in mind when he wrote *Robinson Crusoe,* since most of his descriptions of Crusoe's island fits Tobago. Visitors have described Tobago as an enchanting island with friendly, hospitable people, thatched-hut simplicity, and jet-modern hotels. There are miles of deserted white-sand beaches which are fringed on one side by acres of coconut trees and on the other by warm, clear water. Many of the reefs surrounding the island are unexplored.

## SKIN DIVING INFORMATION

Buccoo Reef is a well-known shallow reef on the northwest coast. A trip over this major tourist attraction can be arranged through any hotel and is recommended for beginners. Nonswimmers are given sneakers and can stand in the waist-deep waters, bend over, and observe the varied marine life through a face mask. This system provides an excellent introduction to undersea life.

Buccoo Reef is a National Underwater Park, as noted below. The most commonly seen tropical fish here are grunts, parrot fish, snappers, angelfish, trumpet fish, butterfly fish, jewel fish, and squirrelfish.

Buccoo Village is photogenic, with a number of colorful boats drawn up on the sand, drying fishnets, extensive coconut groves, banana trees, and small islanders' homes completing a picture of a South Seas village.

**Laws:** Buccoo Reef is a National Underwater Park. Taking marine life of any kind, spearfishing, or even the possession of a spear gun is unlawful in this area. Island constables constantly patrol the area to enforce this law. Spearfishing is not prohibited elsewhere.

Do not take female lobsters with eggs.

**Trips, Guides, Boats:** Captain Allen offers spearfishing, photography, and Buccoo Reef trips. Contact him or his partner, Carl Williams, in Scarborough, Box 204, or at the Buccoo Reef Marina, or through any hotel.

Jerry Brynjulson (Brin-hill-sun), an American, operates the 45-foot twin diesel *Fiesta*, as well as some smaller boats. He specializes in guiding experienced divers but also offers scuba instruction to novices. He can be reached through any hotel or at the Golden Grove Lagoon (Tel: 2260), near Buccoo Bay. For advance reservations, write to P. O. Box 234, Scarborough, Tobago, W.I.

Bill Craig, an Englishman, offers diving trips, scuba instruction, and photography trips. Address: c/o the Crown Point Hotel, Tobago, West Indies.

**Diving Gear for Sale:** Snorkeling equipment can be purchased at Sports and Games, Ltd., Burnett Street, Scarborough and at Miller's Department Store, in Scarborough.

Rental equipment is not available.

**Compressed Air:** Tank refills can be obtained through Bill Craig at the Crown Point Hotel. Divers planning to bring tanks are advised to write in advance to make sure air will be available.

**Currents, Winds:** The South Equatorial Current attains a velocity of up to four knots around the northeast and southwest tips of the island. Diving here is only for strong, experienced swimmers, who are followed closely by a diving boat. Local divers enter the water "upstream" and drift with the current.

Along the coasts, currents are usually weak, especially in the many protected bays.

The southeast side of the island continually experiences a heavy swell. A ground swell is also experienced along the north coast in winter.

The easterly trade winds prevail.

There are plenty of fish around Tobago. Little spearfishing has been done, so far, so the fish are not yet spooky. The most commonly seen game fish are tuna, albacores, barracuda, kingfish, wahoos, crevalles, various jacks, dolphins, tarpon, mackerel, groupers, and snappers. While sharks are sometimes seen in deeper water, there have been no recorded shark attacks.

## SOUTH COAST

This coast trends roughly from northeast to southwest. The sea normally breaks heavily on this coast and diving is difficult. When the seas moderate, as they do occasionally, this coast is a first-class area for diving, along almost the entire length. Plenty of game fish are seen here, in varying depths. The following is a description of some of the better areas, from east to west.

From Tyrells Bay, at the eastern end of Tobago, southwest to Pedro Point, the coastline is steep and rocky. Experienced divers will find plenty of fish here. Plan to dive close to the shoreline since the cliffs rise steeply from a deep bottom. A road leads to Speyside, in Tyrells Bay, where boats can be hired.

Farther to the southwest, the area around Black Rock and King's Bay is excellent for spearfishing. Depths vary from awash to one hundred feet. Access is by boat.

Queen's Island lies south of Black Rock. Depths vary from awash to over one hundred feet. There is plenty of coral and fish here. Access is by boat.

The entire coastline from Queen's Island southwest to Barbados Bay is a maze of reefs, rocks, and shoals. During calm seas, diving along this shore is very good. Plenty of fish can be seen here.

Great River Shoal is an especially large area of reefs which extend to seaward for over a mile south of Goldsborough Bay. Depths vary from awash to thirty feet. Access is by boat from Scarborough.

## NORTH COAST

This leeward coast is best for diving, especially for beginners. The entire coastline has excellent diving conditions and to describe each portion would be repetitious and unnecessary. The following describes some of the diving highlights of this superb coastline.

From Crown Point (at the western end of the island) northeast to Buccoo Reef the water is clear, the reefs are shallow (from awash to fifteen feet), and the underwater formations are interesting. This is the best place on the island for beginners. Pigeon Point has an especially lovely, palm-studded beach. The nearby shallow reefs offer perfect snorkeling conditions. Access is by swimming from shore or, especially to Buccoo Reef, by boat.

Excellent spearfishing conditions are, from southwest to northeast, the areas around Anse Formagier, Culloden Bay, the rocks offshore from Culloden Bay, King Peter Bay, the area between King Peter Bay and Englishman's Bay, and the two groups of offshore rocks, The Sisters and The Brothers. Man of War Bay, near the north point, is a large, protected bay with many offshore rocks; ideal for spearfishing.

A secondary road runs along the north coast. The adventurous diver can drive to the various diving areas and swim off the shore or hire a local fishing boat. The most reliable way is to make the trip on a boat chartered from one of the island's professional guides.

### WASP SHOAL

The following applies only to divers with experience in diving in rough, fast-moving waters in the open sea. Each of the professional guides on Tobago offers a trip to Wasp Shoal, which lies about two and a half miles southwest of Crown Point.

The current is very strong here so the procedure is to enter the water "upstream" and drift across the reef with the current. The diving boat follows closely.

Wasp Shoal has just about any kind and size game fish seen in the Caribbean. Huge barracuda, kingfish, amberjacks, groupers, mackerel, and others are present in quantity. Sharks are also all over the place, and speared fish must be boated immediately to minimize the possibility of an attack.

Bill Craig regularly visits this area to renew his acquaintance with "Big Ben," a jewfish about the size of a Volkswagen microbus!

### LITTLE TOBAGO ISLAND

This is the only place in the world where Birds of Paradise live in a wild state except in their original New Guinea home. For this reason this islet is also called Bird of Paradise Island. It can be reached by boat from Speyside.

It is dangerous to dive around this island and around nearby Goat and Melville islands because of the four-knot current which sweeps through the narrow passages.

*Chapter 31*

# TRINIDAD

**How to Get There:** By Pan Am Jet Clipper in five and three-quarter hours' elapsed time from New York. Also by Pan Am service from Miami.

**Customs Regulations:** Personal clothing and one quart of liquor may be brought in duty free. A maximum of £10/- sterling, or the equivalent in West Indian dollars, may be brought in or taken off the island.

**Travel Documents Required:** U.S. citizens must have proof of identity and nationality. Visitors arriving from infected areas must have a certificate of inoculation against yellow fever.

**Currency:** T.T. (Trinidad and Tobago) dollars are exchanged at $1.68 T.T. to $1.00 U.S.

**Hotels:** There is a wide variety of hotels and guesthouses with over nine hundred rooms at winter rates ranging upward from $5.00, single, American plan.

**Transportation:** Taxis and rental cars are available. Drive on the left. Most roads are in good shape.

**Medical Facilities:** There is a general hospital in Port of Spain, the capital.

**Other Information:** Trinidad and Tobago are independent members of the British Commonwealth. Tourist information and a list of hotels can be obtained from the Trinidad and Tobago Tourist Board at 56 Frederick Street, Port of Spain.

The Pan Am office, at 12 Abercromby Street, Port of Spain (Tel: 6161), is another excellent source of general tourist information.

## SKIN DIVING INFORMATION

The waters around this island are continually muddied by the
discharge of the nearby Orinoco River. Consequently, diving is not
recommended here except for really top spearfishermen, highly
experienced, who do not mind diving in rough, dirty, dangerous
water. Visibility is often nil around the entire coastline. Sharks and
barracuda are plentiful, although divers have never been attacked
(probably because there are so many fish to eat). There are no
organized diving facilities here because of the poor diving conditions. A local club exists, but they have had such bad experiences
with visiting, self-styled expert divers that they prefer not to be
listed.

Therefore the following information is for the true expert only.
Beginners are advised to visit nearby Tobago, or some other Caribbean island, where diving conditions are excellent.

**Diving Gear for Sale:** Sports and Games, Ltd., 26 Henry Street,
Port of Spain, offers a wide selection of diving equipment.

Rental gear is not available in Trinidad.

**Boats:** Fishermen's boats can be rented by negotiating directly
with the fishermen. A few boats are available for charter, at times,
through the Yacht Club. Any boats available for charter will be
listed with the travel agency in the Trinidad Hilton Hotel.

**Compressed Air:** The only nonprivate source of air on the island
is Industrial Gases, Ltd., Aranjuez Estate, San Juan.

**Currents, Winds:** Tidal currents are strong and unpredictable.
Along the south coast the ocean current is to the east. The east
and west coasts have a northwest-going current. The north coast
has unpredictable currents, with the direction and velocity depending on the tide and the flow of the Orinoco River.

The west and south coasts are too dirty for diving, and so is the
east coast most of the time. One of the best places for spearfishing
on the east coast is around some abandoned offshore oil rigs about
eight miles off Mayaro Beach, toward the southern end of this
coast. The depth here is one hundred feet. Giant barracuda, grou-

pers, and snappers are seen here. Two of the local spearfishermen consistently bring up one thousand pounds of fish a day on trips to these rigs. About one hundred yards east of the rigs is a forty-foot-deep reef, loaded with large snappers and groupers.

Visitors should make sure that the boatman is familiar with this area and will stay close to the divers. The boat should not be anchored but should always be ready to receive speared fish to minimize the danger of shark attack. Scuba divers must surface frequently to let the boatman know all is well and to prevent becoming separated from the boat. Further, the bottom current here frequently flows in a different direction from the surface current.

The water around the rigs is extremely dirty for the first ten to twenty feet. Below that depth, it clears up to about thirty-foot visibility. The exception is during the rainy season, in early fall, when there is even more silt in the water from the Orinoco River runoff.

The most commonly used spear guns here are the six-foot-long "shark" guns. These rubber-powered arbaletes and powerful $CO_2$ guns are necessary for the uncommonly large fish that live in this area. It is suggested that spear guns be equipped with a heavy-duty reel with one hundred feet of 500-pound-test nylon line. A six-foot steel cable is sometimes used to connect the spear shaft with the line, to prevent the line from breaking because of chafing against coral. Gloves are a must here, to protect the diver's hands against cuts when handling the nylon line or the large fish.

The clearest water is found along the north coast. Most of this shoreline rises almost vertically from the sea, so a boat is essential. Stay close to the shoreline, because the bottom drops off steeply. A variety of large fish are found here, particularly barracuda, groupers, and sharks. Spearfishermen should be able to snorkel down at least to fifty feet and stay there long enough to shoot a fish. Few large fish are found in less than fifty-foot depths.

A peculiarity of this coast is the drifting patches of alternately clear and murky waters. The best system is to find a clear patch of water and drift along with it as it moves with the current. Make sure the diving boat is always nearby.

*Chapter* 32

## CURAÇAO

**How to Get There:** By Pan Am Jet Clipper from New York. Flight time is six hours.

**Customs Regulations:** Personal clothing and small quantities of tobacco and liquor for personal consumption are allowed duty free.

**Travel Documents Required:** U.S. citizens must have proof of identity and nationality, plus a smallpox vaccination certificate issued within three years and a ticket to another destination.

**Currency:** The guilder, or florin (written: Fl.), is exchanged at Fl. 1.85 to $1.00 U.S. There are 100 cents in a guilder. Most stores accept U.S. currency.

**Hotels:** The most convenient hotel for visiting divers is the air-conditioned Hotel Curaçao Intercontinental, which is near the center of Willemstad. Other hotels offer a wide variety of accommodations at winter rates ranging upward from $6.00 per person. Reservations are essential during the winter.

**Transportation:** Taxis, rental autos, and buses are available. All major roads are well paved.

**Medical Facilities:** There are excellent doctors and hospitals on the island.

**Other Information:** The official language is Dutch, but the multilingual Antilleans almost all speak English fluently. S. E. L. Maduro and Sons, de Ruyterplein 4, are agents for Pan Am and are happy to offer whatever information or assistance may be required. The Curaçao Information Center in Willemstad, and at 604 Fifth Avenue, New York, can supply general tourist information and a hotel list, with current rates.

## SKIN DIVING INFORMATION

Since the trade winds are normally from the north, Curaçao's north coast is quite rough and most diving is done on the calm southern coast.

**Diving Gear for Sale:** The most comprehensive selection of equipment, including scuba gear, is at the Curaçao Oxygen Factory, at the Curaçao Dock Co. on New Harbour Road (Tel: 3-6623). Cap Lenderink, a veteran diver, is the managing director. Snorkeling equipment is also available at various sporting goods shops in Willemstad.

**Diving Gear for Rent:** Curaçao Aquatics, Inc., Hotel Curaçao Intercontinental, Willemstad (Tel: 1-1358), has snorkeling and scuba equipment for rent. The manager is Mr. Papy Martínez.

**Scuba Instruction:** Antillian Scuba Diving Association, P. O. Box 578, Curaçao, can arrange for diving lessons. Contact the president, Mr. Ole Hansen (Tel: 3-5679 or 1-2600, ext. 50), or Mr. Dick Hoogerwerf (Tel: 3-6546), or Mr. Cap Lenderink (Tel: 3-6623).

**Diving Trips, Boats:** Mr. Papy Martínez of Curaçao Aquatics is an excellent diver and conducts reef trips for photographers, spearfishermen, tropical fish collectors, or fish watchers.

Boats can also be obtained from Mr. Robert Schouten, Taber Tours, Inc., Hotel Intercontinental, who organizes trips on a diesel cruiser completely equipped with snorkeling and scuba gear. Camera rentals are also available.

**Compressed Air:** Air is available at the Curaçao Oxygen Factory.

**Currents, Winds:** The currents usually flow from east to west. Along the north shore and the east and west points of the island, the currents are stiff. Along the south coast, especially in the bays, currents are no problem.

Trade winds blow from northeast to southwest, causing almost constant heavy seas along the north coast.

## NORTH COAST

The sea on this coast is rough and should be explored by expert divers only, while accompanied by a local diver. The method of entry is to jump into the sea from a cliff. It is difficult to leave the water because of the seas and the cliffs, and the sharp coral ledges.

There is not much underwater coral and quite a lot of kelplike seaweed, so divers must be careful not to become entangled. Close to shore, the depth is about three feet. About one hundred or more yards offshore, the bottom angles to about fifty feet, then drops off steeply into very deep water. On an exceptional day, visibility can reach 150 feet. It averages about seventy-five to one hundred feet.

The heaviest seas and strongest winds occur during June, July, and August. The best months for diving are September, October, and November. The rainy season is in December, January, and February. Access to this coast is by road.

## SOUTH COAST

From Oostpunt (the eastern tip) west to the Mining Company at Fuik Baai, the seas are usually heavy. Spearfishing is good here. There is a strong east to west current in this region. Entry must be by boat since the land is private property and trespassing is prohibited. This area is for expert divers only.

From Fuik Baai west to Kaap St. Marie, conditions for diving are not very good because of poor visibility.

From Kaap St. Marie to the western tip of the island the conditions are very good for snorkeling, especially for novices. There are a number of protected bays with hundred-foot-plus visibility and very calm water. There are few game fish except at very deep levels. A favorite is Laguna Beach, where entry is easy, the coral is attractive (especially along the sides of the bay), and the water is well protected from winds by the high hills.

*Chapter* 33

# BONAIRE

**How to Get There:** By Pan Am Jet Clipper to Curaçao with a connecting flight to Bonaire.

**Customs, Travel Documents, and Currency:** See Curaçao.

**Hotels:** There are two hotels and two small guesthouses with winter rates ranging upward from $6.00 per day. Reservations are recommended during the winter.

**Transportation:** Taxis and rental autos are available.

**Medical Facilities:** There is a doctor on the island. Serious medical cases are sent to Curaçao, only half an hour away by air.

**Other Information:** S. E. L. Maduro and Sons, in Kralendijk, are Pan Am agents and can provide local tourist information. The main office of the Bonaire Tourist Bureau is in Kralendijk. In New York the address is 1270 Avenue of the Americas.

## SKIN DIVING INFORMATION

**Diving Gear for Sale:** Little is available here. It is best to bring in gear from elsewhere.

**Rental Gear, Trips, Guides, Boats, Compressed Air:** The Flamingo Beach Club offers all these facilities.

**Currents, Winds:** Ocean currents are from east to west and are not strong except at the extremities of the island.

The trade winds are from the northeast. The north coast is almost continually pounded by heavy seas.

Bonaire rises steeply from the ocean depths and offers few

shallow snorkeling areas. For an experienced diver this island is excellent because of the large number of game fish here.

The best area for snorkeling is in front of the Flamingo Beach Club. A variety of coral in depths of ten feet or more and a good number of small reef fish are seen here.

Another snorkeling spot is inside Lac Bay, which, though on the windward side, is protected by a barrier reef and is calm. A stiff outward current is felt at ebb tide. Divers should be careful not to get caught in this. Spearfishing is good here and visibility is around one hundred feet. Barracuda, tarpon, dolphins, and groupers are plentiful.

Virtually anywhere along the protected west coast is good for diving, with the bottom dropping off into very deep water a short distance offshore.

The north and east coasts are usually pounded by heavy surf and are not recommended except during periods of light winds and calm seas.

Klein Bonaire is a small island lying just a short distance off Kralendijk. Since this island is to leeward of Bonaire, the seas are usually calm. Fringing reefs are situated along the east coast and the northwest and southwest points of the island. Excellent spearfishing is found around this small island and visibility is well over one hundred feet.

*Chapter 34*

# ARUBA

**How to Get There:** By Pan Am Jet Clipper from New York in seven hours.

**Customs, Travel Documents, and Currency:** See Curaçao.

**Hotels:** Six hotels offer a total of 223 rooms at winter rates ranging upward from $12.00, single, American plan. A new, 200-room hotel should be completed in 1967.

**Transportation:** Taxis and rental cars are available. All major roads are paved.

**Medical Facilities:** There are two hospitals and many doctors.

**Other Information:** English is spoken everywhere. S. E. L. Maduro and Sons, Nassaustraat 88, in Oranjestad are Pan Am agents. General tourist information and a hotel list is available from the Aruba Tourist Bureau in Oranjestad or from the Aruba Information Center, 609 Fifth Avenue, Suite 705, New York.

## SKIN DIVING INFORMATION

**Diving Gear for Sale:** A limited selection of basic equipment can be purchased in Oranjestad.

**Diving Gear for Sale and Rent, Trips, Guides, Boats, Compressed Air:** These services are available from Mr. Art LaMour, water sports manager, the Aruba Caribbean Hotel.

**Currents, Winds:** Ocean currents are from east to west, and are stiff along the north shore and the eastern and western extremities of the island. Strong currents are not usually found along the south coast.

The trade winds are from the northeast. Accordingly the north-coast waters are usually too rough for diving.

### NORTH COAST

Due to almost constant heavy seas, diving is not recommended here.

### SOUTH COAST

A large oil refinery is situated at the southeastern end of the island. It is a bit dangerous to dive here because of the heavy ship traffic.

A reef extends from Spanish Lagoon northwest to Oranjestad about a half mile offshore. Depths on the reef vary from ten to thirty feet. Outside the reef the bottom drops off to more than one hundred feet. Spearfishing is pretty good on this reef.

Most diving is along the area from Westpunt, the western tip of the island, to Noorwest Punt, the northern tip. Depths vary from eight to forty feet. Three wrecks are located here. One is in about fifteen feet of water about half a mile north-northwest of the Aruba Caribbean Hotel. Another is in about twenty feet of water not quite a mile west of the Basi Ruti Hotel. The third is farther north, about one and a half miles north of the second wreck mentioned. It is about forty feet deep and is marked with a light buoy.

# PART TWO

# THE MEDITERRANEAN

*Chapter* 35

# INTRODUCTION TO THE MEDITERRANEAN

It is possible to go skin diving in any good-sized body of water. However, unless the water is transparent enough for the diver to see clearly underwater, and unless there are some interesting underwater sights, and unless the water is calm enough to swim in without becoming tired quickly, diving will not be much fun. Therefore sport divers—whether spearfishermen, fish watchers, or photographers—look for ideal conditions: calm, clear, warm water, interesting underwater formations, and fish.

Ideal diving conditions seldom exist near harbors or large coastal settlements because the surrounding water is almost always murky and polluted. Underwater visibility is usually poor near the mouths of rivers because of the silt discharged into the sea. Fish are seldom found in any quantity where a lot of people congregate— such as near bathing beaches. Sandy areas underwater resemble deserts and are ordinarily inhabited only by flat fish such as flounder.

The problem, then, of the diver—novice or expert—is how to evaluate a given area in terms of its suitability for diving and where to find the optimum conditions for diving without having to travel any farther than necessary. The purpose of this book is to solve this problem.

In the Mediterranean, and in other oceans and seas not warm enough for the growth of coral reefs, the terrain underwater will closely resemble the terrain of the bordering shoreline. Thus, the sea bottom off a sand or gravel beach is usually sandy, while a rocky shoreline usually indicates that the sea bottom nearby will also be rocky. Similarly, a steep and cliffy coastline is usually continued underwater and the sea bottom near such a shore is likely to be deep (there are a few exceptions to this, such as a rocky, shallow reef lying at some distance off a sandy beach). It is because of the fact that the underwater terrain can be judged according to the configuration of the shoreline that the shorelines of the Mediterranean countries are described on the following pages. From the descriptions given, the visitor can judge where the best diving areas are in relation to his holiday headquarters.

The following comments will help the reader select a good spot for diving. If the water near the shore looks even slightly opaque, the chances are that the underwater visibility will not be very good. If the water is clear and blue right up to the shore, it is likely that underwater visibility will be good. An exposed, rocky, steep shoreline on a windward shore will probably not be an exceptionally good area for fish, even when the seas are calm, since the scouring action of the heavy waves pounding against the rocks prevents the growth of seaweed and other marine life upon which some fish depend for food.

The best places for diving, whether for spearfishing or fish watching, are around rocky areas that are at least partially protected from heavy winds and seas and strong currents. It is here that marine growth can thrive and attract the small, herbivorous rock dwellers which attract the larger predators that are considered fair game for spear guns or cameras.

The most commonly seen game fish in the Mediterranean are groupers, amberjacks, bass, bream, dentexes, mullet, mackerel, and tuna. Although some species are more likely to be seen in a given area than other species, the above list covers those fish most likely to be seen. Accordingly, to avoid repetition, these fish are not listed for each diving area described.

The best time of year for diving in the Mediterranean is from June through September. Since most Europeans take their annual vacations in August, visiting skin divers are likely to find coastal areas quite crowded during that month.

Water evaporates from the Mediterranean at a rate greater than the water discharged into it by rivers. To offset this evaporation loss, a compensating supply flows from the Atlantic into the western Mediterranean through the Strait of Gibraltar and from the Black Sea through the Bosporus and the Dardanelles into the Aegean. The tremendous inflow through the Strait of Gibraltar accounts for the general easterly direction of the current in the western Mediterranean. The flow of water from the Black Sea accounts for the southwesterly set of the current in the eastern Aegean. Generally speaking, except near Gibraltar and the Dardanelles, currents in the Mediterranean are not strong enough to affect divers except around the tips of peninsulas or prominent headlands. Wherever there are strong currents, it will be mentioned in the text.

In many places there are underwater caves large enough to explore. It is suggested that cave diving be attempted only by experienced scuba divers, and never alone. An underwater flashlight should be carried along. The most colorful part of caves is the ceiling, rather than the walls or floor.

Ships of all kinds have voyaged across the Mediterranean for thousands of years. Accordingly, wrecks can be found along many shorelines. Most wrecks are found accidentally. Even with a description of the location, as given in this book, currents, winds, visibility problems, and the difficulty of precisely measuring distances across the water are factors which make it difficult at times to locate sunken ships. Frequently, local fishermen can help in this task since their fishing nets become fouled on wrecks resting on an otherwise flat bottom.

Amphorae were the all-purpose containers of the ancient mariners. These jars were made of baked clay, were oval or egg-shaped, usually pointed at the bottom, and had a curved handle on each side. They were used for carrying and storing cargoes of wine, grain, or anything else that could be poured into them. The ancient Greeks coated the inside surfaces of their wine amphorae with a resinous compound to retard evaporation of the wine. This coating imparted a resinous flavor to Greek wine which is still preferred by many Greeks and accounts for the popularity of the resinous retsina wine.

Amphorae, ballast stones, pottery, and stone or lead anchors are all that remain of most ancient wrecks. However, the discovery of a single amphora does not necessarily indicate a nearby ancient wreck. Amphorae were frequently thrown over the side after the contents had been consumed, in much the same way that a modern ship's cook will throw paper wrappings, tin cans, and other empty food containers into the sea after preparing a meal. Amphorae were also thrown into the sea to lighten the ship in a gale and as an offering to the sea gods—a type of trip insurance.

Ancient wrecks are now recognized as important, sometimes previously unknown, pieces in the mosaic of history. This is largely because the archaeologist can study a complete slice of life as it was lived at the time of the ship's disaster. Since everything manufactured in the Mediterranean of any value was transported by sea, the careful, professional study of ancient wrecks has contributed greatly to our understanding of ancient history.

For this reason, if for no other, divers are urged to leave ancient wrecks strictly alone. It is only by studying each fragment of a wreck in relation to the whole that archaeologists can arrive at an accurate evaluation. Amphorae, or other fragments, removed carelessly and at random, make it difficult to study a wreck methodically.

Most of the Mediterranean countries have laws prohibiting the removal of amphorae or other artifacts from the sea. In some places, notably Greece, this law is strictly enforced and violators are severely punished.

The words "sunken port" or "sunken town" sometimes conjure up images of drowned cities, delicately draped with a bit of seaweed, which appear much as they did before they became submerged. Unfortunately this is not true. In many cases, building stones, marble columns, and occasional statues can be seen. The majority of these sites, though, are a jumble of almost un-identifiable lumps joined together by cementlike concretions, and require considerable methodical study by archaeologists before any real sense can be made of them.

In our automated jet age, there are few opportunities for most of us to experience the profoundly gratifying experience of personal exploration and discovery. The museums, cathedrals, and monuments of Europe are classified, road-mapped, and, literally, overrun by improbably dressed camera toters frantically cramming several millennia of European history into a hectic and grueling two-week vacation.

Lucky indeed are those who will even briefly return to the primordial sea and discover, in tranquil silence, the uncatalogued beauty, serenity, and well-ordered life which has remained fundamentally unchanged during the uncounted ages since our first ancestor emerged from its depths.

# Chapter 36

## PORTUGAL

**How to Get There:** By Pan Am Jet Clipper from New York to Lisbon, nonstop, in six and a quarter hours; ten and a quarter hours from Miami; two hours from Paris; one hour from Madrid.

**Customs Regulations:** Personal belongings and 250 grams of tobacco or fifty cigars or two hundred cigarettes are admitted duty free.

**Travel Documents Required:** U.S. citizens must have passports; however, a visa is not necessary unless a stopover is made in the Azores.

**Currency:** The escudo is worth about 3½¢ in U.S. currency. There are 100 centavos in an escudo. Thirty-five escudos, fifty centavos is written 35$50. There are no currency restrictions.

**Hotels:** Lisbon and other larger cities have a wide variety of hotels, from low-priced pensions and pousadas (State Tourist Inns) to magnificent luxury hotels. Rates range upward from $5.00 per day with all meals.

**Transportation:** Taxis are quite inexpensive. Rental autos are readily available. Internal rail and air transportation also provide access to many coastal areas.

**Medical Facilities:** In the larger communities, there are good hospitals. First aid stations are found throughout the country. Visitors to Lisbon requiring medical aid can arrange for it through their hotel, or dial the emergency medical number: 77-51-71.

**Other Information:** The Pan American office is at Praça dos Restauradores 46 and is an excellent source of general tourist information. The Secretariado Nacional de Informação (Portuguese

Tourist Office) is also on Praça dos Restauradores, across the plaza from the Pan Am office. Their New York office is Casa de Portugal, 570 Fifth Avenue (Tel: 581-2450). General tourist information and the pamphlets "Portugal Hotels" and "Portugal Welcomes You" are available through these offices.

## SKIN DIVING INFORMATION

Centro Português de Actividades Submarinas (CPAS) is the national diving club of Portugal. They welcome foreign divers and offer as much assistance and information as possible. It is suggested that visiting divers contact the club either at Avenida Almirante Reis, 106 (Tel: 73-42-28) or at Rua Egas Moniz 43-A (Tel: 71-15-05) before embarking on any major diving trips.

Portugal has two coastlines; the Atlantic coast to the west, and the Algarve coast to the south. Diving conditions on the Atlantic coast are subject to rapid change, depending on the rather variable weather. The Algarve coast is very much like the Mediterranean and the water is more consistently calm. Diving conditions are generally better along the western portion of the Algarve for this reason. Since the Algarve is about 180 miles south of Lisbon it has not been visited by a great number of skin divers and there are still plenty of fish and lobsters to be seen.

The best diving areas on the Atlantic coast are at Sines, Peniche, Berlenga Island, and Sesimbra. On the Algarve coast, the best diving areas are found between Cabo de São Vicente and Lagos. These areas will be discussed in detail later in this chapter.

**Laws:** Spearfishing while wearing scuba gear is prohibited. The daily shellfish limit is two per diver. There is no limit on fish. Visitors must obtain a license (through CPAS) if their stay in Portugal exceeds two months.

**Diving Gear for Sale:** Spril Sports, Rua do Carmo 21 in Lisbon, is the most dependable source of good-quality French and Italian diving equipment. A limited selection of snorkeling gear can be found in some of the sporting goods stores in Lisbon as well as in the smaller coastal towns, particularly Estoril and Cascais. Rental equipment is not yet available.

**Guides, Boats:** The best method of obtaining guides is through CPAS in Lisbon. A professional dive shop has yet to appear in Portugal. Boats can be hired from fishermen in most coastal towns.

**Compressed Air:** Compressed air for scuba tanks is available in Lisbon only through CPAS or through Ar Liquido, rua Quinta do Almargem 14 (Tel: 38-27-72 or 38-32-65).

**Currents, Winds:** Currents are usually not strong enough close to shore to affect divers, except as noted in the following text. The prevailing winds are from the north and the northwest.

The water temperature varies between 60° and 70°, depending on the season, location, and weather conditions.

### DIVING SITES ON THE ATLANTIC COAST

Peniche is a fishing village about seventy miles by road north of Lisbon. This is one of the best areas on the west coast for loafing along in shallow water, exploring among the rocks, or spearfishing. There are two small pensions in town, and several good beaches nearby. The shallow waters northwest of the breakwater are excellent for novice divers.

The Portuguese Government is considering establishing an underwater park here which will extend from Peniche northwest to the village of Remédios. Visitors to this area should check on this before spearfishing in this area.

Divers can enter the water from the rocky shoreline or can rent fishing boats from the villagers. The bottom is alternately sandy and rocky. The bottom gradually deepens from two to six feet near the shore.

In summer the visibility here is thirty to fifty feet. In winter, visibility is variable depending entirely on weather and sea conditions.

There are plenty of fish here. In addition to the small reef fish found in shallow water, there are corbinas, sea bass, mackerel, tuna, dolphins, groupers, mullet, bream, and an occasional swordfish. There are also lobsters, clams, oysters, and crabs.

Only on the clearest days is underwater photography feasible here. However, one can usually obtain good photos of fish and underwater formations with flash if the photographer concentrates on close-ups. Film should be brought from Lisbon since it is scarce in Peniche. There are no dive shops here.

Berlenga is a small rocky island about an hour offshore from Peniche. There are a few cottages and a fourteen-room pousada, the Pousada de São João Baptista.

Berlenga is an ideal place to spend a few days spearfishing, exploring the underwater terrain, or just resting. Aquatur, Rua Egas Moniz 43-A, Lisbon, is a well-organized travel agency specializing in skin diving tours to Berlenga. This island can be reached by boat service from Peniche.

The sea bottom here is rocky and visibility in summer is fifty feet or more. In winter, visibility is variable, depending on sea conditions. The same variety of fish can be seen here as in Peniche; however, the fish are usually larger around Berlenga.

For the keen spearfisherman, Berlenga is a good diving spot. It is best to plan on staying at least two days here since it wouldn't be worth the trouble of getting here otherwise.

From Peniche south to Estoril the coastline is alternately rocky and sandy. During strong winds the seas are rough and diving is impossible.

The coastline is rocky along the Estoril area (just north of Lisbon) and the waters are protected by a peninsula from the north winds. Snorkelers should stay close to shore because of the heavy boat traffic here. There are few, if any, large fish in this area.

From Lisbon south to Cabo Espichel the water is dirty and unsuitable for diving because of the outflow of water from the Rio Tejo (Tagus River). The Tejo brings down quantities of silt.

Sesimbra is a picturesque fishing village and resort about fourteen miles south of Lisbon. This is the best place for diving near Lisbon. Since the area is sheltered by cliffs from the northwest winds and Atlantic swells, the region is ideal for both beginners and expert divers. The 1958 World Championship Spearfishing competition was held here. This village can be reached by good road from Lisbon.

The bottom is rocky with some sandy areas. Depths close to shore are variable and range from shallow water to sixty feet or more. A kelplike seaweed covers much of the sea bottom. There are several fairly large caves where groupers may be found.

In summer, underwater visibility varies between forty and seventy feet. Visibility in winter varies with the weather. Visibility is usually better here than along most of the Atlantic coast since the water is relatively calm because of the protecting cliffs.

Groupers, sea bass, mackerel, mullet, bream, and some tuna are seen here. Lobsters and crabs can also be found.

A limited selection of snorkeling equipment is available in local stores. It is better to obtain gear in Lisbon, where the selection is greater. There are three hotels in the village.

From Sesimbra the coast is sandy and uninteresting for several miles, as far south as Sines. Sines is a small fishing village about ninety-seven miles south of Lisbon. Cabo de Sines is a rocky point jutting out into the Atlantic which offers excellent spearfishing and underwater sightseeing conditions. Game fish are usually found around a group of rocky islets lying off the southwestern side of the cape. Sines can be reached by auto from Lisbon. There is train service from Lisbon, but auto travel is quicker.

The bottom here is mixed: sand, rock, and seaweed. The bottom shelves off from a couple of feet near the coast to about ninety feet not too far offshore. Visibility underwater ranges between thirty and fifty feet in the summer and is usually less than thirty feet in winter, depending on the weather.

Corbinas, groupers, mullet, bream, mackerel, tuna, dolphins, sea bass, and various species of reef fish are seen here.

The Sines area has the reputation among Portuguese divers as having the best conditions for spearfishing on the west coast. Seas are very heavy here with strong westerly winds. There are five small pensions in the village.

The sea bottom is mostly sandy from Sines south for eighteen and a half miles. In this area the only feature of interest to divers is Ilha do Pecegueiro, a small island about three hundred yards offshore about eight and a half miles south of Cabo de Sines. The bottom is rocky for over four hundred yards around the island and game fish can be found here. A ruined castle sits atop this islet.

About eighteen and a half miles south of Sines the coast becomes rocky and steep and affords good diving conditions as far south as Cabo de São. Vicente, the southwestern tip of Portugal. The area is not too heavily populated and is battered by heavy seas when strong winds prevail. Fishing boats can usually be hired at low cost in the isolated coastal villages.

### THE ALGARVE COAST

The western portion of the Algarve coast is the best area for diving. There are areas for various levels of diving ability, and various interests: from beginner to expert and for snorkeling in shallow water to deep-water spearfishing. This part of the Algarve is usually calm and the water is fairly clear with summer visibility fifty to seventy feet. Visibility varies in winter but is usually between twenty-five and fifty feet.

This area can be reached by a 165-mile drive from Lisbon or by train from Lisbon or Faro or by air from Lisbon to Faro and automobile to Lagos.

Small boats can be rented from fishermen for offshore diving. The water can be entered in many places directly off the rocks.

Dolphins, mackerel, groupers, tuna, sea bass, corbinas, and mullet are seen in this region. The bottom is alternately sandy and rocky. Snorkeling equipment can be purchased in Lagos and in Portimão.

There are plenty of fish in the area between Sagres and Cabo de São Vicente. Divers are cautioned to stay away from the extremities of Cabo de São Vicente and Ponta de Sagres because the water can be quite rough and the currents very strong.

The waters between Lagos and Portimão can be murky due to the outfall of a river. There are a variety of hotels, pousadas, and pensions in Lagos and Portimão. There is a hotel and a pousada in Sagres.

From Portimão east to Faro the coastline is varied, with high cliffs separated by many long stretches of beach. The variety of fish to be found here may not equal those found in the area to the west, but the rocky portions of the coastline here are good spots for various underwater activities.

Near Portimão there is an especially convenient area for snorkeling at Praia de Rocha. The rocky, steep coastline at the eastern end of the bay offers attractive underwater scenery and fair spearfishing.

There has been a recent building boom in this region and hotels of various types have been erected. Consequently the region is good for the casual diver—the one who is interested in snorkeling as a part of a holiday but is not particularly interested in journeying to some of the more remote, wild areas of the coast.

From Faro east to the Spanish border the coastline is mostly low and sandy. Although many lovely beaches can be found in this region, there are few underwater attractions.

The only recompression chamber in Portugal is in the town of Alfeite, across the Tejo from Lisbon. It is kept in the Portuguese Navy headquarters. In case it is needed, telephone 27-09-53. It is in charge of: Direcção do Serviço de Submersíveis, Alfeite.

*Chapter* 37

# MOROCCO

**How to Get There:** By Pan Am Jet Clipper direct from New York to Rabat in eleven hours or from Lisbon or Paris by direct flights. A passenger train runs between Rabat and Tangier (Tanger). Tangier may also be reached by ferry from Gibraltar or from Algeciras, Spain.

**Customs Regulations:** Personal clothing, two hundred cigarettes, or fifty cigars, or a pound of tobacco and a bottle of liquor are admitted duty free.

**Travel Documents Required:** U.S. citizens must have passports. Visas are not required.

**Currency:** Moroccan dirhams (written: DH) are valued at 20¢ each, or DH5 to $1.00 U.S. Importing or exporting Moroccan currency is prohibited. Visitors must declare all currency in their possession when entering and leaving the country.

**Hotels:** A wide variety of hotels and guesthouses is found in the larger cities. The National Tourist Office maintains a chain of comfortable hotels throughout the country.

**Transportation:** Taxis, rental autos, domestic air flights, and trains provide internal transportation. Be sure to settle the fare in advance with drivers of nonmetered taxis. Roads are good. The Government sells gasoline coupons which enable tourists to buy gasoline duty free. The coupons are purchased by tourists for seven dirhams each and redeemed at gasoline stations at a value of ten dirhams each. These tax-free coupons are sold at the various ports of entry and by all branches of the Banque National pour le Commerce Exterior.

**Medical Facilities:** Good in all cities. English-speaking doctors are available. Visitors are advised to arrange for medical service through hotels, when possible.

**Other Information:** French and Arabic are spoken everywhere. English is spoken by many in the larger communities. Royal Air Maroc is general agent for Pan Am. Their Rabat office is on Avenue Mohammed V (Tel: 246-04/07).

Tourist information of a general nature is available from the Moroccan National Tourist Office, 341 Madison Avenue, New York (Tel: 679-4570), or from the National Moroccan Tourist Office, 19 rue Maurice Pascouet, Rabat, Morocco.

## SKIN DIVING INFORMATION

Morocco has two coastlines: the Atlantic and the Mediterranean. Diving on the Atlantic coast is not possible most of the year due to heavy ground swells which break on the shore with considerable force.

Divers planning a trip to Morocco are advised to contact Monsieur Henri Tolila, 12 Boulevard d'Oujda, Casablanca. He is the director of the Fédération Royale Marocaine d'Études et de Sports Sous-Marins (Federation of Moroccan Skin Diving Clubs) and can assist with arrangements for trips, diving boats, etc.

**Laws:** Diving at night is prohibited. Spearfishing may not be practiced within one hundred meters of permanent works and fishing nets and within fifty meters of beaches and bathing places. Spear guns powered by explosives or compressed gas (air or $CO_2$) are prohibited. Spearfishing while wearing scuba equipment is prohibited. Spearfishing with an underwater light source is prohibited. Spear guns must be unloaded when out of the water. Speared fish may not be sold. Spearfishermen must hold a valid spearfishing license. Application for this license may be made to the "Chief, Direction de la Marine Marchande et des Pêches Maritimes," located on the ground floor of the buildings facing the Bridge Station (Gare du Port) in Casablanca. Applicants must present a medical certificate and an insurance policy. Permits are issued to persons eighteen years old or over (or to sixteen- and seventeen-year-olds with written permission from parents or a legal guardian). The fee is DH25 ($5.00 U.S.). Permits are valid for the calendar year in which they are issued.

Alternatively, and more easily, an international spearfishing permit valid in Morocco, Portugal, and France may be obtained from the headquarters of the World Underwater Society (Confédération Mondiale Activité des Subaquatique). The address is: C.M.A.S., 34 rue du Colisée, Paris 8ᵉ, France.

**Diving Gear for Sale:** Limited quantities of equipment can be found in Rabat and Tangier. Vidal Sport Shop, at the entrance to the Old Port in Tangier, offers French diving gear for sale. Visitors are advised to bring their own gear. Rental equipment is not available.

**Boats and Guides:** Boats may be hired in most coastal towns from fishermen. The cost depends on the ability of the bargainers. It is best to make arrangements through the Moroccan Skin Diving Federation.

Professional guides are not available except for guests of the Club Méditerranée at their camp in Al Hoceima.

**Compressed Air:** *Agadir:* M. Boichut, Enterprises Portuaires. *Casablanca:* Groupe Epi-Vignaud des Recherches Sous-Marines or at l'Usine d'Air Liquide, Route des Ouled-Ziane. *Rabat:* Groupe des Activités Sous-Marines, Quai Léon Petit. *Tétouan:* Dépôt d'-Air Liquide. *Meknès:* Dépôt d'Air Liquide.

**Currents and Winds:** The Mediterranean coast presents many excellent opportunities for diving. However, the area from Tangier west to Cap Spartel (the northwest point of Morocco) and east to Ceuta should be approached with caution because of the strong current of the Strait of Gibraltar. Within this area, diving is safe in the bays and inlets that are sheltered from the main force of the current.

East of Ceuta, little, if any, current is felt except around peninsulas or salient headlands. Tides are not a problem since the Mediterranean is virtually tideless.

Along this coast the winds are from the northeast from about

March until October. The rest of the year they are from the quadrant northwest to southwest. A rule of thumb used by local divers is that east winds bring cold, clear water and west winds bring warm, murky water.

The Mediterranean coast is described below in geographical order, from west to east, commencing with Tangier.

### TANGIER TO CEUTA

The Bay of Tangier is not suitable for diving because there is little to see on the sandy bottom. Beyond this bay the coastline is extremely steep and rocky. Access is by boat since the few existing roads are inland except at Malabata Point and Ceuta, which is a Spanish possession.

Depths close to shore are about ten feet and gradually deepen. The bottom is rocky and quantities of game fish can be seen. Lobsters are not too plentiful. Sea crabs are sometimes found in early summer. The visibility varies widely and unpredictably. Some of the better spots in this region are: Cala Grande (a road is under construction which will link this bay with the main east/west road), Rosh Bourre, and Punta Cires. Wrecks may be found as follows: a stranded wreck is in water about fifteen to twenty feet deep toward the eastern end of the bay just east of Punta de Alcázar; another wreck is submerged in about fifteen feet of water about four hundred yards north of Punta Blanca (which is about three miles west of Ceuta); two more wrecks lie in ten and thirty feet of water about one hundred and two hundred yards, respectively, north of Punta Santa Catalina (just east of Ceuta). It is suggested that divers visiting Ceuta contact the local diving club: Club de Actividades Submarinas y Maritimo Deportivas Ceuta, Espino no. 16, Ceuta (Tel: Ceuta 3753).

### CEUTA TO TETÓUAN

The coast trends southeast here, and is low and sandy. A few offshore rocks are found but the area is not as suitable for diving

[25] *Above.* The "flowers" of the sea bottom are sea anemones. A tube sponge is shown at the upper left.   [26] *Below.* A school of striped grunts swims over brain coral *(right)* and fire coral *(left).* Fire coral will give a painful skin "burn" if touched and should be avoided. It is about the color of mustard.

[27] *Above.* The stingray spends much of his time on the sandy bottom and frequently burrows into the sand so that only his eyes and nostrils show above the bottom. A sharp, serrated stinger is attached to the base of his tail. It can inflict a painful wound; however, the stingray is ordinarily a nonaggressive creature and uses the stinger only for defense. [28] *Below.* The leopard ray is one of the most graceful and beautiful of sea creatures. It is harmless and should be left alone by spearfishermen.

[29] The basket sponge is one of the unusual forms of life found in tropical seas.

[30] The trunkfish has an almost completely rigid body, composed of hard scales fused together. This one is swimming above a few black sea urchins. Divers should avoid contact with urchins since their spines are sharp, brittle, and barbed. They cause a painful puncture; however, the pain will usually disappear in half an hour or so.

[31] Spiny lobsters, or langoustes, normally spend the daylight hours in a hole or cave and venture out at night to feed.

[32] *Above.* In addition to fish, there are several forms of sea life shown here: a sea anemone and tube worms *(bottom, just left of center)*, seaweed *(lower right)*, brain coral *(center)*, gorgonians *(upper right)*, and hard reef coral *(upper left)*. [33] *Below.* Small reef fish live in the remnants of a sunken ship. The deck winch can be seen on the right.

[34] Two French angelfish hover over a coral reef.

[35] A shy banded butterfly fish heads for the protection of a coral cave. Stonelike reef coral and brain coral can be seen here.

[36] A green parrot fish is seen among a forest of gorgonians. This creature has a fused beak which is used to bite off bits of coral, a principal item of diet. Parrot fish are harmless.

[37] *Above*. The triangular tip of an anchor fluke is visible to the right. This relic is one of the few traces of a sunken ship to survive the corrosion of the sea. [38] *Below*. Small reef fish and a blowfish cluster near the protection of a coral cave. When frightened, the blowfish inhales quantities of water. This causes sharp spines to stand out on his distended, balloonlike body—an effective discourager of predators. Blowfish are timid and harmless creatures and are very slow-moving when blown up.

[39] *Above*. Three trunkfish "flying" in formation over a Caribbean reef.  [40]
*Below*. Green turtles are surprisingly fast swimmers and can outdistance a
diver. Unfortunately for them, their flesh is delicious and their numbers have
been severely reduced by the Caribbean turtling fleets—and by spearfishermen.

[41] Diving guide Papy Martínez, of Curaçao, left, escorting a group of visitors to one of the many coral gardens around that island.

[42] The author's wife about to enjoy an underwater tour of Bahamian reefs aboard the dry submarine operated by Lloyd's Spearfishing Resort on Spanish Wells.

as the one just described. The most salient feature is Cabo Negro (Cap Noir), which is a bold, rugged, promontory. Since sunken rocks lie offshore of this cape for about half a mile, it would seem to be suitable for diving. However, currents here can be quite strong; therefore, diving is sometimes dangerous and is not advisable.

Also included in this region is Restinga, a popular resort. The beaches are excellent but diving conditions are mediocre.

### TETÓUAN TO THE ALGERIAN BORDER

As far as Melilla, the coastline is predominately rugged, rocky, and steep. The area is almost inaccessible except by boat since roads lead from inland points only to Al Hoceima, Melilla, and Maidia. Within this area very good conditions for spearfishing are found: clear water, and plenty of game fish. This is true particularly at Al Hoceima and Cabo del Agua (north of Melilla). The bottom slopes off gradually from shallow depths near the shore. The best plan for diving in this area is to headquarter at either Al Hoceima or Melilla, where boats can be hired for exploring the outlying areas.

From Melilla east to the border the coast is low and sandy with shallow water extending as far as two miles offshore. There is little of interest for the diver here.

*Chapter 38*

# SPAIN, Including Gibraltar

**How to Get There:** By Pan Am Jet Clipper to Barcelona from New York in about nine hours or by Clipper to Lisbon, with connecting flights to coastal points in Spain.

**Customs Regulations:** Items for personal use and a bottle of liquor, a bottle of wine, and a carton of cigarettes will be admitted duty free.

**Travel Documents Required:** U.S. citizens must have a passport. A visa is not required. The departure tax is 50 pesetas (85¢).

**Currency:** The peseta is divided into 100 centimes and is exchanged at 60 pesetas to $1.00 U.S. There are no restrictions on taking money into or out of the country.

**Hotels:** Hotels are plentiful all over Spain, with a wide variety except in the remote areas. The most up-to-date listing of hotels, and rates, is in the book *Guide to Spanish Hotels*. It is available at newsstands all over the country. Pan Am agents will be glad to assist with hotel reservations where possible.

**Transportation:** Taxis, buses, airplanes, rental autos, and trains provide an excellent system of internal transportation. The main roads are paved and usually in good condition.

**Medical Facilities:** Excellent in the larger communities.

**Other Information:** The Pan Am offices are at Calle Mallorca 250 in Barcelona (Tel: 215-20-58); in the Edificio España (Tel: 241-42-00); and in the Palace Hotel lobby in Madrid.

Spanish National Tourist offices are located at: 589 Fifth Avenue, New York; 453 Post Street, San Francisco; 23 West Jackson Boulevard, Chicago; and 1418 Commerce Street, in Dallas. The head office is Subsecretaría de Turismo, Ministerio de Información y Turismo, Madrid, Spain. There are branch offices in most of the large towns.

## SKIN DIVING INFORMATION

The southern Spanish coastline is divided into two parts: the Atlantic coast, from the Portuguese border to Gibraltar; and the Mediterranean coast from Gibraltar to the French border. Each section is discussed separately in geographical order, from west to east. Mallorca and Menorca are discussed separately, after the section on the Spanish Mediterranean coast.

Although Gibraltar is British, it is included in this chapter because of its geographical location.

**Laws:** Spearfishing while using scuba gear is prohibited. Disturbing or removing amphorae or other ancient artifacts is prohibited. The removal of coral is prohibited. Speared fish may not be sold.

Although most tourists, and many Spaniards, are not aware of it, Spanish law requires a license for spearfishing. The license can be obtained from the Spanish Admiralty in Barcelona, or from the Marine Commandant in other ports, by presenting your passport.

### THE SOUTHERN ATLANTIC COASTLINE

A road parallels the coastline from Cádiz to Algeciras. However, due to the cliffy nature of this coastline, the best way of approaching a diving area is by boat. April through August is the best time of year for clarity of water and temperature. For dives lasting longer than an hour, a wet suit will be useful. Underwater visibility is usually fifty to seventy-five feet in summer, lower in winter. The most common game fish seen here are tuna, corbinas, sargos, dolphins, and groupers.

**Diving Gear for Sale and Rent:** Spanish diving equipment is available in limited quantities in sporting goods and marine supply stores in Cádiz and Algeciras. Maxie's Dive Shop, 272 Main Street, Gibraltar, is the best source of equipment in this region. Rental equipment is not available.

**Boats:** Spanish-speaking divers can hire fishing boats in the coastal villages. There are two boat-rental agencies in Gibraltar: Mediterranean Marina Sports, Ltd., and Beverly Boats, Ltd., in the Marina.

**Compressed Air:** Maxie's Dive Shop in Gibraltar.

**Currents, Winds:** Ocean and tidal currents in the area of the Strait of Gibraltar are quite strong. For this reason, diving is not recommended in this area for novices or weak swimmers. Local divers limit their activities to rocky areas where it is possible to dive in the lee of the rocks. Along the coastline, the tidal currents flow from east to west, and from west to east. The tidal range is six to eight feet.

The prevailing winds are as follows: From December through March, east winds prevail; from April through August, west winds are most common; and from September through November, the winds are usually from the south and southeast.

From the Portuguese border to Cádiz, the coastline is low and sandy, with few rocks. The water is murky in most places due to silting from the rivers in this area. A wreck, which is marked with a buoy, lies about one and a third miles north of the Castillo de San Sebastián Light near Cádiz Harbor. A recompression chamber is stationed at the Naval Arsenal de la Carraca, San Fernando, Cádiz.

From Cádiz east to Cabo Trafalgar the coast is mostly sandy and uninteresting for diving. There are numerous reefs from one to five miles offshore, but diving is considered unsafe due to the strong current.

From Cabo Trafalgar to Gibraltar the coastline is, generally, rocky and steep. While diving conditions are usually good in the areas specified below, care must be taken not to get caught in the strong current. The tide is exceptionally strong off Cabo Trafalgar. Local divers dive at slack tide. The best diving areas in this region are: Cabo Trafalgar to Barbate; Punta Paloma; Punta de la

Pena; Isla de Tarifa to Punta Carnero. The bottom drops off steeply in most places.

A wreck is situated in shallow water about one-third mile down the coast from Punta de Zahara.

Los Cabezos Reef is about two miles south of Punta Paloma. Expert divers will find this a good hunting ground for pelagic fish. A wreck is on the north side of the eastern tip of this reef in shallow water.

Another wreck lies between Punta del Acebuche and Dos Hermanas (two large rocks northeast of Punta del Acebuche). Spearfishing in this area is good.

Further along the coast, in a northeasterly direction, is another reef, La Perla, where another wreck may be seen in shallow water. Nearby, Isla de las Palomas is a favorite area for local spearfishermen.

Spanish divers from Algeciras spend most of their time in the area from Tarifa to Punta Carnero. The northeasterly trend of the coastline protects the swimmers from the main force of the Gibraltar current.

The most protected area near Algeciras is around Punta Carnero. Many grouper are found here in the rocky bottom and in caves. The depths close to shore vary from ten to twenty feet. This area is certainly the most convenient, and safest, diving spot for visitors to Algeciras or Gibraltar. A wreck is situated about a quarter mile north of the point. Due to its depth, over thirty feet, it will be easier to find with the help of a local fisherman.

A dispute now exists between the Spanish and the English over possession of Gibraltar. As a result, automobile traffic, through Spanish La Línea, has been severely curtailed because of lengthy and deliberately tedious Customs examinations. Visitors are advised to take the ferry boat to Gibraltar from Algeciras. At the time of writing, this means of entering Gibraltar still operates smoothly.

The currency on Gibraltar is sterling. There are no particular immigration requirements except that visitors must have a passport. Only Soviet-bloc citizens must have visas.

Gibraltar has over thirty miles of tunnels and many more miles of caves, some of which contain artifacts indicating that they were inhabited by early man.

Gibraltar Bay itself is of little interest to the diver, except for the Punta Carnero area. The current in the bay is variable and is affected principally by the wind. Current velocity can reach one knot. Southwesterly winds create heavy seas in the bay.

The visibility of the waters around Gibraltar varies widely and unpredictably from ten to over one hundred feet. Groupers, wrasses, bass, and corbinas, as well as a few lobsters, are seen in these waters.

Beginners will find a good snorkeling area on the west side of Gibraltar, north of Rosia Bay, in a rocky area called the Seven Sisters. Few large fish are seen here, but the underwater terrain is interesting for snorkelers. On the eastern side, another good snorkeling area extends from Alisa Craig southward almost to Europa Point. Within this last-named area are some caves, including Gorham's Cave, which contains numerous artifacts from Neolithic man.

About three hundred yards north of Europa Point, on the east side, there are two Sherman tanks in about fifteen feet of water.

Avoid diving on Europa Point. The current is extremely strong.

Along the south mole, between stations 37 and 42, there is a wreck lying in seventy-five feet of water. This wreck is on the west side (outside) of the mole. It is about thirty feet to the top of the deck.

Another wreck lies upside down on the west side (outside) of the detached mole. It can be found by swimming west about seventy yards from the center of the mole. It is about seventy feet to the wreck. The bottom is one hundred feet deep. There are three large holes near the bow. The wreck, a casualty of World War II, is still unidentified.

Two wrecks, about thirty-five feet deep, can be found about a half mile due east of the Gibraltar airport runway. They are about one hundred yards northwest of the innermost yellow flashing buoy. Two more wrecks are in fifteen feet of water about three hundred yards north and slightly east of these first two. Closer to shore, there is a wreck in about ten feet of water about one hundred yards due east of the British/Spanish border.

## THE MEDITERRANEAN COASTLINE

The Mediterranean coast of Spain, about 770 miles in length, is varied in appearance. Rocky, steep shores alternate with long sandy beaches. The best diving areas are around the rocky headlands. Fish most commonly seen are groupers, tuna, mullet, bass, and dolphins.

The availability of diving equipment and compressed air is discussed in the text below. Rental equipment is, to date, only available on the Costa Brava from the following two firms: Hostal Estel, Gerona 5a, Palamós, and from Louis J. Villa, Ctra. Gerona, B-1, 4th Floor, San Felieu de Guixols.

Fishing boats can be hired from any of the many coastal villages.

From Gibraltar eastward, currents are not usually strong, except at a few points which will be mentioned in the text. A road parallels the shoreline all the way to the French border.

From Gibraltar to Málaga the coastline is generally rocky, with deep water close to shore. The bottom drops almost straight down to fifteen to thirty feet, then shelves off steeply to more than one hundred feet about two hundred to three hundred yards offshore. For this reason, this region is not especially good for beginners. Equipment is not available in this region except for a limited selection in Torremolinos and Málaga. Around the rocky headlands the spearfishing is pretty good, with the usual assortment of Mediterranean fish.

A wreck, which shows at low tide, is about seven miles northeast of Gibraltar. It can be found about a quarter mile north of La Tunara, or one and a half miles south of Punta Chullera.

Farther east, just beyond Estepona, another wreck lies about sixty feet deep about one hundred yards offshore from Punta del Castor.

Torremolinos is a booming tourist area. Accordingly there are fewer fish here than along other sections of the coastline. Limited quantities of snorkeling equipment are available for sale, but a diving specialty shop has yet to appear. Boats can be rented on the beach.

The coastline from Torremolinos eastward to Málaga is low and sandy, with little of interest to divers. Also, the water is murky due to the discharge of the Río Guadalhorce.

Compressed air is available in Málaga at Oxhídrica Malagueña, Paseo de los Tilos, 46 (Tel: 23243). Diving equipment is available in some of the sporting goods shops.

The coastline from Málaga east to Almería is similar to the region just described. From Málaga to Punta de Vélez-Málaga, the shore is sandy, with little underwater to attract divers. Punta de Vélez-Málaga itself is at the outlet of the Río Menoba. As a consequence, the water is usually murky. The bottom is sandy and uninteresting.

From Punta de Vélez-Málaga, another beach stretches to Punta del Torrox. Punta del Torrox itself is rocky and offers some interesting underwater terrain.

From Punta del Torrox to Punta de la Concepción the coastline is alternately rocky and sandy. The bottom is sandy for the most part and shelves off quite steeply. The bay of La Herradura has a rocky shoreline with some groupers lurking in caves.

From Punta de la Concepción east to Salobreña the coast is rocky and is suitable for spearfishing. Most of this coast is difficult to approach by land, due to cliffs, and it is suggested that a boat be rented in one of the fishing villages.

From Salobreña to Cabo Sacratif, the water is murky and the bottom uninteresting due to the discharge of the Río Guadalfeo.

Cabo Sacratif is a rugged promontory offering very good spearfishing. The area directly below the ruined castle atop the cape is especially good.

From Cabo Sacratif east to Adra, the coastline is rocky and cliffy with a few intervening sandy beaches.

The Río de Adra empties in the vicinity of Adra and muddies

the water in that vicinity. The coast from Adra to Punta de los Baños is sandy and not recommended for diving.

A mile offshore of Punta de los Baños is Banco Culo de Perros, which is a good spearfishing reef with a least depth of thirteen feet. A wreck is located about one and a half miles southeast of Punta de los Baños, on the same reef.

The region from Punta de los Baños to Punta de Sabinal is a fair diving area. The bottom is alternately rocky and sandy.

From Punta de Sabinal to Cabo de Gata, diving conditions are not generally good due to the discharge of some small rivers, sand and mud bottoms, and the presence of shipping lanes for Almería-bound vessels. However, there are some rocky areas, particularly west of the city of Almería where cliffs rise abruptly from the sea.

A skin diving club is headquartered in the Club del Mar in Almería; the Sección de Pesca Submarina y Escafandrismo. Compressed air is available at Oxhídricas Malagueñas, General Saliquet, 12 (Tel: 1598).

Cabo de Gata, a rocky promontory east of Almería, is an excellent diving area. The bottom is rocky and shallow for about three quarters of a mile offshore. Diving conditions are very good from the southwest part of the Cape to Punta de Loma Pelada.

From Loma Pelada east to Punta Cope the coastline is mostly cliffy, with occasional beaches. Diving around the rocky areas is good, especially in the waters around Punta Cope which are clear, shallow, and have good quantities of fish. From Punta Cope to Cabo Tiñoso, the bottom is mostly sandy and uninteresting.

The entire region from Cabo Tiñoso east to Cabo de Palos is an excellent area for beginners as well as expert divers. The exception to this is the area in the immediate vicinity of Cartagena. The coastline in this region is high and rocky, the bottom is mostly rocky, with some sandy areas, and there are good quantities of fish. The bottom drops off to fairly deep water close to shore, so most snorkeling is done close-to.

Currents off the south coast of Cabo Tiñoso are strong. They usually set to the east, but can be influenced by strong winds.

Isla de las Palomas, south of Cabezo de Roldán, is a good diving spot, with clear water, a rocky bottom, and plenty of fish.

The area around Cabo de Palos is an excellent diving area: here, the diver will find many reefs, rocks, and shoals, in a variety of depths. As with most of the diving spots on this coastline, a boat is necessary here.

Compressed air is available in Cartagena at Sociedad General del Oxígeno, Jara 53 (Tel: 1227). Diving equipment is sold in sporting goods stores here. A recompression chamber is located at Arsenal de la Marina in Cartagena.

A wreck lies in about one hundred feet of water about four thousand feet south-southeast of the Cabo de Palos light, which is about twenty miles east of Cartagena. Good spearfishing conditions are found in the chain of rocks and reefs extending seaward from the Cape, and terminating in a group of islands and rocks named Las Hormigas.

From Cabo de Palos several miles east to Cabo de Santa Pola the coast is mostly low and sandy with several rocky points. This area is not a good one for diving, due to the sandy, muddy bottom.

Isla de Tabarca is a small island a few miles southeast of Cabo de Santa Pola. It is surrounded by rocks and the water around the island is shallow, seldom exceeding thirty feet. The island can be reached by boat from either Alicante or Santa Pola. This is an excellent place for beginners or experts. Spearfishing conditions are very good. Ancient Roman and Arab wrecks are found here, particularly around the rocks off the southern point of the island. Accommodations are simple and inexpensive, consisting of a small two-room pension and a few small cottages. Fishing boats can be rented from the village fishermen. This is an idyllic spot that has, so far, escaped the onrush of tourism and commercialism that is rapidly spoiling the Spanish coast.

From Cabo de Santa Pola to Alicante the coastline is sandy and unsuitable for diving.

There is a diving club in Alicante: S.E.D.E.S., Dr. Frías 27 (Bar Bonet). Compressed air is available from Autógena Martínez, S.A., Carretera de Ocaña (Tel: 20244).

The region from Alicante northeast to Punta de la Escaleta is alternately rocky and sandy. A long beach, Playa de las Huertas, extends north from Cabo de las Huertas for several miles. In the rocky sections beyond this beach, diving conditions are good.

The shoreline between Punta de la Escaleta and Punta del Albir is high and rocky. Diving conditions are good here with clear water, offshore rocks, and game fish. Depths vary from a few feet near shore to deep water a few hundred yards offshore. Game fish can also be found around Islota Mediana and Islota de la Pila, two small offshore islands in this area.

The region between Punta del Albir and Punta Ifach is not recommended for diving since the Río Algar discharges into this bay, bringing quantities of silt into the sea.

Good diving conditions exist between Punta Ifach and Cabo de San Antonio. The coastline is rocky and the bottom is mixed sand and rock.

The coast recedes to the west from Cabo de San Antonio, then northeast, to form the Gulf of Valencia. The city of Valencia is at the head of this bay. The entire region is sandy and not particularly good as a diving area. This region includes over 110 miles of the coastline.

There is a diving club in Denia (a few miles northwest of Cabo de San Antonio): C.I.A.S., Avenida José Antonio 28.

Diving equipment is available in a few sporting goods stores in Valencia. There are three diving clubs in this city: (1) Agrupación Juvenil de Actividades Subacuáticas (A.J.A.S.), Pascual Genis 20. (2) Centro de Investigaciones y Actividades Subacuáticas (C.I.-A.S.), Avenida Marqués del Turia 12. (3) Grupo de Investigaciones Submarinas de Educación y Descanso, Literato Azorín 17. Compressed air is available at Deportes Fernando, Sorni 13, and at Abello, Oxígeno-Linde, S.A., Colón 13, in Valencia.

For the more than sixty miles from Cabo de Oropesa northeast to Cabo de Tortosa the coast is low and sandy, with swampy portions, except for a cliffy area located between the village of Capicorp and Peñíscola. The Río Ebro empties into the sea at

Cabo de Tortosa. Large quantities of silt brought down the river make diving virtually impossible in this region.

Near the village of Amapolla, just a short distance northwest of Cabo de Tortosa, the coastline becomes steep and rocky and remains so as far as the city of Tarragona. Diving conditions are variable in this region, depending on the direction and velocity of the currents, which, at times, bring silt from the Río Ebro into this region. A diving club is situated in Tarragona: Sociedad de Exploraciones Submarinas (S.E.S.), Plaza José Antonio 41. Compressed air is available at: Abello, Oxígeno-Linde, S.A., Apodaca 27.

Between Tarragona and Barcelona, over fifty miles away, the coastline is mostly low and sandy, with occasional rocky areas. The best diving area in this region lies between La Trinidad and Torre Barona. A wreck, marked by a yellow buoy with a red flag, lies in forty feet of water about a mile directly offshore from a radio station mast, south of Barcelona, about one and a half miles south of the Lóbregat light.

Barcelona is the center of diving for the Spanish Mediterranean coast. Visiting divers will be well received at C.R.I.S. (Centro de Recuperación y Investigaciones Submarinas), Provenza 284, third floor. Detailed information on diving, boat rentals, etc., can be obtained here.

Compressed air is available at the following places in Barcelona: (1) C.R.I.S. air station, Rocafort 191 (Tel: 230-30-90). (2) Abello, Oxígeno-Linde, S.A., Bailén 105. (3) Vilarrubis y Sagué, Sagrera 44 (Tel: 251-44-04). (4) Sociedad Española de Carburos Metalicos, Puigcerdá, s-n (Tel: 225-60-77). Vilarrubis y Sague are manufacturers of the well-known Nemrod brand of diving equipment.

A recompression chamber is stationed in Barcelona at Rocafort 191 (Tel: 230-30-90) and is maintained by C.R.I.S.

It was C.R.I.S. who supplied the author with most of the information on diving clubs, air stations, and recompression chambers for this chapter.

The Costa Brava (translation: Wild Coast) extends from Blanes (about thirty miles northeast of Barcelona) to the French border.

This is the very best diving area along the entire Spanish Mediterranean coast. The shoreline is rocky, with cliffs dropping straight down into the water to depths varying from ten to two hundred feet. There are many rocky bays, inlets, islets, and reefs to explore. A boat is almost a necessity here for spearfishing, although beginners can find many good snorkeling spots in the rocky areas adjacent to the bathing beaches.

Visibility averages ninety to one hundred feet in the summer and forty-five to sixty feet in the winter. Visibility is reduced near the mouths of the rivers that empty into the sea here: Río Ter, Río Fluviá, and Río Muga.

Groupers, mullet, sole, mackerel, wrasses, and occasional swordfish as well as lobsters and edible crabs can be seen here.

The Islas Medas, offshore islands a short distance from Estartit, provide good conditions for both beginning divers and experts.

Currents here are not usually strong except at Cabo de Creus, where extreme caution must be observed.

Boats can be rented from fishermen at most fishing villages. The usual charge is 400 pesetas for five hours.

About three quarters of a mile offshore of the village of Malgrat is a wreck lying in sixty feet of water. It is marked with three buoys.

A half mile offshore (south) of Palamós is a reef named Laja de Palamós. This is a good area for spearfishing. A wreck, part of it showing above water, lies on this reef.

A Club Méditerranée holiday camp is situated at Cadaqués. This camp is completely equipped with scuba gear, a compressor, boats, instructors, and all other necessary diving equipment.

Compressed air is available at the following locations along the Costa Brava; *Blanes:* Puerto de la Maestranza, 66 Casa Creixell, (Tel: 207). *San Feliu de Guixols:* Colón, s-n, Varadero. *Palamós:* Gerona 50, Hostal Estel (Tel: 203). *Cadaqués:* Higinio Llach (a garage), and the Club Méditerranée camp.

Cabo de Creus was an exceptionally dangerous point for ancient (and modern) sailing ships because of the strong winds from the north sweeping across the Bay of Biscay. Consequently many

Roman and Greek galleys were lost in this wild region. These wrecks are usually over one hundred feet deep.

In the muddy bottom of the Golfo de Rosas there are numerous ancient wrecks. The Greeks established outposts on both the north and south sides of the gulf and amphorae from their ships are occasionally dragged up by fishermen.

*Chapter* 39

# MALLORCA AND MENORCA

**How to Get There:** By Pan Am Jet Clipper to Barcelona with a
connecting flight to Palma, Mallorca. The Compañía Transmediter-
ránea also provides ferry services to Palma and Menorca from
Barcelona, Valencia, and Alicante.

**Customs, Travel Documents, Currency:** See the chapter on
Spain.

**Hotels:** Over 900 guesthouses and hotels are available on Mallorca and accommodations can be found in all price ranges. Menorca also has ample hotel space. Reservations are necessary in
summer, particularly in August.

**Transportation:** Taxis, buses, and rental autos are available. Mallorca has a train, with passenger service. Interisland travel is by
scheduled ferry.

**Medical Facilities:** Medical facilities are good, with English-
speaking doctors available.

**Other Information:** The Tourist Information Office of the Subsecretaría de Turismo is at Avenida de Jaime III, no. 56 (Tel:
12216), in Palma. Tourist information can be obtained from this
office or from the Spanish National Tourist offices in the United
States, which are listed in the chapter on Spain.

## SKIN DIVING INFORMATION

The northern coasts of Mallorca and Menorca are, in most places,
steep and rocky. The southern coasts tend to be low and sandy.
**Laws:** See the chapter on Spain.

**Diving Gear for Sale:** Spanish diving gear can be purchased at low cost in sporting goods stores. Rentals are not available.

**Boats:** Boats can be hired in most fishing villages for 50 to 60 pesetas per hour. For larger, more comfortable yachts, contact "Palcoa" at Edificio Paseo Marítimo, Palma, Mallorca (Tel: 30190).

**Compressed Air:** Sociedad General Oxígeno, Avenida A. Rosello 112, Palma. A recompression chamber is stationed at the Submarine School in Mallorca.

The following is a description of the coastlines of the islands, commencing at the north points and progressing clockwise around the islands.

## MALLORCA

Mallorca is an excellent place for diving for both beginners and experienced divers. Beginners will find good snorkeling conditions at Cala Millor, Cala Bota, Colonia San Jorge, and Colonia San Pedro. These are shallow, easily reached areas with interesting underwater terrain. For experienced divers, the best places are around Isla Dragonera, and at Cala de Estallenchs, and Calobra. The northeastern peninsula from Cabo Farruch to Cabo del Pinar is excellent for spearfishing. At some places in this region the cliffs drop down almost vertically to a sea bottom thirty to seventy-five feet deep.

Currents are variable and depend largely on the wind. They are usually not strong enough to affect skin divers. Groupers, sargos, corbinas, dolphins, tuna, and cigalas (similar to small lobsters) are seen around the island.

Visibility is seventy-five to one hundred feet in summer. In winter, the visibility is usually fifty feet or more.

In the summer, southerly winds are frequent. Northerly and northwesterly winds predominate in winter.

Many diving sites mentioned below can be reached by road, then by swimming off the rocks. However, a boat is necessary in a number of the sites, particularly along the steep northern coast.

## DESCRIPTION OF THE COASTS

Cabo de Formentor, the northern tip of the island, is a bold promontory with steep sides. Close to shore, the water is sixty-five feet deep or more. From this cape south and east to Isla de Formentor, good diving conditions exist.

From Isla de Formentor around the bay to Cabo del Pinar the coast is unsuitable for diving with sandy beaches and a sandy bottom.

Cabo del Pinar and Cabo de Menorca are steep and rocky and good spearfishing sites. Bahía de Alcudia is southeast of Cabo de Menorca. This entire bay, beginning just south of Cabo de Menorca, is sandy and uninteresting underwater as far as Cabo Farruch, at the eastern entrance to the bay.

Between Cabo Farruch and Cabo del Pinar the coastline is high and rocky and excellent for spearfishing. The steep cliffs here drop down into just a few feet of water. The bottom shelves off steeply a few hundred yards offshore. This entire area is indented with bays and rocky headlands, excellent conditions for hunting fish, especially groupers.

The east coast, from Cabo del Pinar south to Punta Salinas, the most southerly tip of Mallorca, is mostly low, with shallow water close to shore. The bottom is alternately sandy and rocky. The shoreline is fairly straight and the indentations are shallow coves. Though diving conditions are not as good here as in other parts of Mallorca, beginners will find this a safe and moderately interesting coastline to explore. Most points can be reached by road.

The south coast extends westward from Punta Salinas to Punta Galera. The eastern portion of this coast, from Punta Salinas to Cabo Blanco shelves off gradually and is a good area for beginning snorkelers. The bottom is alternately sandy and rocky. The better areas for snorkeling are Colonia San Jorge, and around Isla Moltona and Isla Llarga.

South of this area is a group of islands lying from five to over seven miles offshore. They are good diving sites but should be explored only by experienced divers since the current here can be quite strong. The northernmost of these islands, six islands plus rocks and reefs, are excellent diving areas. They rise steeply from the ocean floor, over one hundred feet deep. The largest of the islands, Isla Cabrera, is controlled by Spanish military authorities. Their permission must be obtained before this island can be visited.

From Cabo Blanco northwest to Cabo Enderrocat the shoreline is high and cliffy. The coastal waters are shallow close to shore then shelve off to about seventy-five feet. Diving is good here and this area has the advantage of being within boating distance of Palma. About two miles beyond Cabo Enderrocat, the shoreline becomes low and sandy with little of interest underwater.

Punta de San Carlos is west of Palma and forms the northern shore of Ensenada de Cala Mayor. Within this bay, steep shores alternate with dandy stretches of shoreline. Fish, mostly groupers, are found among the rocks in this section. Las Isletas and Isla de la Caleta lie at the southern end of Ensenada de Cala Mayor. These islands are good areas for beginners as well as advanced divers. This region is also easily reached from Palma.

Between Las Isletas and Punta de la Torre the coast is low and the diving conditions indifferent.

South of Punta de la Torre is Isla de la Porassa which offers good diving conditions. Depths of sixty feet or more are found on the southern face of this island. Between Porassa and Punta de Cala Figuera, the southwestern entrance to the Bay of Palma, the coast is rocky and steep, with several coves. Diving is good in this area.

Between Punta de Cala Figuera and Punta de Sas Barbinas, a few miles northwest, cliffs line the shoreline and drop vertically into 60 to 120 feet of water. El Toro is the outer of four small islands of Punta Barbinas. These islands are fringed with rocks and offer excellent diving conditions for experienced divers.

From Punta de Sas Barbinas northwest to Playa de Paguera the shore is steep but the water is shallow near the shore, and averages ten to fifteen feet. Small bays indent deeply into the shoreline.

Most of these bays have small beaches at their heads. Islas Mala-grats and Conejos lie just offshore in this region. Their steep sides drop into water varying from less than five to about ninety feet. From Playa de Paguera northwest to Punta Galinda, the southwest-ern tip of the island, the shoreline is quite rugged and rocky with good diving conditions. This last named area is an excellent one for experienced divers; however, currents between Punta Galinda and Isla Dragonera, just offshore, can be strong.

The islands in this region are Islas Pantaleu, Mitjana, and Dragonera. The first two are smaller and are close to shore. They are ringed with rocky reefs and are excellent diving spots.

Isla Dragonera is a large island about a half mile off Punta Galera. The northwest coast is extremely steep with cliffs dropping into over one hundred feet of water along the shore. The southeast coast is not quite so steep and, in most places, the bottom is less than fifteen feet deep next to the shore. When northwesterly winds make other sections of the northwest coast of Mallorca too rough for diving, the sheltered southwest coast of Isla Dragonera can be used.

The northwest coast extends from Punta Galera northwest to Cabo de Formentor. This region is characterized by high cliffs, rocky headlands, numerous bays, and deep water close to the shoreline. The entire area, except near the coastal villages, is rec-ommended for experienced divers. Novices will find the east coast better for snorkeling since the coastal waters are shallower and the diving sites are more easily accessible.

Roads lead to several points along the northwest coast where divers can swim off the rocks. Boats can be hired in the several fishing villages along this coast.

## MENORCA

Menorca is about twenty miles northeast of Mallorca. The north-ern coast is fairly steep and rocky, although not as rugged as the north shore of Mallorca.

Snorkeling gear can be purchased in sporting goods stores. Visibility is about the same as the waters around Mallorca. Northerly winds prevail here for most of the year, although southerlies are frequent in summer. In winter, northerly winds sometimes blow with considerable force for several weeks without let up. Currents are variable and are greatly influenced by the wind.

As in Mallorca, fishing boats can be hired at most fishing villages.

### NORTH COAST

Due to heavy northerly winds, particularly in winter, this coast is frequently battered by heavy seas and diving is impossible. When seas are calm, this coast is an excellent one for diving, both for beginners and experienced divers. There are several bays and rocky headlands fringed with offshore rocks and reefs which contain grouper and other Mediterranean game fish.

Off Cabo Nati, there is a small island and a reef worth exploring. The reef extends offshore for about a quarter mile.

From Cabo Nati east to Punta del Escuá the coastline is precipitous, with depths of about fifty feet close to shore. Between Punta del Escuá and Punta Fantinat the bottom varies from five feet or less to twenty-five feet, close to shore, then slopes off to over one hundred feet. There are beaches at the heads of the many bays, but the rocky headlands are well worth exploring underwater. There are several offshore reefs and islands in this region. Cabo Caballería, a peninsula extending northward, is a good spearfishing area, as is Isla Nitge, about a quarter mile northwest of the cape.

The north coast is accessible by boat which can be hired in Mahón or in Fornells.

### EAST COAST

This shoreline is deeply indented with bays. Parts of the coast are high and cliffy with fifty or more feet of water close to the shore.

Punta Fantinat, the northwestern point on this coast, is low with shallow water close-to. Southeast of this point is Punta Codolada where grouper can usually be seen among the rocks. A mile south of this point are Islas Addaya, a group of small islands surrounded by an excellent reef for diving. Farther south, about four miles, is Isla Colom which rises rather steeply from the sea bottom. This is a good island for spearfishing, as is the fifteen-foot-deep rocky shoal about 450 yards off its eastern point.

Mahón, the capital of Menorca, is near the southern end of this coast. Fishing boats can be hired here. From Mahón south to Punta Prima, the coast is low and diving conditions not as desirable as in the region north of Mahón.

Isla del Aire lies close off Punta Prima. Be careful of the strong current in the channel between this island and the mainland. A smaller island is off the northeast point and the area between is worth exploring. The southern side of this island is rocky and steep. West of the north point of the island is a wreck about thirty-five feet deep.

### SOUTH COAST

This coast is low, with streams emptying into the sea at several points. Generally, diving conditions are not as good here as around other portions of Menorca, but there are a few spots worth looking into.

From Punta Prima west to Cala Biniparraitx the coastline is indented and rocky and fairly shallow water is found close to shore. Fish can be seen around the offshore rocks and along the rocky coast.

From Cala Biniparraitx west to Cala San Llorens, there are fewer indentations in the steep coastline. Several streams discharge into this area and visibility is lowered after a rainfall.

From Cala San Llorens west to Cabo Dartuch the bottom slopes off from shallow depths near shore to forty feet or more a quarter mile offshore. The bottom is mixed sand and rock and several streams discharge into the area. Except after rains, visibility is usually good and quantities of fish can be found. A wreck is located over half a mile southeast of Punta Gobernado in about seventy-five feet of water.

### WEST COAST

This coast is low and steep. Two rivers discharge into the sea here. The town of Ciudadela, located in the middle of the coast, is linked to Mallorca by ferry. Fair diving is found along this shoreline except off the beaches. The principal beaches here are Santandria, Algairanes, and Cala Blanca. For the most part, the bottom drops off into depths of forty feet or more near the shoreline. There isn't much here to attract the novice fish watcher, although spearfishermen will find good quantities of game fish.

*Chapter 40*

# FRANCE

**How to Get There:** By Pan American Jet Clipper nonstop to Paris in seven hours from New York or Boston. From New York to Nice via Lisbon and Barcelona, the flight time is about ten and three-quarter hours. Flights from Los Angeles via New York are about fifteen and a quarter hours, or ten and a half hours via the polar route to London with connecting flights to France.

**Customs Regulations:** A bottle of opened liquor, two pounds of foodstuffs, and 400 cigarettes or 125 cigars or a pound of tobacco are admitted duty free.

**Travel Documents Required:** U.S. citizens must have a passport. A visa is not necessary.

**Currency:** The French franc (written: N.F.) is valued at 20¢ U.S. and is divided into 100 centimes. A maximum of 750 francs may be taken out of the country. Some stores offer goods at up to twenty percent discounts to visitors paying in U.S. or Canadian dollars or travelers checks. Duty-free shopping is available in some stores in Paris and Nice and at Orly airport in Paris and at the Nice airport.

**Hotels:** Accommodations of all types are available in France, from simple pensions to luxury hotels. Advance reservations are suggested during the summer, particularly in August.

**Transportation:** Rail, bus, air, and boat transportation is excellent. Rental autos and taxis are readily available almost everywhere. Taxi rates double after 11 P.M. Roads are good.

**Medical Facilities:** Good everywhere.

**Other Information:** Pan American offices are in the Hôtel Negresco, 37 Promenade des Anglais, in Nice (Tel: 88-99-11). The Paris offices are at 138 Champs Élysées and at 1 rue Scribe (Tel: BAL 9200 for reservations or BAL 8800 for Administrative offices).

A hotel guide and general tourist information is available from the French Government Tourist Office at 610 Fifth Avenue in New York. In France, tourist information can be obtained from the Syndicat d'Initiative offices in each city and, in Paris, from the Direction Commissariat Général au Tourisme, 8 avenue de l'Opéra or from the National Office for Tourist Information at 127 Champs Élysées and at 7 rue Balzac.

## SKIN DIVING INFORMATION

Snorkeling is not prohibited or regulated, but scuba diving and spearfishing are much more rigidly controlled in France than in the United States. Because of the many regulations and the license necessary for spearfishing, visiting divers are advised either to contact a diving club in advance to make arrangements for diving trips with club members or to use the services of one of the many professional guides. The latter must be nationally certified instructors (in French: moniteurs) and have boats, equipment, and a good knowledge of conditions in their particular locality.

The waters around most of the points (caps) of land are suitable for snorkeling, except in the vicinity of harbors or rivers. In the summer, visibility along the French Riviera averages about sixty to seventy-five feet and sometimes approaches one hundred. The visibility in winter is usually forty to fifty feet, depending entirely on the weather.

Snorkelers will not need diving suits in summertime because the water is warm on the surface. However, scuba divers will find the water pretty cold below thirty to forty feet, even in summer, and will need a suit. Some of the dive shops can supply suits along with the other equipment.

The headquarters of the World Confederation of Divers (Confédération Mondiale des Activités Subaquatiques) is at 3 rue du

Colisée in Paris (Tel: 359-22-15). All divers visiting Paris are welcome to visit the clubhouse and can obtain a spearfishing permit valid in France, Portugal, and Morocco.

**Laws:** It is prohibited to: spearfish while wearing scuba equipment; use $CO_2$ or powder-propelled spear guns; spearfish at night with lights; spearfish near public beaches and ports.

A license is necessary for spearfishing in France. This can be obtained by applying to a club belonging to the French Federation of Diving Clubs (FFESSM). A list of these clubs is found at the end of this chapter. The international spearfishing permit issued by C.M.A.S. in Paris can also be used.

**Diving Gear for Sale:** Equipment can be obtained in almost any community along the south coast of France. French-made equipment is of excellent quality and is not very expensive. A complete list of dive shops is appended to this chapter.

**Diving Gear for Rent:** Snorkeling equipment is so inexpensive it is hardly worth while to rent it. Scuba equipment can be rented by divers demonstrating a thorough knowledge of scuba diving. Most of the dive shops listed at the end of this chapter have rental equipment.

**Diving Trips, Guides, Boats:** Diving trips can be organized by the dive shops listed at the end of this chapter. If they are contacted in advance, the members of most diving clubs will welcome visiting scuba divers on club diving excursions.

**Compressed Air:** A list of compressed air stations for the south coast of France is appended to this chapter. Recompression chambers are also listed.

**Winds:** The mistral (northerly and northwesterly wind) cools off the water, especially in wintertime, but seldom affect underwater visibility. The east winds are warm but frequently create cloudy water.

### SPANISH BORDER TO MARSEILLES

This western portion of the French coastline is mostly low and sandy and the underwater scenery is uninteresting. The exceptions are the extreme eastern and western ends of this area which are rocky and steep.

At the western end, near the Spanish border, there are three wartime wrecks 150 feet deep just off the harbor entrance to the town of Port Vendres. Many of the townspeople saw the vessels sink after having been torpedoed.

Underwater visibility at the eastern end is limited near the mouth of the Rhône River which discharges large quantities of silt into the sea.

### MARSEILLE TO THE ITALIAN BORDER

This is the best diving area in France. The coastline is mostly steep and rocky and the bottom is rocky with some sand or mud patches. Fish are not too plentiful except in some of the less frequented regions east of Marseille.

Visitors to Marseille can contact Mr. François Clouzot, president of Club Amis d'Archimède, 116 Cours Liautaud. The Club maintains a diving center, with hotel accommodations, on Île Maire, a small island south of Marseille. Diving conditions in the region of Île Maire are excellent and a sunken ship lies a short distance offshore.

A little over five miles west-southwest of Île Maire is the tiny islet of Île du Planier. Directly off the lighthouse in about one hundred feet of water lie the remains of a sunken freighter.

Le Grand Congloue is a small islet less than two miles southeast of Île Maire. A team of divers directed by Captain Jacques Cousteau recovered thousands of amphorae and other artifacts from a wrecked Greek wine ship of the third century B.C. The wreck was found 130 feet deep off the northwest point of the island. An Italian freighter was wrecked a few hundred yards off Île Riou, a larger islet, on September 29, 1953, while the Greek ship was being excavated. The crew was rescued from Île Riou by Cousteau's research ship *Calypso*. The recent wreck lies seventy-five feet deep.

Diving conditions along the coastline from Cap Croisette (south of Marseille) east to La Ciotat are excellent. Calm, clear water is found in the deep fjordlike indentations, called calanques, which characterize this shoreline. Access is by boat from Île Maire, Marseille, or Cassis. The bottom drops off rather sharply close to shore to fifty feet and deeper.

From La Ciotat east to Toulon, the coast is varied, with bold, steep headlands and low sandy bays. The bottom off the headlands is mostly rocky.

Bandol, a small town about twenty-five miles west of Toulon, could be called the cradle of scuba diving. It was here in June 1943 that Captain Jacques Cousteau tested the first Aqua Lung, together with the legendary Frédéric Dumas and Philippe Taillez.

It is perhaps fitting that the most complete diving center in southern France is located here, on the small island of Bendor, a few hundred yards offshore. Bendor can be reached by scheduled ferry every half hour from the pier at Bandol. The Centre International de Plongée (C.I.P.) is an official training establishment for France and it is here that civil servants (policemen, firemen, etc.) receive instruction in underwater techniques. Visitors are welcome and can enroll in courses in Aqua Lung diving, underwater photography, underwater archaeology, and other underwater activities. Complete pension (including room and board, guides, boats, and equipment) costs little. The address is C.I.P., Île de Bendor, Bandol (Var), France. Reservations are advised in summer and should be made through: The Secretary, C.I.P., 27 rue Trébois, Levallois-Perret, France.

The coastline from Toulon to the Italian border is mostly steep and rocky. Beaches of sand or pebbles are found in most of the bays. The sea bottom off the rocky headlands is rocky and suited for snorkeling and scuba diving. Deep water is found a few hundred yards offshore in most places, so diving is usually best close in along the shoreline.

East of Toulon about fifteen miles are the Îles d'Hyères, a group of small, rocky islands where scuba divers will find good diving conditions. These islands can be reached by chartered boat from Toulon or by ferry from Toulon, La Capte, Port Pothuau, Le

Lavandou, or Cavalaire. A few hundred yards south of small Île Grand Ribaud is a wreck in over one hundred feet of water. Another deep wreck is found a few hundred yards west of the northeastern point of Île de Porquerolles. Another wreck, about sixty feet deep, is in the channel between Île de Port-Cros and smaller Île de Bagaud, due west of the village of Port-Cros. These wrecks may be difficult to locate because of their depths and because of the advanced deterioration of the remnants.

Northwest of Îles d'Hyères there is a peninsula on the north coast of which is the resort of St. Tropez. With the exception of Pampelonne Beach (Anse de Pampelonne), this coast offers good diving conditions. Near shore, the bottom is about twenty feet deep and shelves off to deep water a few hundred yards offshore. The bottom is rocky and the water is usually clear. Access is by swimming out from shore or by boat from Cavalaire or St. Tropez.

From St. Tropez northeast to Cannes the coastline is generally steep and rocky except for beaches south of St. Raphaël and Cannes. The road (the Corniche d'Or) hugs the coastline, providing access to diving areas. About twenty miles south of Cannes by road is an interesting underwater formation named Notre-Dame Cathedral. It is south of Miramar, just off La Trayas. The Cathedral is an unusually formed cave with vertical and horizontal passages through which the light passes, giving a cathedral-like appearance.

East of Cannes is Cap de la Croisette. Diving conditions are not especially good here. Île Ste. Marguerite lies less than a mile south of Cap de la Croisette. Diving here is best around the rocky eastern portion of the island. Access is by boat from Cannes or Juan-les-Pins.

A peninsula, terminating in Cap d'Antibes, lies about ten miles northeast of Cannes. Diving conditions here are best between the two lighthouses: the first one is just south of Juan-les-Pins (on the southern side); the other is southeast of Antibes (on the northern side). An entry point into the water is found near the Eden Roc Hotel. A reef extends for about one-third mile northwest of Pointe Bacon, on the north side.

Diving is not very good from Antibes to Cap de Nice (which

is east of the Nice harbor, Port de Nice). The coastline is low, with pebble beaches, and the underwater visibility is not good.

Cap de Nice is steep and rocky. Access is best by boat due to the steep cliffs. This is the diving area closest to the resort of Nice. Few fish will be seen here. The best plan is to arrange for a diving trip through André Portelatine, l'Exploration Sous-Marine, 14 Quai des Docks, Port de Nice, Tel: 85-42-44. Portelatine is a true professional whose diving exploits were featured in the motion picture *World Without Sun*. He and his partner, Michel Feix, know the underwater terrain of the south of France intimately.

Cap Ferrat is a short distance east of Cap de Nice. The best diving area on this cape is at the tip and along the tip of nearby Pointe de St. Hospice. The cliffs plunge straight into the sea at Cap Ferrat so the best access to the water is by boat or by swimming off the boat landing place on the southwestern end of the cape. Depths of six to ten feet surround Pointe de St. Hospice for a couple of hundred yards offshore, where the bottom slopes off to fifty feet and deeper.

Another rocky diving area begins a few miles east of Cap Ferrat at Pointe Mala Cabuel and continues around to Cap d'Ail. This section has deep water close to shore. The best access is by boat. Underwater visibility between Cap d'Ail and Monaco is frequently poor.

Visitors to this part of France should be sure to visit the Oceanographic Museum at Monaco where many interesting mementoes of the sea and diving are on exhibit. An aquarium houses a wide variety of fish and other sea life. The Museum, directed by Captain Jacques Cousteau, was the nerve center of the Conshelf III experiment in which six men lived for a month at 330 feet off nearby Cap Ferrat in 1965.

## SKIN DIVING CLUBS IN SOUTHERN FRANCE

The following are active clubs which welcome foreign divers. They are primarily interested in scuba diving but can offer advice, if needed, to visiting snorkelers. They are all members of the French Federation of Diving Clubs (Fédération Française d'-Études et de Sports Sous-Marins) at 24 Quai de Rive Neuve, Marseille (7e), Tel: 33-39-96.

**Port de Bouc:** *Club de Plongée "Le Phoque."* President: M. Boscolo, Avenue F. Mistral, Plage de Bottai, Port de Bouc.

**Marseille:** (1) *G.P.E.S.* Pres.: M. Lasalarie, 4 Place Sadi-Carnot, Marseille (2e). (2) *Association Sportive des P & T.* 12 Boulevard Charles Nédelec, Marseille (1er). (3) *Sports Nautiques de l'Estaque.* Fontaine des Tuileries, Estaque Plage, Marseille (16e). (4) *Club de la Mer de Sormiou.* Pres.: M. Durroux, 308 Avenue de la Capelette, Marseille (10e). (5) *Les Amis de la Méditerranée.* Pres.: M. Gautier, 51 rue Gillibert, Marseille (5e). (6) *Club Sous-Marin Provence-Côte d'Azur.* Pres.: M. Battistini, 6 Avenue des Lilas, Marseille (9e). (7) *Association des Amis d'Archimède.* Pres.: M. François Clouzot, 331 Boulevard de Ste. Marguerite, Marseille (9e). (8) *Yachting Club Pointe Rouge—Section Activités Sous Marines.* Baie de la Pointe Rouge, Marseille (8e).

**Cassis:** *Centre Cassidain de Plongée.* Pres.: M. Manganelli, Lotissement Le Loano, Cassis.

**La Ciotat:** *Groupement d'Exploration Sous Marine de La Ciotat.* Pres.: M. Lucas, 14 Boulevard Lamartine, La Ciotat.

**Toulon:** *Groupe de Plongées et d'Études Sous-Marines.* Pres.: M. Assaiante, Immeuble l'Aviso—Entrée C. Avenue Lazare Carnot Prolongée, Toulon.

**Hyères:** (1) *Yacht Club d'Hyères.* Pres.: Dr. Robin, 4 Place de la République, Hyères. (2) *Club des Loisirs et Nautiques "Les Îles d'Or."* 26 Avenue François Arène, Hyères.

**La Londe les Maures:** *Club Nautique Londais.* Pres.: Dr. Goiran, Les Bormettes, La Londe les Maures.

**St. Tropez:** *Club de la Mer de St. Tropez.* Pres.: M. Gérard Happel, Les Granges St. Cannat.

**Ste. Maxime:** *Club Nautique de Ste. Maxime.* Pres.: M. de Germond, 7 Boulevard Beau Site, Ste. Maxime.

**St. Raphaël:** (1) *Club Nautique de St. Raphaël.* Pres.: M. Deschamps, 71 Boulevard d'Alsace, St. Raphaël. (2) *Groupe d'Ex-*

*ploration Sous Marin.* Pres.: Dr. Delonca, 35 Avenue Victor Hugo, St. Raphaël. (3) *Cercle des Nageurs de St. Raphaël.* Lycée A. de St.-Exupéry, Avenue du Commandant-Charcot, St. Raphaël.

**Cannes:** *Subaquatic Club de Cannes.* Bateau de Plongée l'Idéal, Quai St. Pierre, Cannes (Tel: 39-91-58).

**Antibes:** (1) *Club Sous-Marin de France.* Pres.: Dr. Piroux, 2 rue de la République, Antibes. (2) *International Sporting Club de la Côte d'Azur.* Pres.: M. LaPorte, Ponte de la Rivière Brague, Antibes.

**Nice:** (1) *Club d'Activités Subaquatiques.* Pres.: M. Prette, 24 rue Cassini, Nice. (2) *Société Sportive de Pêche à la Nage.* 8 rue du Congrès, Nice. (3) *Club des Explorateurs Sous Marin.* Pres.: M. Duclos, 77 bis, Boulevard Gambetta, Nice.

**Beaulieu:** *Groupe Subaquatique du Yacht Club de Beaulieu.* Pres.: M. Nobilitato, Beaulieu S/Mer.

**Menton:** *Sporting Club de Menton.* Pres.: M. Lamoureux, 1 Avenue Félix Faure, Menton.

## SKIN DIVING FACILITIES IN SOUTHERN FRANCE

Listed below are sources of compressed air, shops selling diving equipment, and recompression chambers. The following code is used: *D*—dealer. *A*—Compressed air. *R*—recompression chamber. These facilities are listed in geographical order, from west to east. The following information is presented through the courtesy of Mr. Pierre Marie, president of La Spirotechnique in Paris.

| TOWN | CODE | NAME AND ADDRESS |
|---|---|---|
| Banyuls | D | Sport-Ménager, rue St. Pierre |
| | D | Jude, Avenue Charles de Gaulle |
| | A | Club Nautique Banyulenc |
| | A | Laboratoire Arago |
| Port-Vendres | D, A | La Flotille, Sur le Quai (on the quay) |

| TOWN | CODE | NAME AND ADDRESS |
|---|---|---|
| Collioure | D, A | Pierre Girodeau, 45 rue de l'Égalité, Tel: 395 |
|  | D | Michajliczyn, Route Nationale |
| Perpignan | R | Single Chamber at the Fire Station |
|  | A | LaCombe, rue de la Paix |
|  | D | Nauti-France, 21 rue du Lycée |
|  | D | Sport Radio, 1 Place Jean-Jaurès |
|  | D | Perpignan Sport, 18 Place de la Loge |
|  | D | Voltaire-Sport, 4 rue Voltaire |
|  | D | Mille-Sport, 25 Boulevard Fernand-Mercader |
|  | D | Chantier-Naval Gondolys, 88 bis, Avenue Victor-Dalbiez |
|  | D | Henri Ducommum, 23 rue Louis-Blanc, Tel: 34-35-61 |
| Canet | D | Tout Pour le Sport |
| Narbonne | D | Prud'homme, 3 rue du 1er Mai |
| Gruissan | A | Club de Plongée |
| Béziers | A | Sabineau, Face au Cimetière |
|  | D | Taillardat, 9 rue de 4 Septembre |
|  | D | Rouilly, 29 Allée P.-Riquet |
|  | D | La Hutte, 10 Allée P.-Riquet |
| Agde | A | Fonquerle, rue Alsace-Lorraine |
|  | D | Bernard, rue Meuratet |
|  | D | Compère, 5 rue Jean-Roger |
| Sete | A, D | Duffour et Igon, Route de Montpellier |
|  | D | La Hutte, 14 Quai De-Lattre |
|  | D | Cabanon, rue Henri-Euzet |
|  | D | Rives, 12 rue Gambetta |
|  | D | Doutre, Quai de la Consigne |
| Frontignan | D | Frontignan-Sport, Place Jean-Jaurès |
| Montpellier | A, D | Montpellier-Auto, 5 rue Maguelone |
|  | D | Suttel Marine, rue du Grand-Saint-Jean |
|  | D | La Hutte, 9 Boulevard Victor-Hugo |

| TOWN | CODE | NAME AND ADDRESS |
|---|---|---|
| Palavas | D | Hall Nautique du Golf |
| Le Grau-du-Roi | A | Nautica, La Croix du Sud |
| Port-de-Bouc | A, D | A.R.M.A., Port de Bouc |
| Martigues | D | Boscolo, 6 rue Gambetta |
| Marseille | R | Multiplace chamber at the Marine Firehouse, Tel: 37-56-71 |
| | A, D | La Plongée, 26 Quai Rive-Neuve, Tel: 33-23-43 |
| | A, D | Bernard-Sport, 21 Boulevard L-Salvator |
| | A, D | La Vieux Plongeur, 116 Cours Lieutaud |
| | D | Raphaël, 5 Cours d'E.-d'Orves |
| | D | Sporamic, 31 rue Vincent Scoto |
| Cassis | A, D | Robion-Sport, Cassis |
| La Ciotat | A, D | Groupe de Pêche et d'Étude, 19 Quai Ganthaume |
| St. Jean la Ciotat | A, D | Nautic-Service, 13 Boulevard Beaurivage |
| Bandol | D | Meister Sport, 5 Quai de Gaulle |
| Bendor | A, R | C.I.P., Tel: 129. Single Chamber |
| Sanary | D | Au Petit Tube, Sanary |
| La Seyne | A | Air Liquide, La Seyne |
| Toulon | R | Multiplace Chamber at G.E.R.S.—Arsenal |
| | D | Tamisier, 103 Quai de la Sinse |
| | D | Plein Air, 48 rue d'Alger |
| | D | Berlet, 23 rue d'Alger |
| Hyères | A, D | Yacht Club d'Hyères |
| | A, D | Mare Nostrum, Sur le Port (in the port) |
| Le Lavandou | A | Léo Milliand, l'Exploration Sous-Marine |
| | D | Delage, 5 Avenue Charles Guzin |
| Cavalaire | D | Mer et Soleil, Les Hespérides |
| St. Tropez | A, D | Vermiglio, St. Tropez |
| | D | Navi-Service, St. Tropez |

| TOWN | CODE | NAME AND ADDRESS |
|---|---|---|
| St. Raphaël | A, D | Masselli, 112 Avenue du Commandant-Guilbaut |
| | A, D | René Girodon, "La Plongée," 29 Place du Maréchal-Gallieni |
| | R | Single Chamber at the Fire Station |
| Anthéor | A, D | Zoi, Sous le Pont |
| Cannes | R | Single Chamber at the Fire Station |
| | A, D | H. Broussard, 10 Place du Commandant-Lamy |
| Golfe-Juan | D | Moria, Boulevard de la Plage |
| Juan-les-Pins | A, D | Louis Lehoux, Avenue Guy de Maupassant, Tel: 34-13-19 |
| Nice | R | Single Chamber at the Fire Station |
| | A, D | l'Exploration Sous Marine, 14 Quai des Docks, Port de Nice, Tel: 85-42-44 |
| Beaulieu | A | Club de Plongée, Sur la Plage |
| Monaco | A | Yacht Club, Avenue de Monte Carlo, Tel: 30-58-39 |
| | D | Monaco-Shilplander, 9 Quai des États-Unis |
| | D | Monaco-Sport-Nautique, Le Ruscino, Quai Antoine-1$^{er}$ |
| Menton | A, D | Lamoureux, 1 Avenue Félix-Faure |

*Chapter 41*

# CORSICA

**How to Get There:** By Pan Am Jet Clipper to Paris or Nice. From Paris there is a direct ninety-minute flight to Corsica. From Nice visitors have a choice of air or steamer service, and from Toulon and Marseille overnight steamer service is available. Scheduled hydrofoil service links Corsica with Elba and Leghorn, Italy.

**Customs, Travel Documents, and Currency:** See the chapter on France.

**Hotels:** There are plenty of hotels in various price ranges, with new ones being built each year. Reservations are strongly advised in summer, especially in August.

**Transportation:** Taxis and hired cars are available in Ajaccio and Bastia. Roads are paved. Scheduled bus and train service links the larger communities.

**Medical Facilities:** Good in Bastia and Ajaccio.

**Other Information:** General tourist information is available from the French Government Tourist Office, 610 Fifth Avenue, New York.

## SKIN DIVING INFORMATION

Corsica is a good place for skin diving for both beginners and advanced divers. The water here is warmer than it is along the French Riviera (during the summer, especially) and many French and Italian divers visit the island for this reason. The best living conditions are found from June to September. A wet suit is almost a necessity after October. The usual assortment of Mediterranean fish is present. Monk seals are also seen. In summer, underwater visibility is usually ninety to one hundred feet or more. Visibility varies during the winter with the weather.

Access to the diving areas is either by boat or by swimming from the shore. A road circles the island and provides access to many diving areas for visitors who rent a car.

A multiplace recompression chamber is situated in Ajaccio at C.I.N.C., Aspretto-Ajaccio, Tel: 16-67.

Quite a few artifacts from ancient Greek and Roman wrecks have been dredged up by fishermen.

**Laws:** See "Laws" in the chapter on France.

**Diving Gear for Sale:** *Calvi:* l'Aquarium (near the port). *Bastia:* Nautic-Sport. *Ajaccio:* Ajaccio Sport. *Propriano:* Gutknecht. All these dive shops have a good selection of French equipment.

**Diving Gear for Rent:** l'Aquarium, in Calvi. Some of the newer beach hotels also have equipment for their guests.

**Boats, Trips, Guides:** Arrangements can be made through the dive shops listed above. Motorboats and sailboats can be hired at the Ajaccio Harbor and from many of the nearby new beachfront hotels. Fishing boats can also be hired in the small fishing villages.

**Compressed Air:** The dive shops listed above, as well as the Sub Aqua Club in St. Florent, have compressors.

**Currents, Winds:** Currents are negligible except in the Strait of Bonifacio which separates Corsica and Sardinia. In the Strait the current generally sets eastward, but is greatly influenced by the winds.

Winds are variable but are frequently from the west or northwest, especially in winter.

### EAST COAST

From Cap Corse south to Bastia the coastline is rocky and steep and is excellent for diving. The shoreline is rather straight, with few bays or headlands. Close-to-shore depths vary from ten to fifty feet. Depths of more than seventy-five feet are found less than a half mile offshore in most places. The waters around the Îles Finocchiarola, off the northeast tip of Cap Corse, are rocky and good for diving.

From Bastia south to Marine de Solenzara (over fifty miles) the coastline is low, sandy, and swampy. Several streams empty into the sea in this region. Not recommended for diving.

The region from Marine de Solenzara south to the south point is well suited to diving, with some exceptions which are noted below. The Solenzara River brings down silt, making the area near the village of Solenzara too murky for enjoyable diving. From Solenzara south to the Gulf of Porto Vecchio the coastline is rocky and steep and depths of thirty to fifty feet are found near the shore in many places.

The Gulf of Porto Vecchio is at the mouth of the Stabiacco River. Accordingly the water in this area is murky.

From Porto Vecchio south to Bonifacio diving conditions are very good. Bold headlands plunge vertically into the sea and depths close to shore vary from thirty to seventy-five feet, except in the Gulf of Santa-Giulia where depths of less than ten feet are found.

Numerous rocks and islands are found in this area. The best ones for diving are Islas Forana, Isla de la Vacca, Îles Cerbicales, and Île du Toro, all of which are southwest of Pointe de la Chiappa. Sometimes, naval ships use Île de la Vacca as a target during gunnery practice, so make sure that warships are not in the vicinity before diving in the area.

The southern tip of the island and the islands in the Strait of Bonifacio are excellent for diving except when strong winds create choppy seas and surface currents. The remains of several ancient wrecks have been found in the Straits.

The best islands in the Strait for diving are Île Poraggia, which is surrounded by shallow, rocky water; Île Ratino, also surrounded by rocks; Île Perduto; Île Cavallo, one of the best diving areas in the Strait; and Île de Lavezzi, just south of Île Cavallo. The Italian islands in this Strait are described in the section on Sardinia. Since the water around most of these small islands is shallow, this area is suitable for both snorkelers and scuba divers. Near Bonifacio, a sunken submarine lies in shallow water on the western side of Calanque de la Catena.

## WEST COAST

There are innumerable bays and inlets along the west coast and the shoreline is mostly rocky and steep. Thus, almost all of this coast is ideal for skin diving. Winds from the west or the northwest can cause heavy seas, so check on the weather before planning a diving trip to this coast. Even in heavy weather, however, calm water can be found in the lee of the peninsulas and rocky headlands. Around the mouths of some of the larger streams low, muddy shorelines have resulted from silt deposits.

North of Cap de Feno (at the southern end of the island) are Îles de la Tonnara which are excellent for spearfishing. Farther north, Pointe de Figari offers very good diving conditions. Îles Bruzzi, north of Figari, are a group of small, rocky islands and shallow reefs and are well worth a visit.

About seven and a half miles north of Cap de Feno is an extensive reef named Grand Ecueil d'Olmeto. This reef varies in depth from barely awash to twenty-five feet and affords excellent spearfishing and exploring.

About one and a half miles south of Cap de Roccapina is another offshore reef named Les Moines. Spearfishing is good here.

Farther north, Cap Senetosa is fringed by shallow reefs for almost a half mile offshore.

The southern side of the Gulf of Valinco from Pointe de Campo-Moro to Pointe Cardicciani is recommended. Shoal water alternates with deeper areas close to shore. The remainder of the gulf is not as well suited to diving due to sandy areas and some rivers which discharge here. The town of Propriano is at the head of this gulf.

In Ajaccio Bay diving is especially good around Cap Muro, Pointe Castagna, and Pointe Sette Nave. These are rocky promontories surrounded by rocky, shallow reefs.

Pointe Parata, west of Ajaccio, is fringed by sunken rocks and shoals which extend more than one and a half miles offshore in a southwesterly direction.

From Pointe Parata to Cap Corse the best areas are the rocky headlands, most of which are surrounded by shoals and rocky reefs. These areas are found near Cap de Feno, Pointe de Cargese, Pointe d'Omignia, Cap Rosso, Pointe Rossa, Pointe Bianca (from which a reef, Les Scoglietti, extends northwest for about a quarter mile), Cap de la Morsetta, Cap Cavallo, and Pointe Revellata.

Calvi is the headquarters for divers for the northwestern section of Corsica. It is situated along a superb coastline, rocky, rugged, and steep, and offers diving equipment and compressed air. It is connected with Nice by steamer and Nice, Marseille, and Tunis by air.

Other good diving spots on the west coast, north of Calvi, are Pointe d'Espano, Pointe Vallitone, Îles Rousses, Pointe de l'Alciolo, Pointe de Mignole, and Pointe de Curza. The underwater terrain around each of these areas is similar: rocky, steep, clear water, and plenty of game fish.

The western shore of the Gulf of St. Florent has a peculiar flat ledge about five or six feet deep which extends to seaward for about two thousand feet. Beyond the ledge, the bottom drops off steeply to thirty-five to fifty feet.

From the Gulf of St. Florent to Cap Corse (the north point), the coastline presents much the same appearance as the rest of the west coast, except that it is less deeply indented. The underwater terrain here is similar to the rest of this coast.

*Chapter 42*

# SARDINIA

**How to Get There:** By Pan Am Jet Clipper to Rome, with a two-hour direct connecting flight to Sardinia, at Cagliari. Ferry boats ply between Civitavecchia, Italy, and Olbia and Cagliari, Sardinia.

**Customs, Travel Documents, Currency:** See the chapter on Italy.

**Hotels:** There are quite a few hotels of various types on the island. Reservations are advisable in summer.

**Transportation:** Taxis, rental autos, and buses. Main roads are well paved.

**Medical Facilities:** Good in Cagliari.

**Other Information:** Travel and tourist information can be obtained at the Pan Am office, Via Bissolati 46, in Rome (Tel: 47-69-51). The New York office of the Italian Government Information Center is at 626 Fifth Avenue.

## SKIN DIVING INFORMATION

Sardinia offers many excellent diving spots, suitable for beginning snorkelers or for scuba divers. The coasts are irregular and indented with many protected bays, suitable for lazy snorkeling. Visibility is normally ninety feet or better in summer, and varies widely in winter, depending on the weather. Game fish can be seen here but not in as large numbers as around neighboring Corsica.

The best places for diving are:

1 – The entire north and northeast point from Capo Testa east and south to Capo Coda Cavallo. The best base is the town of

Olbia which is linked by ferry to Civitavecchia, Italy. There are a number of hotels of various types in this region, and a famous, and luxurious, hotel north of Olbia built by the Aga Khan.

2 – The east coast between Capo Comino and Capo Sferracavallo is a good spearfishing area. The best place to stay here is in the village of Tortolì.

3 – The southeast tip of the island, from Punta deis Cappuccinus south and west to Torre del Finnochio is another good diving area. Because many portions of this section have shallow water close to shore, it is a good area for beginners. These diving areas can be reached by boat or road from Cagliari.

4 – The southwest corner of the island, from Capo Spartivento west, then northwest to Capo Altano, has everything for the beginners as well as the experts: roofs, fish, islands, offshore rocks, and clear water. It can be reached by boat or road from Cagliari, but divers may wish to stay in a pension in Carbonia.

5 – Isola di Mal di Ventre, in the center of the west coast, is an excellent spearfishing area. It can be reached by boat from Bosa or from Oristano.

6 – One of the best diving areas on the island lies in the northwest corner of the island from Capo Caccia north to Isola Asinara. Just inside the point at Capo Caccia is a large cave, about sixty-five feet high, which tunnels into the mountain for 1200 to 1500 feet. It is well worth exploring. A prison is situated on Asinara Island and permission to land on the island must be obtained from the head jailer.

Sardinian coastal waters abound with ancient wrecks from almost every maritime power. Most of them are in depths exceeding one hundred feet and are difficult to locate. Divers are reminded that it is against Italian law to disturb these wrecks or remove anything from them.

**Laws:** See the chapter on Italy.

**Diving Gear for Sale:** A list of diving specialty shops is at the end of this chapter. In addition to the shops on this list, many stores in the larger towns have snorkeling gear for sale.

**Diving Gear for Rent:** Rentals are not available. Some of the luxury hotels have a few sets for use of guests.

**Boats, Guides:** Most dive shops can arrange for boat trips. Fishing boats are available everywhere. Arrange with the dive shops for diving guides.

**Compressed Air:** See the list of diving specialty shops.

**Currents, Winds:** Except in the Strait of Bonifacio, where currents are sometimes stiff, the currents around Sardinia are normally weak.

Winds are mostly from the west and northwest on the west coast. On the east coast the winds are from southwest to northwest except from October through March, when they are variable. Rough seas can be expected from late autumn to early spring.


### EAST COAST

The region from Punta Falcone southeast to Capo Coda Cavallo is especially suited to diving both for beginners and experts. The islands and rocks in the Strait of Bonifacio are steep, rocky, and usually have game fish in their surrounding waters. The best islands in the Strait for diving are Razzoli, Santa Maria, Spargi, La Maddalena, Caprera, and Delle Bisce. The Club Méditerranée holiday camp and diving center is on Isola Caprera.

A wreck can be found in about thirty feet of water about four hundred yards northwest of the north point of Isola Razzoli. Another wreck is sixty feet deep slightly over nine hundred yards from the southeastern coast of Isola Spargi. Another wreck can be seen in about thirty-five feet of water slightly over six hundred yards west of Punta Stagnali on Isola Santo Stefano. About three hundred yards north of Cala Portese is a wreck in about fifty feet of water. It is marked with three buoys.

The coastline plunges straight down to a bottom sixty to seventy-five feet deep between Punta Sardegna and Cap d'Orso and at Capo Ferro. Spearfishing is excellent here. The nearby rocky islands of Nibani Poveri, Mortoriotto, Mortorio, and Soffi are also well worth exploring.

Capo Figari is a bold headland jutting out in a westerly direction. Depths of fifty to one hundred feet are close along the shore. Many caves, and groupers, are in this area.

From Capo Figari south to Capo Coda Cavallo the coast is rocky, irregular, and steep. Shoals extend offshore for up to half a mile. North of Capo Coda Cavallo is Isola Tavolara, which has a rocky, shallow reef extending northwest from the southwest tip. Isola Molara, south of Tavolara, is ringed with reefs and rocky shoals. Isola Molarotto, a small island east of Molara, is an excellent diving area with reefs all around the coastline.

From Capo Coda Cavallo over a mile south to Punta Sabbatino the shore is rocky and diving conditions are good. Offshore diving spots here are Isola Rossa and Scoglio Testa di Moro. From Punta Sabbatino south for several miles to Capo Comino the coastline is sandy and marshy and not suited for diving. The exception to this is Isola Rossa, a rocky island off Capo Camino.

From Capo Comino south to Punta deis Cappucini (near the southern tip of Sardinia) the coastline is not as deeply indented as it is farther north. However, fair quantities of fish are seen here and most sections of the coast are rocky with offshore reefs. There is also an occasional sandy stretch of coast. The Cedrino River discharges into the northern end of the Gulf of Orosei, causing murky water. About a half mile southeast of Torre San Giovanni di Saralla (a white cylindrical tower three miles south of Capo Sferracavallo) is a wreck in about sixty feet of water. The masts show above the surface. Another wreck lies in about forty-five feet of water about one thousand yards south of the tower.

Punta deis Cappucini is a rocky headland with steep cliffs dropping down to a sea bottom seventy-five feet deep. Offshore about two miles south of Cappucini is the island of Serpentaro. A reef is located off the north shore of this island.

The area around Capo Carbonara, the southeast tip of Sardinia, is rocky and varies in depth from a few feet to over one hundred feet. Diving is good here and around Isola Cavoli (southeast of the cape) and Secca Caterina (a shoal southwest of the cape).

## SOUTH COAST

From Capo Carbonara west about nine miles to Torre del Finnochio (a cylindrical tower atop a hill) the coast is rocky and indented. Water depth varies from ten to thirty feet close alongside the shore. This is a good diving area.

The coast from Torre del Finnochio to Capo Spartivento, which includes the city of Cagliari, is mostly low, sandy, and marshy. Diving conditions are poor here.

The entire region from Capo Spartivento east to Capo Altano (the southwest corner of Sardinia) is rocky, with steep cliffs and offshore reefs and islands. Good quantities of fish are found here. Boats can be hired in Cagliari or in the coastal fishing villages. A wreck is in fifteen feet of water not quite three hundred yards north-northeast of Porto de Teulada (which is at the head of the Gulf of Teulada).

Isola de Sant'Antioco and Isola di San Pietro are two large islands a short distance off the southwest corner of Sardinia. The bottom between these islands and the mainland is shallow and mostly weed and sand. Their outer shores are the preferred diving areas. Good diving conditions are also found around Isola Piana (off the north tip of Isola di San Pietro), and Secca Grande (a reef northwest of Isola Piana). Off the western sides of these two last-named places, the water shelves off abruptly to over hundred-foot depths.

Diving is good around Capo Altano, a rugged, rock-fringed promontory, and the nearby Isola dei Meli. The sea bottom in this vicinity is rather shallow and drops off abruptly a few hundred yards offshore.

## WEST COAST

The 3¼-mile stretch from Capo Altano north to Porto Paglia is rocky. In most places vertical cliffs drop down to sixty-foot depths. This is a good area for experienced divers.

A beach stretches northward from Porto Paglia for about two miles. The coast as far north as Golfo di Oristano is not particularly interesting underwater.

The Golfo di Oristano, in which the town of Oristano is situated, is not too good for diving, especially after rains, since the Tirso River empties into the sea here. The shoreline is mostly sandy. From Capo San Marco, at the northern end of Golfo di Oristano, to Capo Mannu, the shoreline is mostly sandy with a few rocks.

North of Capo San Marco is Isola di Mal di Ventre, about four miles off the mainland. This small island is surrounded by many rocky areas and is well worth a visit as many fish are found here. It is one of the favorite spots for Italian divers from the mainland. It can be reached by boat from Oristano or Bosa.

From Capo Mannu a few miles north to Porto Caguragas the depths near shore vary from five to twenty feet and gradually deepen a few hundred yards offshore. The underwater scenery is only moderately interesting.

From Porto Caguragas northward for about seven and a half miles steep cliffs drop vertically to a bottom forty to seventy-five feet deep. Spearfishing is fair here.

The waters near the town of Bosa are dirtied from the discharge of the River Temo.

The region between Capo Moro, north of the Temo River, and Capo Caccia is indented with numerous bays. This is a good diving area. Boats can be hired from fishermen in Bosa or in Alghero.

The northwest coast from Capo Caccia north to Isola Asinara is one of the best diving areas on Sardinia for experienced divers. It is not suitable for beginners because the shoreline is very steep with cliffs that drop to a sea bed forty to sixty-five feet deep. The large cave just inside the point on Capo Caccia is well worth a visit. It can be reached only by boat.

Northwest of Capo Caccia lies Isolotto Foradada, a steep, rocky island where game fish are usually found. Two miles farther north is a slightly larger island, Isolotto Piana, where fish are also seen.

Isola Asinara is off the northwest corner of Sardinia. Almost the entire coastline is excellent for spearfishing. A boat can be hired at Porto Torres or at Alghero. Remember to obtain permission from the head jailer of the prison before attempting to go ashore on this island. The prison is located on the cove named Cala d'Oliva, which is on the east coast, near the north point. The west coast is extremely rocky and steep, while the east coast is alternately rocky and sandy.

### NORTH COAST

From Punta Negra east to Punta Tramonta the coastline is low and sandy. There is little of interest here. Porto Torres, the seaport for the town of Sassari, is in this region.

From Punta Tramontana east to Castel Sardo, the coastline is rocky and steep, with fair diving conditions.

Between Castel Sardo and Isola Rossa the coast is sandy. The river Coghinas discharges into the sea here. Diving is poor.

From Isola Rossa northeast to Punta Falcone the shore is mostly rocky and steep and diving conditions are good. Capo Testa, southwest of Punta Falcone, is a rocky headland surrounded by reefs and rocks in varying depths. Care should be observed when diving along the north face of this cape because of the currents, which can be rather strong.

## DIVING SPECIALTY SHOPS AND COMPRESSED AIR STATIONS ON SARDINIA

The following information is presented through the courtesy of Dr. Sergio Scuderi, Editorial Director of *Mondo Sommerso*.

| *Name of Town* | *Name and Address of Dive Shop* |
|---|---|
| Alghero | Pasquali—Via Vittorio Emanuele 1 |
|  | G. Sassu—Via Sassari 6 |
| Cagliari | G. Cortis—Via Angioi 38 |
|  | SASOI—Via Cimitero 2 |

| Name of Town | Name and Address of Dive Shop |
| --- | --- |
| La Maddalena | P. Dini—Corso Garibaldi 47H |
|  | B. Ugazzi—Cala Gavetta |
| Olbia | G. Piro—Corso Umberto |
| Oristano | A.R.I.L.—Via Cagliari 18 |
| Santa Teresa di Gallura | Vincentelli—Via Italia 8 |
| Sassari | Chessa—Piazza Tola 6 |
|  | Pasquali—Via F. Cavallotti 9 |
| Tortolì | Esso service station |

*Chapter* 43

## ITALY

**How to Get There:** By Pan Am Jet Clipper flight time is eight hours from New York direct to Rome. Service is also provided via Paris or via Lisbon, Barcelona, and Nice.

**Customs Regulations:** Personal clothing and four hundred cigarettes or a pound of tobacco, and one bottle of liquor or two bottles of wine, and a still camera with five rolls of film, and a movie camera with two reels of film are admitted duty free.

**Travel Documents Required:** U.S. citizens must have passports. Visas are not required.

**Currency:** Italian lire are exchanged at approximately L. 625 to $1.00 U.S.

**Hotels:** Italy has a wide range of hotels, from the very finest to the inexpensive pension. Reservations are advisable in the summer, especially in the large cities and the seaside resorts.

**Transportation:** Taxis, rental autos, air, bus, and train transportation are excellent and well organized.

**Medical Facilities:** Excellent, except in the small villages.

**Other Information:** Pan Am offices are at Via Bissolati 46 in Rome (Tel: 47-69-51) and on Torre Valasca (Tel: 89-88-15) in Milan. Tourist information is available from the Italian Government Information Center, 626 Fifth Avenue, New York.

## SKIN DIVING INFORMATION

The best skin diving spots are along the west coast of Italy which is steep and rocky in many places. Few game fish will be seen here except in very deep water. The east coast is predominately low and sandy and unsuited for diving. The exception is the rocky "spur" on the "boot" of Italy and around the nearby Tremiti Islands.

Italian diving equipment is of excellent quality, inexpensive, and is sold in every seaside town.

**Laws:** The removal of amphorae or other artifacts from the sea is prohibited.

**Diving Gear for Sale:** Snorkeling equipment is sold almost everywhere. A list of skin diving specialty shops along the west coast is at the end of this chapter.

**Diving Gear for Rent:** Since snorkeling equipment is so inexpensive, it is hardly worth renting. Some of the larger seaside hotels have a few sets for use of guests. The best place for renting equipment, obtaining scuba instruction, or arranging diving trips is Centro Subacqueo Nervi, via Eros da Ros, in Genova (Genoa), Nervi, Tel: 37-89-91 (c/o Hotel Savoia Beeler). This well-equipped diving center is highly recommended. It offers a complete range of services, including special hotel arrangements, and is the State-approved certification center for all diving instructors in Italy.

**Boats, Guides:** Rental boats are available in every seaside resort. Also, fishermen's boats may be hired for around 3000 lire per day for small boats without engines or from 15,000 to 20,000 lire per day for motor boats. Make arrangements for diving guides through the diving specialty shops.

**Compressed Air:** Compressed air stations are listed at the end of this chapter.

**Currents, Winds:** With a few exceptions, noted below, currents are usually weak and not a serious factor in skin diving except for stiff currents in the Strait of Messina, between Italy and Sicily.

In summer the winds on the west coast are mostly southwesterly or westerly in the northern regions and northwesterly in the southern portion.

Winter winds are mostly northerly and northeasterly as far south as Naples. South of Naples, southerly winds are more frequent.

## WEST COAST

From the French border south to Genoa, diving conditions are not especially good. The bottom is mostly sand, with several beaches along the shoreline. Occasional portions of the coastline are rocky with some areas of interest to shallow-water snorkelers, and there are a few wrecks for exploration.

A sunken vessel, thirty-five feet deep, lies a half mile south of the Capo Berta jetty (which is a little over a mile east of the town of Imperia).

Farther along the coast, another wreck is in seventy feet of water a little over one and a quarter miles southwest of Capo Mele. Another wreck lies forty-five feet deep south-southwest of Capo Mele, about 1300 yards offshore. Exercise caution when diving in the vicinity of these last two wrecks, since currents, usually setting southwestward, are frequently strong.

Several miles north of Capo Mele is the village of Borghetto Santo Spirito. A wreck lies offshore here about three quarters of a mile south-southwest in seventy-five feet of water. The village of Loano is about one and a quarter miles northeast of Borghetto and a wreck lies 150 feet deep one mile east of this village. A second wreck can be found in about forty feet of water about 1200 yards southeast of this village.

One fairly good diving spot in this region is Bergeggi Island, about three hundred yards offshore, near the town of Vado. Rocks surround this island to a depth of about 120 feet.

The Portofino Peninsula, a few miles east of Genoa, is the best place near Genoa for diving. It can easily be reached by car or by train to Camogli, where boats can be hired. The southwestern face of this peninsula, accessible only by boat, is the best part. Cliffs rise almost vertically from the sea and depths over one hundred feet are found close to shore. Game fish are scarce here but the region is suitable for exploring and underwater photography. Boats are readily available in Camogli, San Fruttuoso, Portofino, Santa Margherita, and other seaside towns.

In San Fruttuoso Bay the statue of Christ of the Abyss can be seen. The sea bottom is about fifty feet deep at the base of the statue. Duplicates of this famous bronze sculpture have been sent to Grenada, West Indies, and to Florida for installation in the Pennekamp Underwater State Park.

The coastline from the Portofino Peninsula south to Punta di Sestri (over twelve miles) is sandy and not suited for diving.

From Punta di Sestri southeast to La Spezia, diving is good around the rocky headlands. In the intervening bays, the bottom is usually sandy and is not good for diving. The best areas in this forty-mile region are Punta di Monte Grosso and Punta del Mesco.

A partially submerged breakwater extends across the Gulf of Spezia. The region from the eastern end of the breakwater, at Punta di Santa Teresa, southeast to Punta Bianca is deeply indented, rocky, and fairly interesting underwater.

The coastline is low and sandy and the underwater terrain uninteresting for diving from Punta Bianca south for over forty miles to Livorno (Leghorn). There are some offshore islands west and southwest of Livorno. These will be discussed at the end of this section on Italy's west coast.

For ten miles south of Livorno, the coastline is rocky with fairly interesting diving around the rocky headlands. However, the bays here are low and sandy with uninteresting underwater terrain.

From about ten miles south of Livorno the coastline is again sandy with poor diving conditions as far south as Promontorio di Piombino. Around this promontory there are several rocky, steep areas where interesting diving is available. The bottom falls off steeply here.

A reef named Secche di Vada lies a short distance off Capo Cavallo (which is north of Promontorio di Piombino). Four wrecks rest on the bottom just off this reef. The first is about fifty feet deep about 1200 yards due south of the navigational light. Another one is in seventy feet of water almost two miles southwest of the light. A third one is two miles south-southwest of the light in 120 feet of water. The last one is 175 feet deep about two and a quarter miles southwest of the light. These wrecks will be difficult to find without local assistance. The best plan is to hire a fishing boat on the mainland and ask the advice of the skipper. A 2000-lire wreck-finding bonus can work wonders.

From Promontorio di Piombino to Promontorio Argentario, thirty miles south, the coastline is mostly low and sandy, with only a few rocky areas. There is little of interest here for skin divers except the offshore islands described later.

Promontorio Argentario is a prominent headland with steep, rocky cliffs which rise vertically from the sea. Depths close-to vary from ten to fifty feet. The area is a good one for diving and can be reached by car from Rome, ninety-two miles south. Boats can be rented at the towns of Porto Santo Stefano, Port Ercole, or Orbetello.

From Promontorio Argentario south for about thirty miles to the city of Civitavecchia the coast is low and sandy. Diving conditions here are poor. An interesting historical landmark, though, can be seen just south of Promontorio Argentario where the ruins of an ancient city of Roman times sprawl atop the hill above Punta Ansedonia.

South of Civitavecchia about four miles is a low, rock-fringed point where depths of less than thirty feet can be found up to half a mile offshore. From here south to Anzio (below Rome) the coastline is low and sandy and the visibility is not generally good due to the discharge of the Tevere (Tiber) and other rivers.

Capo d'Anzio is a good diving area and can be reached by bus or car in about two hours from Rome (depending on traffic, which can be congested beyond all belief on summer weekends). Depths of fifteen to twenty feet are found for three hundred yards offshore. There are caves in the rocky cliff for exploration. A wreck lies about 175 yards south of Capo d'Anzio. An ancient sunken harbor is a few hundred yards offshore, about a quarter mile northwest of the offshore beacon marking a group of offshore rocks named Sconciglio.

About twenty-three miles southeast of Anzio is Capo Circeo. The coast in between is sandy and the waters uninteresting. Capo Circeo is moderately good for diving, with offshore rocks and depths of ten to thirty feet found close to shore. It is easily reached by good road from Rome.

The coast curves in a general easterly direction from Capo Circeo for over twenty miles to Gaeta, which is another rocky promontory with several sandy coves. Diving conditions are good around the rocky spots. A boat can be rented in the town of Gaeta.

From Gaeta south to Pozzuoli, the sea bottom is sandy and uninteresting.

A rocky headland with several offshore rocks and reefs is positioned about two miles east of Pozzuoli. Shallow water extends to seaward for a few hundred yards. Few fish are seen here, but it is a fairly good diving area for divers staying in nearby Naples.

Sorrento is a resort a few miles south of Naples. South of Sorrento the coast is high and rocky and there are some caves for exploring. There are numerous hotels here and access to the sea is provided by pathways down the cliffs from the hotels. Two ancient ruins can be seen: the Temple of Hercules on Capo di Sorrento, and the Great Temple of Hercules on Capo di Massa.

From Capo di Sorrento to Salerno the coastline is steep and rocky and diving conditions are good. The area is a popular resort area and is linked with Naples by bus service over excellent roads. Positano and Amalfi are along this coastline. Few fish will be seen here but the area is a good one for snorkeling among the rocks.

From Salerno south for over twenty miles to Punta Licosa the coast is low with little of interest under the water.

The coast trends southeast for about twenty-nine miles to Punta degli Infreschi. Along this stretch of coast good diving will be found since the shoreline is rocky. The Club Méditeranée holiday camp and diving school is situated near Palinuro, toward the southern end of this stretch of coastline. At the southern end of this section is the town of Marina di Camerota. The remains of a wrecked airplane, about thirty-five feet deep, lie about 220 yards directly offshore from the town.

Not quite two miles south of the town of Sapri is Punta delle

Grive, a rocky point. About 325 yards south of this point lies a wreck in about thirty feet of water.

From Sapri to the southern extremity of Italy, the coastline is alternately rocky and sandy. Some fair diving spots are found here, but the region is not interesting enough to make a special trip just for the diving.

Currents are very strong in the Strait of Messina, between Italy and Sicily, and diving is dangerous and not recommended.

The south coast of Italy, between the toe and the heel of the "boot," is not especially good for diving since there are long stretches of sand and several rivers empty into the sea here, bringing quantities of silt into the water.

### OFFSHORE ISLANDS

A number of islands lie off the west coast of Italy and are described here in geographical order, from north to south. Sardinia and Sicily are described separately.

**Elba and Adjacent Islands:** This group extends from Isola di Gorgona, just off Livorno, south to Isola di Giannutri, a few miles northwest of Civitavecchia. They can be reached by ferry from Livorno, Bastia (on Corsica), Piombino, or Civitavecchia.

Isola di Gorgona is a penal colony. It is forbidden to come to within a quarter mile of the shoreline without express authority from the penal authorities in Livorno.

Twenty-one miles south is Isola di Capraia, where excellent diving is found on the rocky western side. Steep cliffs plunge vertically into the sea and deep water is found close in. Fishing boats can be hired in the village of Capraia. A ferry connects this island with Livorno and Elba. Tourist accommodations are limited.

Elba is five miles off the mainland, near Piombino, and is the largest island in this group. The shores are mostly steep and rocky, with irregular indentations around the entire coastline. Clear water and good diving conditions can be enjoyed here except at the heads of the bays, where sandy beaches are located.

Isola Pianosa is about seven miles southeast of Elba. A prison is situated here, and it is forbidden to come within a mile of the shoreline without permission from the penal authorities.

Isola di Montecristo is a rugged granite island about sixteen miles south of Isola Pianosa. Visitors can land there only by permission. Check with the police in Elba. If permission can be obtained, the experienced spearfisherman will find a good assortment of game fish. Accommodations are severely limited. The housing problem is solved most easily by camping out.

Isola del Giglio lies about eight miles off the Italian mainland at Promontorio Argentario. It can be reached by boat from Porto Santo Stefano. It is a densely populated island with a number of fishermen from whom boats can be hired. The coastline is steep, rocky, and has numerous irregular indentations. The underwater terrain is attractive but is rather deep near shore.

Isola di Giannutri lies about eight and a half miles southeast of Isola del Giglio. Transportation to this island is irregular, and it is suggested that divers visiting this small island do so in day trips from the mainland, starting from Civitavecchia or Orbetello. The coastline is high and steep and indented. The water is clear and fish are found in sizable numbers.

**Isole Ponziane:** These three small islands (Ponza, Palmarola, and Zannone) are favorite weekend destinations for divers from Rome. They can be reached by boat from Gaeta or Anzio. Accommodations are limited and should be arranged for in advance.

The coastlines of each of these islets are rocky, steep, and indented. Good diving spots can be found almost everywhere. Shallow water is found close to shore and depths of twenty-five feet extend up to half a mile offshore in some areas.

**Ischia and Capri:** The resort islands of Ischia and Capri are a short distance off the mainland near Naples. Their coastlines are very rocky and rugged, and are interesting underwater. Italian divers, headed by Raniero Maltini, recently recovered a badly eroded ancient statue from Capri's famed Blue Grotto. It is believed that the statue may have been from Emperor Tiberius' collection. There are several underwater caves in the vicinity of the Grotto. Roman ruins are located on Capri, including the ruins of the palace of the Emperor Tiberius.

Diving can be hazardous around these two islands because of the great number of water-ski boats which move at high speeds along the coastlines.

**The Aeolian Islands:** The seven Aeolian Islands (Isole Eolie) are west of the southern tip of Italy and north of the eastern end of Sicily. They are Lipari, Vulcano, Salina, Alicudi, Filicudi, Panarea, and Stromboli.

The principal island, Lipari, can be reached by ferryboat from Naples, Italy, or from Palermo, Messina, and Milazzo, Sicily. Most of the hotels are situated on Lipari, but there is a large hotel on Vulcano and small pensions on the others. There is a small hospital on Lipari.

These islands are rugged and rocky with steep coastlines. The water is quite clear and diving conditions are excellent. Far more game fish (including large groupers and tuna) are seen here than along most of the Italian coastline. Boats can be hired locally for day trips to diving areas. Alternatively, yachts can be chartered in Palermo, Sicily.

Because of volcanic activity in this region, sulfurous bubbles and heated water will be encountered in a few spots: about two hundred yards from the seaside village of Rinella on the north coast of Salina; on the southern end of the bay named Porto Levante on the northeast end of Vulcano; around the three small islets named Lisca Bianca, Lisca Near, and Bottaro which are over half a mile east of the northeast corner of Panarea; and along the northwestern coast of Stromboli. A stream of molten lava enters the sea along the northwest coast of this active volcano. It is not a good idea to dive here.

## EAST COAST OF ITALY

There is little reason for a diver to make a trip to this coast specifically for diving because the entire shoreline is sandy and there is nothing of interest for divers except for Promontorio del

Gargano (the "spur" on the "boot" of Italy) and the offshore Tremiti Islands.

The promontory extends into the Adriatic for twenty miles from the Italian mainland and is across the Italian peninsula from Naples. It is rocky above and below the water except in the coves. The water is usually clear and the underwater scenery moderately interesting. The usual fishing boats are available for hire.

The Tremiti Islands (San Domino, San Nicola, Caprara, and Cretaccio) are twelve miles off the north coast of Promontorio del Gargano. They are low, rocky islands and good diving conditions in their surrounding waters can be expected. There is little ashore to interest visitors, and it is suggested that these diving areas be visited during day trips from the mainland. Currents, which usually set east-southeast, are frequently strong. Winds are usually from the northeast or southeast. A number of offshore rocks and reefs are located around the islands and game fish are sometimes present in good quantities.

## DIVING SPECIALTY SHOPS AND COMPRESSED AIR STATIONS

The following information is presented through the courtesy of Dr. Sergio Scuderi, Editorial Director of *Mondo Sommerso*. This list is in geographical order, from north to south.

| *Name of Town* | *Name and Address of Dive Shop* |
| --- | --- |
| Bordighera | Pesca Sport di Magnano—Via Libertà 11 |
| San Remo | I. Lanza—Corso E. Cavallotti 168 |
| | Ausenda—Via Roma 97 |
| | Sport Club San Remo—Corso dell'Imperatrice |
| Arma di Taggia | Braschi—Via Queirole |
| Imperia | Biga Sport—Via XXV Aprile 74 |

| *Name of Town* | *Name and Address of Dive Shop* |
|---|---|
| Diano Marina | Vincenzo Ugo—Corso Garibaldi 38 |
| Vado Ligure | Renato Baroncini—Via G. Ferraris 10 |
|  | S.I.O.—Via Manzoni 11/13 |
| Savona | Aprile—Via Buscaglia 6 |
| Genova, Pegli | Recaneschi—Via Lungomare di Pegli |
| Genova, Sestri | Pesce Giuseppe—Piazza Aprosio 7R |
| Genova S. Pier d'Arena | Grillo-Sport—Via Cantore 267R |
| Genova, Cornigliano | S.I.O.—Via Cornigliano 49 |
| Genova, Pra | Alfredo Pastorino—Via Pra 158R |
| Genova | Technisub—Via Sam Pio X° 12 |
|  | S.I.O.—Molo Giano |
|  | Angela Poggioni—Via G. Torti, 42 |
|  | Pesca Sub di Chiappini—Via Scurreria 41R |
|  | Janua Sport—Via XX Settembre 144 |
|  | Pasquale Decreti—Corso Sardegna 310 |
| Genova, Quinto | Aer Sub—Via Majorano 19R |
| Genova, Nervi | Centro Subacqueo Nervi—Via Eros da Ros, c/o Hotel Savoia Beeler, Tel: 37-89-91 |
| Sori | Fabbrica Italiana Plastici—Via E. Caorsi 5 |
| Camogli | Andrea Mori—Via Garibaldi 25R |
|  | A. Costa—Via Garibaldi 33 |
| Santa Margherita | A. Figallo—Via Gramsci 107 |
| Rapallo | Mares Sport—Corso Italia 15 |
|  | Nesti—Via Libertà 33 |
| Chiavari | Mazzoni & Baldassarri—Via San Antonio 10R |
| Sestri Levante | Giuseppe Costantini—Via XXV Aprile 56 |
| Moneglia | Tuttosport di Palmero—Via Viesseux |
| Devia | Giuliana Argilla—Via Embriaco 6 |
| Levanto | L. Perrone—Corso Italia 13 |
| La Spezia | R. Galeazzi—Via Oldoini 65 |
|  | S.I.O.—Via Maralunga 1R |

| Name of Town | Name and Address of Dive Shop |
|---|---|
| Viareggio | Z. Lovi—Via Regia 38 |
| Pisa | S.O.L.—Via Fiorentina 173 |
| Livorno | S.O.L.—Piazza XI Maggio |
| Grosseto | Casa della Gomma—Via Manetti 3 |
| | I. Sensini—Corso Carducci 72 |
| Orbetello | Bastogi—Corso d'Italia 21 |
| Civitavecchia | R. Bortolozzi—Piazza Regina Margherita 5 |
| Santa Marinella | Finder Sport—Via Aurelia 405/408 (Mares) |
| Rome | Caracciolossigeno—Via del Macao 4/10, Tel: 47-49-73 or 48-19-81 |
| | E.I.R. Rivoira—Via Tiburtina 271, Tel: 49-18-40 |
| | Eurosport—Viale Europa 90 |
| | F.I.D.O. Locatelli—Via Giovanni da Empoli 8/10, Tel: 59-30-47 |
| | S.I.O.—Via Prenestina 189, Tel: 29-50-75 |
| | S.O.N.—Via Tiburtina 1100 (Km 11), Tel: 41-92-26 |
| Anzio | Navalmotor—Riv. Zanardelli 275 |
| Terracina | Marzullo—Via Roma 162/164 |
| Naples | S.I.O.—Via G. Ferraris 70 |
| | S.N.O.—Via G. Ferraris 144 |
| | Mondial Sport—Viale Kennedy 313 |
| | Mimi—Via Mergellina 210, Tel: 38-00-67 |
| Santa Maria di Castellabate | Ferrero & Perotti—Regione Lago |
| Sapri | "Capitolino"—Corso Garibaldi 20 |
| Fuscaldo Marina | R. Jannuzzi (private home) |
| Paola Marina | L. Babacci |
| Vibo Valentia | S. Cucinotta—Via Razza 23 |
| Reggio di Calabria | V. de Simone Sacca—Via Veneto 60-77 |
| Crotone | D. Carolei—Piazza Vittorio 16 |

| *Name of Town* | *Name and Address of Dive Shop* |
|---|---|
| Taranto | S.A.P.I.O.—Via della Croce 48 |
| | S.I.O. Via Demenise 3 |
| Gallipoli | W & E Reali—Piazza Tellini 6 |

EAST COAST OF ITALY

*The following dive shops are listed from north to south.*

| | |
|---|---|
| Trieste | G. Cobol—Viale Miramare 273 (Barcola) |
| | DIOXA—Via Trento 15 |
| | Fiorito—Viale XX Settembre 4/2C |
| | S.I.O.—Strada di Fiume 20 |
| | So.Co.Gas—Passaggio S. Andrea 98A |
| Monfalcone | So.Co.Gas—Via XXV Aprile 30 |
| Ravenna | F.R.O.—Via Lanciani 4 |
| Rimini | F.R.O.—Via Flaminia 179 |
| Civitanova Marche | S.I.O.—Via Carducci 14 |
| Pescara | S.A.P.I.O.—Via Aterno 5A |
| Tremiti Is., S. Domino (offshore) | V. Santoro |
| Bari | S.I.O.—Via G. Amendola 124 |
| Brindisi | R. Retino—Corso Umberto I 71 |
| | F. Spagnolo—Piazza Sedile 4 |
| | Trisciuzzi—Via Bastioni S. Giorgio 46 |
| Lecce | Nautica Salento—Piazza Mazzini |
| | G. Predicatore—Viale Lo Re 26B |
| | N. Sammartino—Via A. Costa 4 |

OFFSHORE ISLANDS

| | |
|---|---|
| Elba—Carpani | F. Pacini |
| Elba—Marina di Campo | office of the mechanic G. Dini |
| Elba—Procchio | C. Mazzei |
| Ponza | Villaggio E.N.A.L.—Lido di Frontone |
| Lipari | G. Adornato—Corso Vittorio 178 |

# Chapter 44

## SICILY

**How to Get There:** By Pan Am Jet Clipper to Rome with a three-hour direct flight to Sicily. Also, there are direct flights from many European points to Sicily. Ferryboats offer daily service from the mainland of Italy to Sicilian ports.

**Customs, Travel Documents, Currency:** See chapter on Italy.

**Hotels:** There is a wide variety of hotels and pensions on Sicily. Hotels are usually crowded in summer, and advance reservations are suggested.

**Transportation:** Taxis, rental autos, and buses. Main roads are well paved.

**Medical Facilities:** Excellent in the larger towns and cities.

**Other Information:** See the chapter on Italy.

### SKIN DIVING INFORMATION

The best diving spots are on the north coast, especially around Capo San Vito, at the northwestern tip of the island.

**Laws:** The removal of amphorae or other ancient artifacts from the sea is prohibited.

**Diving Gear for Sale:** Snorkeling equipment is sold in most of the larger towns. A list of diving specialty shops and compressed air stations is at the end of this chapter. Rental gear is not available.

**Guides, Boats:** Check the dive shops for guides. Fishing boats can be hired in almost every seaside town. Yachts can be chartered in Palermo.

**Compressed Air:** See the list at the end of this chapter.

**Currents, Winds:** Currents are usually weak and present no problem to divers except in the Strait of Messina where the current can be very strong. In winter the winds usually vary between northwest and southwest. In summer the winds are mostly from the northwest except along the south coast, where southerly winds are frequent.

NORTH COAST

Capo San Vito, the northwestern tip of Sicily, is a rugged, mountainous peninsula. The rocky bottom around most of this steep shoreline is forty feet or deeper. Except for a sandy area between the end of the cape and Punta di Solanto, one and three quarter miles east, the entire eastern face of the San Vito Peninsula is excellent for spearfishing—one of the best on Sicily. Visibility is usually around seventy-five feet or more, in good weather, and a variety of game fish is usually seen. This cliffy coastline extends southward to the town of Castellammare del Golfo.

Poor diving conditions are found east of Castellammare, as the shore is low and sandy.

East of this long beach the shoreline becomes low and rock-fringed from Capo di Rama around to Capo Gallo. Diving is interesting among the fringing rocks. Shallow water is found close to shore. Boats can be hired at the towns of Balestrate or Terrasini.

The shoreline northwest of Palermo is very steep and rocky from Punta Arenella north to Punta di Priola. This is the diving area that is closest to Palermo, but it is not especially suitable for beginners, since depths close to shore vary from twenty-five to forty feet.

Capo Mongerbino, east of Palermo, is rocky and steep, with offshore reefs. This is a good spot for diving and shallow water will be found off the eastern face of the cape. The reef, Secca di Chianca (thirty feet deep), and the rock, Scoglio Formica, lie off the eastern side of the cape.

From this cape east to the town of Termini Imerese, the coast is low, with a few fringing rocks. Diving is not especially good here.

A sandy beach extends eastward from Termini to Capo Plaja, at the eastern end of the Gulf of Termini Imerese. There is little of interest here for divers.

From Capo Plaja eastward for several miles to Punta Caronia (east of the resort of Cefalù), the coast is rocky, indented, and in some places steep-to. Diving is good here for beginners as well as advanced divers. Shallow water is found near the shore in most places and the underwater scenery is interesting. Boats can be rented in Cefalù, Santo Stefano, or Maronia Marina.

From Punta Caronia eastward for over twenty miles to Capo d'Orlando, the coast is low with little of interest except for a few offshore rocks east of Punta Caronia.

Capo d'Orlando is a bold headland with rocks and reefs extending to seaward for half a mile from the west side. Boats can be hired in the town. Diving is good here, and along the coastline to Capo Calavà, several miles east.

The Gulf of Patti, between Capo Calavà and Capo di Milazzo, is not very good for diving because of the sandy bottom.

Capo di Milazzo is a rocky peninsula with good diving conditions around its steep shoreline at the northern end. Boats can be rented in the town of Milazzo. A reef about twenty-five feet deep extends northward from the cape for about half a mile.

From Capo di Milazzo eastward to Capo Peloro, the easternmost point of Sicily, the sea bottom is sandy and unsuitable for diving.

### EAST COAST

The east coast of Sicily forms one side of the Strait of Messina. Strong currents, tide rips, and whirlpools are encountered in the northern portion of the Strait, and diving is not recommended.

The ancient port of Siracusa (Syracuse) is toward the southern end of this coastline. A number of Greek and Roman wrecks have been found here. This far south the Strait's currents are not felt so strongly.

The coastline is mostly rocky from Capo Santa Panagia (less than two miles north of Siracusa) south to Capo Passero, the southeastern tip of Sicily. Numerous caves can be found at Punta Spuntone, just north of Siracusa.

Along this southern shoreline, shallow water is found close to shore. The best diving sites are around the numerous rocky outcroppings. Boats can be rented in Siracusa or Avola.

## SOUTH COAST

Capo Passero, the southeasternmost peninsula on Sicily, is rocky, with several good diving spots. From this cape westward for almost seventy-five miles to Licata the coast is low and sandy, with occasional offshore rocks. This coastline is not recommended for diving.

The shoreline is rocky for about three miles east of Licata. Diving conditions are fair, but not good enough to make a special trip here just for the diving. Divers visiting this area should make a point of exploring the rocky bottom in the vicinity of Rocca Muddafedda, three miles east of Licata.

Punta Bianca is about fifteen miles west of Rocca Muddafedda. A wreck lies in shallow water about eight hundred yards southwest of this point. Another wreck is in fifty feet of water about 1300 yards southwest of the same point.

From Punta Bianca west for over forty miles to the town of Sciacca, the shore is alternately rocky and sandy. Snorkeling is fair in some areas, but this coastline is not as well suited for diving as the north coast. Beyond Sciacca the coast and sea bottom are sandy to Capo Granitola, the southwestern point on Sicily.

## WEST COAST

From Capo Granitola northwest to the town of Trapani the shoreline, and bottom, is sandy and uninteresting. The town of Marsala is in this area.

From Trapani northeast to Capo San Vito, diving conditions are good. Cliffs line much of this coast, the bottom is rocky, and game fish are found in good quantities. Occasionally, tropical fish from the African coast are seen here. Close-to, the water is five to ten feet deep in many places, and the bottom shelves off to over fifty feet a few hundred yards offshore except along the northwestern face of the San Vito Peninsula. Here, the cliffs rise straight out of deep water. Fishing boats can be hired in Trapani. The San Vito Peninsula is the best diving area in Sicily.

West of Trapani are the Aegadian Islands (Isole Egadi): Favignana, Levanzo, Marettimo, and some smaller islets and rocks. Diving conditions around any of these small islands is excellent and plenty of fish can be seen around their rugged shorelines. There is a small community on each of the larger islands. It is suggested that divers visiting this area hire a boat in Trapani.

## DIVING SPECIALTY SHOPS AND COMPRESSED AIR STATIONS ON SICILY

The following information is presented through the courtesy of Dr. Sergio Scuderi, Editorial Director of *Mondo Sommerso*.

| Name of Town | Name and Address of Diving Facility |
| --- | --- |
| Catania | S.A.D.E.—Via Vecchia Ognina 110 |
| Messina | R. D'Angelo—Via Torino, lotto 12, zona industriale |
| Milazzo | F. lli la Rosa—Via Madonna del Lume 4 |
| Palermo | I.S.O.—Via dei Cantieri 8A |
| Siracusa | S.M.O.—Via Ermocrate |
| Taormina | G. Martinez—Lido Mazzaro |
| Trapani | R. La Russa—Via Fardella 309 |

### AEGADIAN ISLANDS

| | |
| --- | --- |
| Favignana | D. Cannizzaro—Via Roma 10 |

*Chapter 45*

# THE MALTESE ISLANDS

**How to Get There:** By Pan Am Jet Clipper to Rome with connecting flight to Malta. The air fare from New York to Malta is only $11.00 more than the Rome fare.

**Customs Regulations:** Personal clothing and belongings and a reasonable quantity of tobacco, cigars, or cigarettes are admitted duty free.

**Travel Documents Required:** U.S. citizens must have a passport. A visa is not required.

**Currency:** The Maltese pound is currently valued at $2.80 U.S. There are 20 shillings (14¢ each) to a pound. A shilling is divided into 12 pence (approximately 1¢ each). There are no regulations on taking currency into or out of these islands.

**Hotels:** There are thirty-one hotels on Malta, five on Gozo, and one on Comino. Rates range from about $3.50 to about $20.50, with meals. Hotels are usually crowded in summer.

**Transportation:** Taxis, buses, and auto rentals. Horse-drawn carriages, called karrozzin, are used for sightseeing trips around Valletta, the capital of Malta. Most roads are in good condition. Drive on the left side of the road.

Regularly scheduled ferryboats connect the three islands. Hydrofoil service is also available between Malta and Gozo.

**Medical Facilities:** There are several hospitals and a number of doctors.

**Other Information:** Pan Am agents, A & V Von Brockdorff, are at 14 Zachary Street in Valletta, and will be glad to provide information and assistance wherever possible.

Tourist information and a current hotel list can be obtained by writing or visiting the Malta Government Tourist Board, St. John Square, Valletta, Malta.

The official languages are English and Maltese. The three Maltese islands—Malta, Gozo, and Comino—became independent in 1964.

## SKIN DIVING INFORMATION

Diving conditions are excellent around the Maltese Islands. Visibility seldom drops below seventy feet and frequently exceeds one hundred. There are plenty of shallow reefs and rocks for exploration by beginners and advanced divers. Game fish are seen here in good quantities, especially groupers. The best time for diving here is between May and October.

Visitors may join the Malta Sub Aqua Club for £1/-. Apply in writing or in person to their headquarters, 137 Old Bakery Street, Valletta, Malta. Visitors belonging to the Club will have an opportunity of meeting and diving with Maltese divers and will also qualify for a special 15 percent club discount on diving equipment purchased here.

**Laws:** Divers planning to hunt for ancient wrecks must first obtain permission from the Director of the Archaeological Section of the National Museum, Valletta. The Director must be notified of all finds.

**Diving Gear for Sale:** Snorkeling equipment from England, France, Italy, and the United States is available in several stores in the larger communities. Diving specialty shops are as follows: M. J. Falla Store, East Lynn, St. George's Road, St. Julian's (Tel: 30004); Bonett Store, 55 Tower Road, Sliema (Tel: Sliema 31165); Edwards Diver's Den, 1 Cathedral Street, Sliema (Tel: Sliema 34709); and Emmanuel Said, 173 Britannia Street, Valletta (Tel: Central 25418).

**Diving Gear for Rent:** Scuba gear can be rented from Joseph Grech, 28/4 Britannia Street, Floriana, Malta (Tel: 21007).

**Guides, Boats:** Trips can be arranged by Joseph Grech, who has several boats, including a twin diesel 58-foot diving boat. Trips can also be arranged through the Mediterranean Aquatic Sports Center, Villa Rosa Beach Club, St. George's Bay, Tel: Sliema 2626. Boats are available for hire at many of the beaches.

**Compressed Air:** Joseph Grech; Bonett Store, 55 Tower Road, Sliema, Tel: Sliema 31165; Simmons Parsons Brewery, Hamrun.

**Currents, Winds:** Currents are normally negligible and not a problem for divers. Winds are mostly from the northwest.

## MALTA

### NORTHEAST COAST

Punta tal Ahrax is the northernmost point on the island. Here, there are cliffs along the shoreline with rocks along the coast above and below the surface. From this point southeast to the entrance to Mellieha Bay, the coastline is excellent for diving. Depths close to shore vary from awash to thirty-five feet for about 150 yards offshore.

The outer ends of Mellieha Bay are rocky and suitable for diving, but the shore (and bottom) becomes sandy toward the southwestern end.

From the southern end of Mellieha Bay southeast to the head of St. Paul's Bay, the coast is low and rocky with many offshore rocks.

The Maltese claim that St. Paul was shipwrecked at what is now named St. Paul's Bay. A statue of St. Paul is situated on small Selmunet Island, at the northwest entrance to the bay. Amphorae believed to have been from St. Paul's ship were recently recovered from an ancient wreck near Selmunet Island. Diving conditions are good around the northwestern and southeastern shores of this bay, except near the head where there is a sandy beach.

From St. Paul's Bay east to Sliema, the coast is heavily indented, rocky, and has rocky shoals extending to seaward for up to four hundred yards. The whole area is a good one for diving except when strong north winds blow. The following offshore reefs in this area are worth checking out by spearfishermen. A thirty-foot-deep offshore shoal is found a half mile northeast of the entrance to Salina Bay. Ghallis rocks are between Ras il Ghallis and Ras il Kreiten. Shallow and rocky, the shoals surrounding these rocks are worth exploring. Twenty-foot-deep Marco Shoal is about a half mile east of Ras il Kreiten. Another offshore shoal, St. George Shoal, lies several hundred yards east.

A sunken warship lies in Marsamuscetto Harbour, Valletta. It is not far offshore, about four hundred yards east of St. Elmo Point, on the southern shore of the harbor. It is about forty-five feet to the top of the wreck. Another sunken warship can be seen about two hundred yards offshore, about half a mile east of Ricasoli Point, east of Grand Harbour. It is about fifty feet to the top of this wreck.

From Grand Harbour east to Punta tal Zonkor, the northeastern tip of the island, the coastline is rocky with cliffs rimming the eastern end. Shoal water extends offshore for about two hundred yards. Depths near shore vary from awash to about twenty-five feet.

## EAST COAST

From Punta tal Zonkor to Binghisa Point, the southeastern tip of the island, the water near shore is shallow with rocky shoals that, off St. Thomas Bay, extend eastward for about a mile. This region is suitable for diving: the water is usually quite clear, there is plenty of interesting underwater scenery, and there are usually plenty of fish to be seen.

Marsaxlokk Bay, situated on the southeastern corner of the island, is divided into two portions by a peninsula at the tip of which is Fort St. Lucian, atop a hill. Conditions can be found here for shallow-water snorkeling or deep-water exploring. A wreck lies in about twenty-five feet of water in the center of the entrance to the northern half of the bay. It is about 540 yards north-northeast of Fort St. Lucian. The village of Marsaxlokk is at the head of this cove.

Binghisa Reef, with minimum depths of about nineteen feet, is about three quarters of a mile south-southeast of Binghisa Point. Spearfishing is good here, but northeastern currents between the reef and the mainland can be strong. The sea breaks heavily on this reef when the winds are from the south or southeast.

### SOUTHWEST COAST

Most of the coastline from Binghisa Point northwest to Ras ir Raheb is very steep. This portion of the coast is not recommended except for experienced divers because of the great depths close to shore.

Quite a number of caves can be seen in this region. The most famous is the Blue Grotto (Wied iz-Zurrieq), about five miles west of Binghisa Point and southwest of the village of Zurrieq. The cave can only be approached from seaward. The light inside the cave is an unusual luminescent blue. The beauty of this cave has been compared favorably with the well-known Blue Grotto on Capri.

Along this coast groupers can be found hiding in caves or ledges in the submarine cliff face. They are usually forty feet deep or deeper.

Hamriah Bank is about a mile west of the Blue Grotto. The Bank extends south for over half a mile in depths varying from a minimum of twenty feet. This is a pretty good spearfishing area.

From Hamriah Bank, the coast trends northwest as an almost unbroken facade of sheer cliffs, some of them eight hundred feet high, to Ras ir Raheb. Depths of more than two hundred feet are found along these cliffs.

### WEST COAST

This coast is backed in most places by high, rugged cliffs fringed with offshore rocks to about four hundred yards. It is one of the best regions on the island for diving since it offers a variety of depths, good quantities of fish, and, usually, calm, clear water.

Golden Bay is an excellent diving spot. The comfortable Côte d'Or Hotel is situated at one end of a wide sandy beach, which is flanked by a cliffy, rocky shoreline. Beginners and advanced divers will find suitable areas for diving in this bay or around the rocks in nearby Ghajn Tuffiema Bay and Gneja Bay.

Paradise Bay is another good diving area for beginners. Not too many game fish are seen here, but the rocky shoreline is a popular one for exploration.

## COMINO

This small island lies between Malta and Gozo. Until recently, less than fifty persons lived here. A new 98-room hotel, the Comino Hotel, provides scheduled ferry service from Marfa, Malta, to Comino.

Diving conditions are excellent around the entire island. To describe the entire coastline would be repetitive and unnecessary since it is all rocky, steep, and indented. Shallow water can be found around most of the coast. The bottom gradually deepens to about fifty feet some two hundred yards offshore in most places. A number of ancient wrecks with amphorae have been discovered in these waters.

## GOZO

Gozo is about four miles northwest of Malta. It too has a steep, rocky shoreline with good diving conditions around the entire island. Gozo can be reached by scheduled ferry which plies between Marfa, Malta, and Mgarr, Gozo. Hydrofoil service is also provided between Valletta (at the Customs Steps) and Mgarr.

The only bus service here is between Mgarr and Victoria (also

called Rabat), the capital of Gozo. Taxis are plentiful and inexpensive.

The eastern two-thirds of the north coast and the eastern third
of the south coast are best for beginning divers. Shallow water is
found close to shore here and there are many rocky formations
underwater for exploration or photography. The rest of the coast
is of steep cliffs with deep water found close-to, except for the
area immediately adjacent to the Inland Sea on the west coast.

### NORTH COAST

From Cape San Dimitri, east to about half a mile east of Ras
Pinu, the coastline is very steep. Depths of up to two hundred feet
are found close to shore. This region is of interest only to spearfishermen, who can usually find groupers in the underwater caves
in the submarine cliff face.

From this cliffy section east to Ras il Qala, the shoreline is not
so steep and is lined with rocks and edged with shallow water.
Ramla Bay is a good snorkeling area with a rocky bottom from
awash to thirty feet. Local legend has it that Ulysses landed in
this bay and was kept captive for seven years by the nymph
Calypso. Calypso's Cave is an interesting spot to visit. It is at the
top of the cliff behind Ramla Bay, not far from the village of
Xaghra.

### SOUTH COAST

From Ras il Qala the coast trends southwest, past the port of
Mgarr, about three and a half miles to Ras il Hobs. This shoreline
is similar to the north coast just described.

From Ras il Hobs west to Cape Bombardo the coast is a sheer
cliff. Depths of well over one hundred feet are found alongside
the cliff face, except at Xlendi Bay where rocks extend to two
hundred yards offshore in shallow water. Amphorae-laden ancient
wrecks have been found in Xlendi Bay.

[43] Except for a handful of astronauts, man is still a stranger to outer space. However, freed from the surface by the aqualung, the diver can explore Captain Cousteau's Inner Space, the sea. He moves three-dimensionally, released temporarily from gravity. His sky is the wave-ruffled surface. His stars are the countless tiny marine organisms, which seem suspended. His domain is the reef-covered sea bottom, at once tranquil and exciting.

[44] Fishing boats such as this one are available for hire throughout the Caribbean. The author's son is returning from a snorkeling trip to the Tobago Cays in the Grenadines. Frigate Island and Carriacou are seen in the distance.

[45] Diving conditions in the Mediterranean can be judged fairly closely by observing the characteristics of the shoreline. Because of the formation of coral reefs, this is not true in the Caribbean. In this photo of a portion of St. Thomas, Virgin Islands, the various reef formations show as the darker, irregularly shaped patterns in the water.

[46] San Francisco Beach is the midday luncheon rendezvous for the diving boats of Cozumel, Mexico.

[47] Bendor, France, is the headquarters for the superbly equipped Centre International de Plongée, or International Diving Center.

[48] Gustavia Harbor, St. Barts. St. Maarten can be seen in the distance.

[49] Sesimbra, Portugal, was the setting of the 1958 International Spearfishing Tournament.

[50] The rugged coastline of Malta offers hundreds of excellent diving areas.

[51] The beautiful, slow-moving turkey fish should be avoided because of its poisonous spines. These creatures inhabit the Indian Ocean and the Red Sea.

[52] Visitors to Mallorca, Balearic Islands, can charter small boats at the yacht basin for diving trips to nearby areas.

### WEST COAST

This entire coast is extremely steep and deep water is found close-to except between South Point and Ras id Dueira. Water fifteen feet deep and deeper is found here. Fungus Rock lies in Cala Dueira (a bay) and is surrounded by a shallow, rocky bottom worth exploring.

Boats can be rented in Xlendi or at the nearby Inland Sea. This small inland salt-water lake is connected by a narrow opening in the cliff to the sea.

*Chapter 46*

# YUGOSLAVIA

**How to get There:** By Pan Am Jet Clipper, flight time from New York to Belgrade, via London and Frankfurt, is eleven and a quarter hours. Scheduled ferryboat services operate from Venice, Ancona, and Bari, Italy, to various Yugoslavian ports. Trains connect Yugoslavia with other European countries.

**Customs Regulations:** Foreign tourists may bring in with them, duty free, items for their personal use. Visitors must register all skin diving equipment in their possession when entering the country and must have it with them upon departure.

**Travel Documents Required:** U.S. citizens must have a passport and a Yugoslav visa which can be obtained at the place of entry. Visas can also be obtained in the United States at the Yugoslav Embassy in Washington, D.C., or at one of the Consulate General offices in New York, Chicago, San Francisco, or Pittsburgh.

**Currency:** There are two kinds of Yugoslav dinars in current use, the old dinar and the new dinar. The old dinar is exchanged at 1250 to $1.00 U.S. The new dinar is exchanged at 12.50 to $1.00 U.S. Foreigners may bring into the country a maximum of 10,000 old dinars (100 new dinars) and may take out a maximum of 5000 old dinars (50 new dinars) in notes up to 100 dinars.

**Hotels:** This country has a very wide selection of hotels of every degree of luxury, from small pensions to elegant luxury hotels. Prices here are generally lower than in most of Europe. Motels are popular here and are also reasonably priced. There are over two thousand seaside resorts.

**Transportation:** Taxis are plentiful. Rental autos are available in the following cities: Belgrade, Ljubljana, Zagreb, Mostar, Titograd, Opatija, and Dubrovnik. Internal air service links the major cities. Rail and bus service are efficient and inexpensive and provide service to almost every town in the country. The main highways are excellent. A 620-mile road parallels the entire Adriatic coastline.

**Medical Facilities:** There are hospitals in the larger communities. There is a hospital or a dispensary in almost every town.

**Other Information:** English is spoken in the main tourist centers. Taking photographs is prohibited within fifteen kilometers of national frontiers. It is also forbidden to take photographs of military installations and troops. Other areas prohibited to photographers are marked with signboards.

The Pan Am offices are in Belgrade (Beograd) at Marsala Tita 18 (Tel: 20949) and in the Hotel Slavija (Tel: 48487). The main office of the Tourist Association of Yugoslavia is at M. Pijade 8 (P. O. Box 595) in Belgrade. In New York the address is Yugoslav Information Center, 816 Fifth Avenue (Tel: TE 8-2300). General tourist information and a complete hotel list, with rates, can be obtained from these tourist offices.

## SKIN DIVING INFORMATION

Yugoslavia has a lovely, varied coastline on the Adriatic which is fringed with 725 islands and over 500 reefs. For skin diving, the coast can be divided into two parts, the northern area from Trieste south to Split and the southern area from Split south to the Albanian border. The northern region is more shallow and has fewer fish than the southern region, which is rockier and more rugged.

The coast road provides access to most coastal diving spots. Ferries ply between the mainland and many of the islands.

In good weather, visibility is usually around fifty feet in the northern region and eighty feet or better in the southern area. Water temperatures on the surface are from 75° to 80° during the summer. Water temperatures gradually drop with an increase in depth.

There are a great number of shallow, rocky areas along this coast for beginners to explore and a number of deeper offshore diving spots for experts. The underwater scenery here is interesting, although not as varied as in some other Mediterranean areas.

Fish are usually seen in greatest numbers on the offshore (western or southwestern) coasts of the offshore islands.

Divers planning a trip to this country are advised to contact the Yugoslavian Federation of Sport Fishing and Underwater Activities (Address: Savez Za Sportski Ribolov Na Moru I Podvodne Aktivnosti Jugoslavije, Rijeka, Ul. Matije Gupca 2, Yugoslavia). This is the Yugoslav national organization for divers and can provide assistance and information to visitors wherever possible.

**Laws:** At the time of writing this, new laws regulating diving activities are being formulated. Therefore, visitors are advised to write to the Underwater Federation for current information. The laws in effect at the time of writing are as follows:

1 – Spearfishing while wearing underwater breathing apparatus of any kind is prohibited.
2 – A permit must be obtained for spearfishing. This can be obtained from the municipality nearest to the diving area. Alternatively, foreigners may join a Yugoslav diving club (through the Federation) and obtain a membership card which replaces the spearfishing permit.
3 – It is forbidden to spear more than five kilos (about eleven pounds) of fish in one day. Rare species may not be speared.
4 – Speared fish may not be sold. The penalty is heavy.
5 – Spearfishing is prohibited in harbors and near beaches.
6 – Rubber, spring, or compressed-air spear guns are permitted. Spear guns powered with gunpowder or using explosive spearpoints are prohibited.
7 – Scuba diving is permitted only in the following areas:

   (a) Near Trieste, the area from the town of Kopar west to Cape Ronek.

(*b*) East of the town of Piran, from Cape Madonski to Fijeso Bay, inclusive.

(*c*) South of Piran, in Croatia, from Cape Katavar (north of the town of Umag) south to the port of Vrsar and the island of Kuvrsad, inclusive.

(*d*) On the island of Cres, from the Cape of Sv. Blaz to Cape Pernat.

(*e*) Island of Sv. Marko; the entire coastline.

(*f*) Island of Krk; the northwest coast of the island from Cape Kijac to Cape Glavotok.

(*g*) On the east coast of Istria, from Crna Punta to Cape Kijac (north of the town of Senj), inclusive.

(*h*) The coast on the southeast part of the Zadar Channel and the Pašman Channel, and the coast from the city of Biograd south to Pirovac Bay, inclusive.

(*i*) Near the city of Šibenik, the coast of the Šibenik Channel and the islands of Prvić and Zlarin.

(*j*) Near the city of Split, the coast of Kaštel Bay.

(*k*) Southeast of the town of Omiš, from Cape Krizica to Žrnovica Bay (south of the town of Gradac), inclusive.

(*l*) On the Pelješac Peninsula, from Cape Lovista to Cape Sv. Ivan (west of the town of Viganj). From Lirica to Prapratna Harbor.

(*m*) Near Dubrovnik, from Slano Harbor south to Zaton Harbor; from Cape Petka south to the town of Mlini; and from Cape Zarubaca (southeast of the town of Cavtat) to Cape V. Pac.

(*n*) The north coast of Hercegnovi Bay from Igalo east to Meljine.

(*o*) The southeast part of the coast of Tivat Bay from the town of Bjelila to the town of Prevlaka, including the island of Stradioti.

(*p*) East of the town of Budva, from Cape Zavala to Debeli Rat.

(*q*) Near the town of Petrovac, from Cape Crvena Stijena to Cape Sapavica.

(*r*) Near the town of Ulcinj, from Cape Mendra east to Cape Djeran.

8 – Underwater photography is permitted only in the areas listed in ⚓6, above.

9 – Visitors must register all diving equipment brought into the country at the place of entry.

10 – A permit must be obtained before searching for or working on archaeological finds (ancient wrecks, etc.). This permit may be obtained at the following places:

(*a*) Institute for Preservation of Monuments of the Socialist Republic of Slovenia, Ljubljana.

(*b*) Conservation Institute, Rijeka.

(*c*) Conservation Institute for Dalmatia, Split.

(*d*) Institute for the Protection of Cultural Monuments of the Socialist Republic of Montenegro, Titograd.

11 – All archaeological finds must be reported to one of the Institutes listed in ⚓10, above. Discoverers of important and previously unknown finds may receive awards, depending on the agreement with the Institute. Depending on the size of the archaeological find and upon the judgment of the Institute responsible for research and protection of the find, the divers making the find may be allowed to keep one object, if there are a large number of duplicates (amphorae, for example).

12 – At the time of writing, it is not possible to purchase artifacts from archaeological finds. Revised regulations are under consideration.

13 – The penalty for damage to, illegal removal of, or exporting of underwater archaeological discoveries or artifacts is five years in prison plus an appropriate fine.

14 – Fishing or spearfishing is prohibited in the following fish preserves: the Lim Channel, the Raša Channel, lakes on the island of Mljet, plus most of the island coastline, and the Ston Channel. Other areas may be set aside from time to time

as fish preserves by the various municipalities. Divers are advised to check with local authorities before going spearfishing.

**Diving Gear for Sale:** A limited selection of Yugoslavian, French, and Italian snorkeling equipment is available in some of the seaside resorts. Visiting spearfishermen should plan on bringing their own spear guns and should also bring an ample supply of spare parts. Parts are not always easy to get in Yugoslavia. Scuba divers will have either to bring in their own equipment or to make arrangements to dive with Yugoslav equipment, through the Fishing and Skin Diving Federation.

**Diving Gear for Rent:** Not available.

**Boats, Guides:** Boats are available almost everywhere and can be hired by the hour or by the day. Daily rates usually range from 2500 to 6000 dinars, depending on the size of the boat, the engine, etc. To date, organized skin diving specialty shops have not appeared. Visitors can frequently find a local diver through their hotel.

**Compressed Air:** Air is available at the following locations: *Portorož:* Institute for Underwater Studies, Portorož 74. *Rijeka:* Center for Underwater Activities, Rozici 1. *Island of Mali Lošinj:* SRD "Udica." *Split:* PIK "Mornar," Plivaliste Spinut. *Dubrovnik:* SRD "Neptun," Brsalje 4. Members of diving clubs, including foreign members, receive a 50 percent discount for compressed air. The average price is $2.00 per tank.

**Currents, Winds:** The general set of the current is to the north; however, among the islands, currents are deflected by the formation of the sea bottom, winds, and other factors. Except in narrow passages between islands and the mainland or around the extremities of the mainland, currents normally are not too strong.

In the summer, winds are usually from the southwest in the morning and shift through west to northwest in the afternoon. During a change in weather, winds are usually from the northeast.

In late autumn and winter, winds are most frequently from the northeast and next most frequently from the southeast.

**Adriatic Fish:** The most commonly seen game fish along the Yugoslavian coast are: sea bass, mackerel, tuna, black drum, mullet, bream, wrasses, dentexes (or toothed bream), and (in the southern waters only) groupers. Moray eels are found in southern waters but not in the north.

Diving conditions are best from May to September, but the coast is quite crowded with European tourists during July and August.

Diving conditions along the Yugoslavian coast are discussed here in geographical order, from north to south.

## NORTHERN REGION—FROM TRIESTE SOUTH TO SPLIT

A few miles south of Trieste are a number of summer resorts on the Istrian Peninsula, the nearest one of which is Koper. Point Gornja (also called Point Savudrija) is a few miles west of Koper and is the northwestern tip of the Istrian Peninsula. A wreck is located in about forty-five feet of water close off the north shore of this Point. The coast between Koper and the Point is uninteresting.

South of Point Gornja for several miles to the town of Pula, the coast is low, with some fringing rocks and a few offshore islets. The sea bottom is mostly sandy. Few fish are seen in the northern portion of the peninsula. The water here is shallow with twenty-foot depths found more than half a mile offshore in several places.

Between the town of Poreč and Nikola Island there are some very old wrecks.

There is an aquarium in Rovinj which houses a collection of fish typical of the Adriatic.

The offshore rocks and small islands north of Rovinj are interesting for snorkeling and are a good place for beginning divers. Some bream can be found about halfway between the towns of Rovinj and Pula, at Dantula Point and at Barbariga Point.

President Tito maintains a home on one of the Brioni Islands, which are north of Pula. Rocks and reefs extend to seaward for about one and a half miles from these islands.

The best spearfishing area on the Istrian Peninsula is from Point Kamenjak northeast to the village of Rabac. This area is not recommended for novices. Steep cliffs rise abruptly from the Adriatic and depths of over one hundred feet are found close alongside this steep shoreline. A variety of game fish can be found here. Currents around the Point can be strong.

The coast from Rabac to the city of Rijeka is an attractive vacation area but has little of interest to divers. From Rijeka south to the Albanian border the coast is steep and rocky in most places.

The sea bottom from Rijeka south to the town of Senj is mostly sandy and uninteresting. Visibility is usually poor in this section.

The offshore islands of Krk, Cres, Losinj, Ilovik, Unije, and several other small islets lie off this coast. Diving conditions are very good around most of these shores. The sea bottom is rocky in most places. Fish are more plentiful here than along the shore of the mainland. The island group is linked with Rijeka and Pula by ferry. Cres and Losinj are served by an auto ferry from Rabac and Rijeka.

An international spearfishing competition was held at Losinj in 1957 because of the quantities of fish in the area.

These wooded islands are beautiful with steep, rocky shores and should be visited by divers traveling through this portion of the country.

On the mainland, the coastline is very steep from Senj for several miles south to Nin. Few fish are seen here and snorkeling is not too enjoyable because of the deep water close to shore. However, the western coasts of the many small islands in this region are interesting for divers who will find shallow water along the shore, good quantities of fish, and a rocky sea bottom.

The best diving area in the northern Adriatic is found among the Kornat Islands and the Central Dalmatian Islands. They lie offshore from approximately west of the city of Zadar, south to a point west of the city of Šibenik.

There are hundreds of small rocks, islets, and reefs in this group. The water is clear, the sea bottom rocky, and plenty of game fish can be seen here—mostly on the southwestern sides of the islands. These islands can be reached by boat from Zadar. Small boats can be rented cheaply in most villages.

There is another group of several islands off the city of Šibenik, with good diving conditions similar to the group just described. Boats from Šibenik can be used to reach these nearby islands. Sponge divers have their headquarters on Zlarin Island, with some on nearby Krapanj Island.

The coastline from Šibenik south to Point Ploča (about halfway to Split) is rocky and indented and is excellent for diving. Good quantities of fish are found here, mostly rock fish found among the sponge- and weed-covered rock bottom.

From Point Ploča south to the town of Trogir there are small caves and crevices in the rocky shoreline. Snorkeling and spear-fishing are good here, with plenty of rock fish. From Trogir east to Split, the bottom is mostly muddy and uninteresting.

SOUTHERN REGION—SPLIT SOUTH TO ULCINJ

The offshore islands opposite and southeast of Split are excellent areas for diving. They have rocky coastlines, the bottom is mostly rock, and there are plenty of fish. They can be reached by boat from Split or by car ferry from the town of Trogir. The principal islands in this group are Solta, Brač, Hvar, Korčula, and Vis.

Here, the sea becomes warmer and clearer than in the region to the north. Coral is occasionally seen. Groupers and moray eels, which are not found in the colder northern waters are seen here in quantity.

On the mainland, the coast is rocky from Split south to the town of Makaŕska. There are plenty of fish among the rocks and weeds on the sea bottom.

The Pelješac Peninsula and the islands of Mljet and Lastovo, north of Dubrovnik, are also excellent diving sites and are similar to the islands just described. There are two lakes on Mljet, with water too cold for diving. Fish are found in quantity along the southern shore of the Pelješac Peninsula and around the islands. There is a ferry service to these islands from Dubrovnik.

Just north of the town of Cavtat (which is south of Dubrovnik), the remains of the sunken city of Epidauros can be seen. These sunken ruins lie on the bottom of Thia Bay north and northwest of the Hotel Epidauros.

The very finest diving area in the Adriatic is along the coast from Dubrovnik south to Ulcinj. Here the water is usually very clear (up to one hundred feet, sometimes more) and warm (surface temperatures reach 80° in summer), and fish and other sea life abound. The coast is rocky and indented and there are caves in many places. The coast between Bar and Ulcinj is accessible only by boat, obtainable in either town.

The beach at Ulcinj is said to be radioactive.

*Chapter 47*

# GREECE

**How to Get There:** By Pan Am Jet Clipper to Rome with connecting flight to Athens. Athens is linked to most of Europe by ship, rail, and highway. An automobile ferry shuttles between Brindisi, Italy, and Corfu and Piraeus, Greece.

**Customs Regulations:** Personal belongings and two hundred cigarettes, a quarter pound of tobacco, or thirty cigars will be admitted duty free.

**Travel Documents Required:** U.S. citizens must have a passport and a smallpox vaccination certificate. A visa is not required.

**Currency:** The Greek drachma is exchanged at 30 drachmas to $1.00 U.S. There are 100 leptas in a drachma. Fifty drachmas, 45 leptas is written: dr 50.45. A maximum of 2000 drachmas may be brought into the country.

**Hotels:** There is a wide selection of hotels in Greece. Rates are generally quite low. The selection of hotels is not quite so wide in outlying areas and on some of the islands, but these hotels are usually comfortable and clean.

**Transportation:** Taxis, buses, and rental autos are available in the cities. Ships connect the various islands, and scheduled buses serve the outlying communities on the mainland.

**Medical Facilities:** There are several hospitals and English-speaking doctors in Athens. There are also hospitals or dispensaries in most of the smaller towns.

**Other Information:** The Pan Am office is at 6 Venizelos Avenue in Athens (Tel: 61-26-95). Tourist information and a complete list of hotels is available from the National Tourist Office, 4 Stadiou Street, in Athens or from the Greek National Tourist Organization, 601 Fifth Avenue, New York (Tel: HA 1-5777).

## SKIN DIVING INFORMATION

Snorkeling is not regulated or prohibited in Greece, but the use of scuba equipment in waters where sunken antiquities (ancient wrecks, sunken temples, etc.) exist, or are believed to exist, is expressly prohibited by the Government. Since the sea bottom here is, in places, cluttered with amphorae and other artifacts, a visitor can unwittingly get into serious trouble by using scuba gear.

Snorkeling is excellent along much of the coast and around most of the Greek islands. The water is clean and, in summer, warm enough to be enjoyed without the protection of a diving suit. Almost any rocky area is worth investigating. As is the case anywhere, there are more fish farther away from the populated areas than near settlements. The deeper one can dive, the more fish one will see.

**Laws:** 1 – Scuba diving on or near known or suspected locations of sunken ancient wrecks or other antiquities, or disturbing or removing any ancient artifact is prohibited. The penalty is severe.

2 – Underwater research can be done only by written permission from the Department of Antiquities and Restoration, Ministry to the Prime Minister's Office, Palaia Anacorta, Athens.

3 – All antiquities discovered underwater must be reported to local port/Coast Guard authorities.

4 – Skin diving is prohibited near the Turkish border and near the Albanian border.

5 – Other areas in Greece are off limits to skin divers, primarily for military reasons. Since regulations concerning these areas are subject to change from time to time, a detailed list is not given here. The best solution is to contact the Coast Guard

installation or the local nautical association nearest the proposed diving site for information. Information can also be obtained from the Greek diving clubs listed at the end of this chapter.

6 – Spearfishing while wearing scuba gear is prohibited.

7 – It is forbidden to shoot fish weighing less than 150 grams.

8 – A diving permit is not absolutely necessary. It is valuable, though, in avoiding minor misunderstandings with local authorities. It is recommended that divers planning a visit to Greece obtain a permit from the Underwater Federation, 9 Venizelos Avenue, Athens. It can be obtained by mail.

9 – Underwater photographers are advised to contact the local Coast Guard authorities for a photography permit.

**Diving Gear for Sale:** Diving gear is freely available in Athens and in Salonica. A limited selection of snorkeling equipment can be purchased in Patras, Corfu, Rhodes, Crete, and Volos. M. Kapellas and Son are importers of French diving equipment on the island of Kalymnos.

**Diving Gear for Rent:** Scuba tanks can be rented from Mr. E. Bouboulis, The Propellor, 1 Akti Moutsopoulou, Passalimani, Piraeus.

**Guides, Boats:** To date, the only training center for diving is located at the St. Kosma Athletic Center, at Hellenikon. Plans are being formulated for providing guides and instruction as well as compressed air through the diving clubs listed at the end of this chapter.

The U. S. Air Force diving club, the Athens Dolphins, is a well-equipped organization which is always willing to provide information to visiting divers and will offer whatever other assistance they can. The club is established on the Air Force base, near the Athens Airport.

Boats can be hired almost everywhere. The average daily cost is $10; however, this is an approximate figure. The rate may vary, depending on the size of the boat and the ability of the bargainer. Boat rentals are usually less on the islands than on the mainland.

Yachts can be chartered for extended trips. Rates begin at about $60 per day for a boat large enough for four passengers. A list of recommended yacht agents can be found at the end of this chapter.

**Compressed Air:** *Athens:* 44 Academias Street; Neon Phaleron, 50 Solomou Street and Fagreos Street.

*Volos:* Pigason and Analipseos №2.

*Salonica:* 13 Vermiou Street; St. George Kypriou №15.

*Hellenikon:* St. Kosma Athletic Center.

**Recompression Chambers:** There are two near Athens: The Royal Hellenic Naval Hospital, Piraeus (Tel: 45-24-66 or 45-27-01); U. S. Air Force Base Dispensary, near the Athens Airport, Tel: 98-21-01.

**Currents, Winds:** Currents in the Aegean Sea are irregular and are considerably influenced by the winds. The general set is to the south. However, in the area adjacent to the Dardanelles, around the island of Limnos, the current is strong to the west. In the channels between the islands to the southeast of Athens (Andros, Tinos, Mykonos, and Naxos), the currents are stiff.

Prevailing winds are from northeast to northwest the year around. There are, though, variations in some localities. In the channel between the islands of Evvoia and Andros, the north winds are quite strong the year around.

Onshore winds usually counteract the north winds along the mainland of Greece and on some of the larger islands. The north wind is felt only infrequently in the Athens area.

In the southern Aegean, southerly winds prevail as frequently as northerlies during the winter.

## THE MAINLAND OF GREECE

Diving information is presented here by following the shoreline south from the Albanian border, then east to the Turkish border. Information about the islands is given separately at the end of this section.

## IONIAN COAST

Diving is not permitted near the Albanian border. From this region south for about twenty miles to Oxia Island, the southwest corner of the mainland, the coast is alternately rocky, sandy, and muddy. Several rivers empty into this region and bring quantities of silt into the sea. Visibility is not as good here as in other areas of Greece.

## SOUTH COAST

The western portion of the south coast of the Greek mainland forms the north shore of the Gulf of Patras. The shoreline here, from the western tip east to "The Narrows" is low, sandy, and not suited to skin diving.

From The Narrows east for over ten miles, to Cape Psaromita, the coast continues low and marshy. From the Cape east to the Corinth Canal, good diving conditions are found around the high, rocky coastline which is fringed in most places with offshore rocks. This includes the Gulf of Alkionidhon, northeast of the Canal. This is a region of small towns and coastal fishing villages. A good road leads from Athens to the city of Corinth, where boats can be hired.

About halfway along this coast is the Gulf of Krissaios. At the northwestern corner of the gulf is the village of Itea. In the bay near Itea are the wrecks of five Turkish warships which were sunk in a naval battle with the Greeks in 1826. Depths vary in the bay from about twenty-five to seventy-five feet.

The Gulf of Athens extends from the Corinth Canal east to Cape Sounion. The city of Athens (and the nearby seaport, Piraeus) is in this portion of the coast.

West of Athens, the coast is generally rocky and steep. An excellent road parallels the coast and the area can be reached by boat, auto, or bus. Fishing boats are readily available. It is suggested that divers planning a visit to this area travel as far away from Athens as possible to avoid heavy sea traffic and water pollution.

East of Athens heavily populated suburbs extend eastward to Vouliagmeni. It is possible to snorkel among the fringing rocks in this area, but the small offshore islands are much more interesting and more fish will be seen around them than along the well-settled mainland. A number of small-boat basins are dotted along these shores and boats are readily available for hire.

From Vouliagmeni eastward to Cape Sounion the coastline is alternately rocky and sandy. This area is the most easily accessible diving area near Athens and may be reached by rented car or by bus. The few small islets that lie off this shore are worth a visit.

At Cape Sounion there are several hotels. The Temple of Poseidon, 2500 years old, is atop the hill here.

### EAST COAST, SOUNION TO THESSALONIKI

To the east of Cape Sounion is the island of Makronisos, a good diving spot. The island is long and narrow and shoals fringe the north, west, and east sides. It can be reached by boat from Sounion.

The mainland coast continues north, then northwest, for over twenty miles to the town of Khalkis. Within this area, the coast is alternately sandy and rocky. There are a number of good diving spots here around the rocky headlands. Good roads lead to this area from Athens and a number of hotels are established around the coast. The Gulf of Marathon, low and sandy and unsuitable for diving, is near the site of the famous battle on the plain of Marathon.

From Khalkis, the coast trends northwest for several miles to the small village of St. Konstantinos. Within this section, the shore is mostly rocky and good diving can be enjoyed. This shore is generally steep. The southeast portion of this section is accessible only by boat. The main road from Athens joins the coast at the village of Skala.

Beyond the village of St. Konstantinos, the coast is indented deeply by two bays near the cities of Lamia and Volos. The water in this region is not very clear.

The best diving area near this region is on the eastern shore of the peninsula which extends southeast from Volos. There, from the village of Platania northwest to the village of Agiokambos, the shoreline is rocky and steep. Diving conditions are good. Volos can be reached by air, ship, or road. Boats can be hired in the fishing villages.

North of Agiokambos, the water becomes murky due to the outflow of several rivers discharging into the Gulf of Saloniki. For this reason, the entire coastline north to Thessaloniki (Salonika) is not especially good for diving.

### FROM THESSALONIKI TO TURKISH BORDER

The Khalkidike Peninsula extends south and east of Thessaloniki. This wide peninsula terminates in three smaller peninsulas: Kassandra (Pallini), Longos, (Sithonia), and Athos (Agion Oros).

The western shore of the Khalkidike Peninsula from Thessaloniki southwest to the Nea Potidaia canal is low and sandy and not very good for diving. The remainder of the peninsula is rocky and steep. Plenty of good diving spots can be found along this irregular shoreline, particularly at the tips of the three peninsulas. Good diving conditions are present also along the eastern shore of Khalkidike Peninsula as far north as the village of Kato Stavros, where the peninsula joins the mainland.

Athos Peninsula is a self-governing region and is inhabited chiefly by religious orders of the Greek Orthodox Church. This is the only monastic state in Europe. Women are not allowed on Athos.

Because of the silt brought by several rivers which discharge into the sea, and because much of the coastline is low and sandy, the area from the village of Kato Stavros east to the Turkish border is not recommended for divers.

The exception to this is the nearby island of Thasos. It is steep and rocky on the eastern and southern coasts, and offers a number of excellent diving areas. The other two sides of the island are sandy. Boats can be rented in the villages. A ferryboat connects this island with the mainland.

## THE GREEK ISLANDS

Most of the Greek islands are excellent for diving. They rise steeply from the sea and feature high cliffs and sunken rocks around their coastlines. To describe each would be repetitive and unnecessary. Consequently, the only ones described will be Corfu, Peloponnesos, Rhodes, and Crete.

Divers can count on finding suitable diving areas around the other islands not specifically mentioned, since they are all rocky. Several of these islands have caves along their shores, and the remains of ancient wrecks, sunken towns, and sunken temples can be found. Visitors are reminded, again, of the strictly enforced laws regarding the exploration of archaeological sites.

All the inhabited islands are connected by steamer service to Athens. Corfu, Peloponnesos, Rhodes, Crete, Lesbos, Limnos, Samos, and Kos have air service. Two of the larger steamship lines in Athens which offer island service are the Typaldos Line and the Epirotiki Line.

## CORFU

Corfu (Kerkyra) is a very popular resort in the Ionian Sea near the Albanian border. It can be reached by boat and by air from Brindisi, Italy, or Athens. An auto ferry operates between Corfu and Igoumenitsa, Italy. There are ten hotels on the island.

On most days a light northwest breeze springs up around noon. Occasionally this breeze develops into a stiff wind.

The north coast is low, sandy, and not suitable for diving. The east coast is mixed, with sandy and rocky areas alternating. Visibility is not so good here, because of the discharge of some rivers on the mainland. The west coast is the best place for diving on the island.

Roads lead across the island to the west coast. Here, the coastline is rugged and rocky. Many above- and below-water rocks can be seen along the irregular, indented shoreline. Boats can be obtained in several of the coastal villages.

## PELOPONNESOS

This is an island, technically, because of the man-made Corinth Canal which separates it from the mainland. It is discussed here, separate from the mainland, because of its size, nearness to Athens, and varied shoreline.

The entire north shore, from Corinth (Korinthos) west to Point Killini, is low and sandy and unsuitable for diving.

About three-fourths of the west coast, from Point Killini south to Proti Island, is also low and sandy.

The shoreline from Proti Island south to Cape Akritas, the southern tip of the western peninsula, is rocky and steep. Good diving can be enjoyed all along this region. A few miles south of Proti Island is Navarin Bay, the largest harbor on Peloponnesos. In 1827 forty-three Turkish ships were sunk in this bay by Admiral Codrington in one of the battles decisive to the independence of Greece. The wrecks lie in from 75 to 120 feet of water and are well worth seeing. It is advisable to check with the local Coast Guard before diving in this area.

Northeast of Cape Akritas a few miles is the village of Koroni. This village is said to be the only place in Greece where amphorae are still produced in the ancient manner, without the use of a potter's wheel. A ruined castle sits atop the hill above Koroni.

East of Cape Akritas are two deep indentations into the southern coast of Peloponnesos: the Gulf of Kalamata and the Gulf of Lakonia. They are separated by a peninsula terminating at Cape Tainaron. Off the southwestern tip of Cape Malea (which forms the eastern shore of the Gulf of Lakonia) is the island of Kithira (discussed separately below). Currents around the southern extremities, particularly between the mainland and Kithira, frequently reach two knots.

The eastern and western shores of both gulfs are rocky, irregular, and rock-fringed. Diving conditions are good here and a number of fish can be seen. The heads of the two gulfs (to the north) are sandy and uninteresting underwater.

Roads from Athens, through Argos, Tripolis, and Kalamai, parallel both shorelines of the Gulf of Kalamata. The usual fishing boats can be rented in the scattered coastal villages. A road leads from Sparta about halfway down the western shore of the Gulf of Lakonia. Another road leads to a few seaside communities on the eastern shore.

About two-thirds of the distance from Cape Tainaron to the head of the Gulf of Lakonia, on the western shore, is small Kato Vathi Bay. A tanker is sunk at the head of this bay. It is about five feet to the top of this wreck.

Across the Gulf, on the eastern shore, is the village of Plitra. The remains of a submerged ancient town can be found next to the village pier.

Kithira (Kythera) Island, southwest of Cape Malea, is another excellent diving area. The coast is rocky and steep except for an occasional sandy beach. The remains of the ancient city of Kithira are at the northern end of St. Nikolaos Bay, which is on the east coast.

From Cape Malea north along the southeastern coast of Peloponnesos about fifteen miles to the village of Monemvasia, the coastline is very irregular, steep, wild, and almost uninhabited. Excellent skin diving conditions are found here, and there are plenty of game fish. Care must be taken not to be caught in rough seas along this coast. The winds from the northeast can build up quite a heavy sea.

From Monemvasia north almost to Nafplion, the coast is rocky and reef fringed. The head of the Gulf of Nauplia, though, is low and not good for diving. The eastern shore of the gulf is rocky, indented, and offers some excellent diving spots. Access is by road from Athens through Argos and Nauplia to fishing villages, where boats can be rented.

A peninsula extends to the southeast from the mainland of the Peloponnesos. The southwestern shore forms one of the shorelines of the Gulf of Nauplia, just described. The northeastern shore forms one of the coasts of the Gulf of Athens. Off the southern coast of this peninsula lies the resort island of Hydra (Idhra), served by regular steamer service from Athens. This entire island is rocky and well suited for diving. Caves and crevices can be found along the indented shoreline, and deep water is found close to the rocks. The village of Hydra (Idhra), on the north coast, is exceptionally attractive and is well worth a visit.

The southern shore of the Gulf of Athens, formed by the northeastern coast of Peloponnesos, is similar to the shoreline of the Gulf of Nauplia; rocky, irregular, and, in places, steep. The town of Epidavros is served by ferry from Athens.

## RHODES

Rhodes (Rodhos), the most easterly of the Greek islands, is the largest of the Dodecanese group and lies just off the coast of Turkey. It can be reached by steamer or plane from Athens. There are over forty hotels of various types on this popular vacation island. Roads reach most spots around its coastline.

The east coast is rocky and steep in places with good diving from the north point south to the peninsula on which the village of Lindos is situated. From this peninsula south to the southern point, the coast is low and fringed with rocks.

The west coast is sandy from the north point south for about twenty-three miles to Cape Kopria. From Cape Kopria south, the shoreline is mostly high and rocky with a few beaches here and there. This latter region is the best one for diving.

## CRETE

Crete can be reached by air or ship from Athens, Piraeus, and Rhodes. There are twenty-three hotels on the island. A good road parallels the north coast. Secondary roads reach some of the coastal villages on the south coast. There are airports at Khania and at Iraklion.

North winds prevail here during the summer and alternate with southerly winds in winter. The north coast is suitable for diving only during calm periods, as brisk northerlies raise a heavy, dangerous sea. The south coast is subject to strong winds during northerly gales, which come howling off the mountains and through the valleys. When southerly winds of any force are experienced along the south coast, the seas are much too heavy for diving.

## NORTH COAST

Most of this coast is exposed to the prevailing northerly winds with the exception of Souda Bay, toward the western end of the island. This bay will be described below.

Cape Vouxa is the northwestern point of the island and is the north end of a peninsula forming the western side of Kisamou Bay. North of this cape is small, rocky Gramvousa Island. From here east for about thirty miles to Point Tripiti, the coast is extremely rocky, irregular, with a number of rocky shoals close-to. Depths close to shore vary from ten to over one hundred feet. The head of Kisamou Bay and the southern shore of Khanion Bay, west of the town of Khania, are sandy and not interesting underwater.

Point Tripiti is the northernmost point of the Kyamon Promontory. From this point south to Souda Bay, the coast is extremely rugged with great depths found close-to. This shoreline is subject to heavy seas during north winds.

Souda Bay is the most protected area on this coast. It extends for about seven miles in an east-west direction, between the Kyamon Promontory and the mainland of Crete. The shoreline is quite rocky. Souda island lies just inside the entrance to the bay. This is the best diving area on this coast. The town of Souda lies at the head of the bay. A naval base is established here.

Point Drapanon is the southeast entrance to Souda Bay. From here south for about seven miles to the head of Almirou Bay, the coastline is rugged and cliffy. Deep water is found close to shore except in a small, unnamed bay two and a half miles south of Point Drapanon. A sunken ship lies in about thirty-five feet of water near the head of this small bay.

Almirou Bay and Rethimnou Bay extend eastward for about twenty miles. This portion of the coastline is sandy and useless for diving except for a section of rocky shoreline extending westward of the town of Rethimnon for about six miles.

The rest of the north coast is extremely rugged and irregular eastward to Point Sideros, the northeastern point of Crete. The only exceptions to this are a marshy, sandy section extending for about five miles eastward of Iraklion, and a short sandy stretch east of the town of Sitia.

In many places along this eastern half of the north coast, shallow, rocky shoals extend to seaward as far as half a mile. Many rocks and reefs fringe the northeastern tip of the island and diving conditions are excellent here, when the winds are light. This area is quite dangerous when the winds are strong. A stranded wreck can be seen on Sideros Reef, just northeast of Point Sideros.

### EAST COAST

This entire coast is steep, rocky, and irregularly indented. Good diving can be found just about everywhere in calm weather. When winds blow heavily, diving should not be attempted.

### SOUTH COAST

From the southeast corner of the island westward for several miles to the village of Ierapetra, the coast is extremely irregular, indented, and rocky with rocky formations found up to five hundred yards offshore. In calm weather this is excellent for diving.

Almost two miles west of Point Ierapetra is the village of the same name. A wreck lies in about forty-five feet of water about half a mile south of the town, in line with Ierapetra Point and an old fort at the southern end of the town.

From Ierapetra west for about thirty miles to Point Tsoutsouros the coast is low and rocky. Some offshore rocks are seen here. This stretch of coast is suitable for shallow-water snorkeling.

The coast is steep and rocky for another thirty miles west of Point Tsoutsouros to Point Lithinon. In calm weather, diving here is excellent, with many shoals and offshore rocks. Groupers can be seen in caves along this shoreline.

The coast turns north at Point Lithinon. Four miles north of this point is Matala Bay, at the head of which is a small village of the same name. There are caves along the shoreline of this bay and tombs in the rock face. According to Homer's *Odyssey*, some of the ships belonging to Menelaus, King of Sparta, were driven ashore here.

For about five miles north, then northwest, of Matala Bay, the shoreline is low and sandy with little of interest underwater.

The coastline from St. Galini Point, near the town of Agia Galini, west to the southwestern end of Crete is rocky. There are numerous deep indentations with occasional beaches found at the heads of small bays. During fine weather, this region is excellent for diving. The most spectacular portion of this coast is a twenty-mile section between Point Mouros and Point Flomes. Here, cliffs rise sheer from the sea, and the whole region has a wild and imposing look. The diving is excellent here and shallow water is found close to shore. Not far from shore, the bottom drops off steeply to well over one hundred feet. There are no coastal villages in this area.

## GREEK DIVING CLUBS

The following is a list of Greek skin diving clubs and nautical and yacht clubs having a diving group in their membership. Their names are listed first in Greek, then in English translation, and are followed by their addresses, if there is one.

*Corfu:* Naftikos Athlitikos Omilos Kerkyras
(Corfu Nautical Athletic Club)

*Ioannina:* Naftikos Omilos Ioanninon
(Yannina Nautical Club)
193 Venezelou Street

*Preveza:* Naftikos Omilos Prevezis
(Preveza Nautical Club)

*Athens area:* Naftikos Omilos Kolpou Elefsinos
(Eleusis Bay Nautical Club)

Omilos Philon Aktis
(Beach Lovers Club)
7 Karageorgi Servias Street, Athens

Omilos Erasitechnon Alieon Peiraios
(Piraeus Pleasure Fishermen's Club)
Pasalimani, Piraeus

Syndesmos Erasitechnon Alieon Athinon
(Athens Pleasure Fishermen's Association)
Tourkolimano, Piraeus

Istioploikos Omilos Peiraios
(Piraeus Yacht Club)

Athens Dolphins Skin Diving Club
U.S.A.F. Base, at Hellenikon Airport

Naftikos Omilos Ellenikou
(Hellenikon Nautical Club)
Hellenikon

Naftikos Omilos Palaiou Phalirou
(Palaion Phaliron Nautical Club)
Palaion Phaliron

Naftikos Omilos Kalamakiou
(Kalamaki Nautical Club)
Kalamaki

Naftiki Enosis Voulas
(Voula Nautical Union)
Voulas

Naftikos Omilos Vouliagmenis
(Vouliagmenis Nautical Club)
Vouliagmenis

*Lavrion:* Syndesmos Erasitechnon Alieon Lavriou
(Lavrion Pleasure Fishermen's Club)

*Khalkis:* Syndesmos Erasitechnon Alieon Khalkidas
(Khalkis Pleasure Fishermen's Association)

*Lamia:* Syndesmos Erasitechnon Alieon Phthiotidos
(Philliotis Pleasure Fishermen's Club)
20 Drossopoulou Street, Lamia

Athlitikos Syllagos Alieon Lamias
(Lamia Fishing and Athletic Club)

*Volos:* Syndesmos Erasitechnon Alieon Volou
(Volos Pleasure Fishermen's Association)

*Katerini:* Syndesmos Erasitechnon Alieon Pierias, Katerini
(Katerini Pleasure Fishermen's Association)

*Thessaloniki*
*(also: Salonika):* Naftikos Omilos Erasitechnikis Alieias Kai
Ypovrichion Drastiriotitos, Thessalonikis
(Salonica Pleasure Fishing and Underwater Activities Club)
Mikron Emvolon, Salonica

Istioploikos Omilos Thessalonikis
(Salonica Yacht Club)

*Drama:* Syndesmos Erasitechnon Alieon Dramas
(Drama Pleasure Fishermen's Club)

*Kavala:* Syndesmos Erasitechnon Alieon Kay Ypovrichion Drastiriotitos Kavalas
(Kavala Pleasure Fishing and Underwater Activities Association)

*Lesbos:*           Syndesmos Erasitechnon Alieon Lesvou
                    (Lesbos Pleasure Fishermen's Association)

*Hydra:*            Syndesmos Erasitechnon Alieon Ydras
                    (Hydra Pleasure Fishermen's Club)

*Peloponnesos:*     Naftikos Omilos Kalamatas
                    (Kalamata Nautical Club)
                    Kalamata (also: Kalame)

*Crete:*            Omilos Erasitechnon Alieon Irakleiou
                    (Herakleion Pleasure Fishermen's Club)
                    Herakleion, Crete

                    Naftikos Omilos Irakleiou Kritis
                    (Heraklieon Nautical Club)
                    Herakleion, Crete

                    Erasitechnikos Alieftikos Syllogos Siteias
                    (Siteia Pleasure Fishermen's Club)
                    Siteia, Crete

## YACHT BROKERS

Yachts can be chartered through the following firms in and near Athens:

Alcyonides
10 Othonos Street
Athens 118

Koutsoukelis
3 Stadiou Street
Athens 125

Archipel Club
25 Loukianou Street
Athens 139

Leggeris
4 Kriezotou Street
Athens 134

Balkania
91–93 Academy Street
Athens 141

Marine Corner
64 Akti Koumoundourou
Tourkolimano

Constantopoulos & Son.
44 El. Venizelou Street
Athens 143

Nautiki Ltd.
1 Alexandras Square
Passalimani

Delmouzos & Louys
Agean Yacht Service
4 Kriezotou Street
Athens 134

Delta Maritime Co Ltd.
1 Streit Street
Athens 111

Hellas Yachting Co
4 Kriezotou Street
Athens 134

The Propellor
1 Akti Moutsopoulou
Passalimani, Piraeus

Yachting Cruises
18 Voulis Street
Athens 126

# Chapter 48

# TURKEY

**How to Get There:** By Pan Am Jet Clipper in twelve and a half hours from New York to İstanbul; forty-five minutes more to Ankara. Air routing can be through London, Paris, Frankfurt, Munich, Belgrade, Vienna, or Rome.

Turkey is linked with Europe by airplanes, steamships, and highway.

**Customs Regulations:** Personal clothing and equipment and fifty cigarettes or fifty grams of tobacco or twenty cigars plus a bottle of liquor and three bottles of perfume will be admitted duty free.

Upon departure from the country, visitors may take out items purchased in Turkey having a total value of up to 5000 Turkish lire. If the total value exceeds this amount, the visitor must produce proof that the amounts paid have been purchased against foreign exchange.

**Travel Documents Required:** U.S. citizens must have a passport. A visa is not required.

**Currency:** The Turkish lira is exchanged at 9 lira to $1.00 U.S. There are 100 kurus to a lira. Fifteen lire, 49 kurus is written 15.49 T.L. The law states that travelers may take a maximum of 200 T.L. from the country.

**Hotels:** The larger cities offer a wide selection of hotels. It is advisable to make sure of reservations in the smaller towns. Some hotels add an extra charge for both service and heat.

**Transportation:** There are two taxi systems in Turkey; regular metered taxis and the Dolmus (pronounced: Dole-*moose*), or shared taxi.

Regular taxis are engaged in the same manner as in any other country in the world. Taxis in İstanbul have meters. In Ankara and İzmir, they are not metered. Instead, the driver uses fixed fares set by the municipality. Ask to see the fare sheet.

The Dolmus is extremely cheap. These taxis travel along a more or less fixed route on the main streets. They are entitled to carry up to five passengers. If they have less than five, they will stop if flagged down. Tell the driver which part of town you want to visit. If he is going in that direction, hop in and pay the fare, which is only 50 kurus (about 6¢) on short rides. Be sure to obtain a map of the city to be certain of the proper destination.

Dolmus taxis are also used for intercity transportation. Be sure to pick a car in good condition and arrange for a specific seat in the taxi. Arrangements can be made through hotels.

There are also city buses in large cities.

Intercity buses are quite inexpensive (about half the train fare), and are, therefore, popular. Make reservations in advance. Buses leave from Sirkeci (Demirkapi) in İstanbul and from the "Garaj" bus station in Ankara.

Trains and an internal air service provide transportation to many parts of the country. Rental autos are available in the cities. The Turkish Maritime Lines has regular coastal service (Tel: 440-133).

**Medical Facilities:** In İstanbul, the Admiral Bristol Hospital (also called the American Hospital) is staffed with English-speaking doctors. Other English-speaking doctors are available in the larger cities. It is best to arrange for medical service through your hotel. There are hospitals in other large cities.

**Other Information:** English is spoken in the cities and by the staffs of larger hotels. In İstanbul the Pan Am office is in the Istanbul Hilton Arcade (Tel: 47-45-30). In Ankara the Pan Am office is at 53 Ataturk Boulevard (Tel: 12-11-20). Tourist information and a complete list of hotels, with current rates, can be obtained from the Turkish Tourism and Information Office, 500 Fifth Avenue, New York (Tel: LO 4-5990).

In Turkey, the Ministry of Tourism has offices at Mithat Pasa Cad. No. 20 in Ankara. Branch offices are in the Hilton Hotel

and at Yeşilköy Airport in Istanbul and at Birinci Kordon in
İzmir. Smaller offices can be found in most other towns of any
size.

## SKIN DIVING INFORMATION

Turkey has four coastlines: the Black Sea, the Sea of Marmara,
the Aegean Sea, and the Mediterranean Sea. Since visibility is
frequently poor along the Black Sea coast, it is not discussed here.
The other three areas offer excellent diving conditions along their
varied coastlines. Of the three, the Aegean Coast offers the best
diving conditions.

Turkey is one of the richest countries in the world in remnants
of ancient history, with some ruins dating back to 3000 B.C.,
perhaps earlier. The Aegean coastline is dotted with ancient artifacts above and below water.

Diving equipment is expensive in Turkey. Therefore, the sport
has not become popular to the extent it has in other countries
and is restricted to the relatively well-off who can pay the high
prices for equipment. It is strongly urged that visitors to this
country bring their own equipment, including spare parts for
spear guns (if used).

Divers planning a trip to Turkey can write to the following
clubs which offer temporary memberships to foreigners:

Mr. Necati Doganbey, President
Turk Balik Adamlar Kulubu
Caddebostan
İstanbul (Tel: 71-69-24)

Cihangir Sormagir Sokak
No. 31/1 Taksim, Beyoglu
İstanbul

Galatasaray Kulubu
Kurucesme, Galatasakay, Adasi
İstanbul (Tel: 63-63-73)

Visibility in the Sea of Marmara is sixty to seventy-five feet or better. Along the Aegean and Mediterranean coasts, visibility is frequently over one hundred feet, except near the mouths of rivers or during heavy weather.

The ancient Greeks had a custom of making sacrifices to Poseidon involving dropping amphorae of oil or wheat, and sometimes golden chains, over the sides of their ships. Thus, isolated amphorae found on the bottom do not necessarily indicate the presence of ancient wrecks nearby. Divers are still looking for the gold chains.

Two places situated at some distance from the seacoast are of interest to divers. Lake İznik is a fresh-water lake a few miles southeast of İstanbul which can be reached by a good road. A sunken village is said to lie in the shallow water at the eastern end of the lake.

Near the inland town of Denizli are the white cliffs of Pamukkale which can be reached by good paved road from İzmir. Here, hot, calcium-filled water bubbles up in great quantity from the earth. The deposits of calcium on the hillside have built up into grotesque, intricately sculptured shapes, resembling frozen waterfalls. The word Pamukkale means Cotton Wool Castle, which aptly describes the appearance of this natural wonder. Nearby are the impressive ruins of the ancient city of Hierapolis. It is possible to dive into the waters of the spring at Pamukkale to explore the sunken ruins of marble buildings which have collapsed into the spring. The water temperature is over 90°. Two motels, Tusan Moteli and Moteli Pamukkale, are nearby.

In İstanbul a recompression chamber is located at the Underwater Salvage Command, Diving School, Çubuklu, Tel: 68-00-01, extension 90. Turkish-speaking representatives from the American Consulate (Tel: 44-49-80) can assist in getting the use of this facility, if needed.

**Laws:** Removing or disturbing any sunken antiquities is forbidden. All treasure found in the sea must be reported to the Government and 25 percent of the value paid to the Government.

**Diving Gear for Sale:** Equipment is difficult to get and is very expensive. Divers are strongly urged to bring their own. Rental equipment is not available.

**Guides, Boats:** There are no professional diving guides. Visitors to İstanbul will be able to meet Turkish divers through the three clubs listed in the introductory paragraphs. Visitors to İzmir can contact Mr. Mustafa Kapkin, who has a photo shop in a large hotel there. He is an expert underwater photographer and diver and knows the Turkish coast well.

Small boats can be hired at most coastal villages. For more extended cruises, and for groups, Turkish sponge boats can be chartered.

**Compressed Air:** In İstanbul air is available from Oksijen Fabrikasi, Kouacilar Caddesi, Vefa (Tel: 27-36-92), and at Omnium Oksijen Fabrikasi, in Balat. In Bodrum, Sokullu Sezen and Co., Underwater Works, Cumhuriyet Caddesi No. 7, has a compressor.

**Currents, Winds:** In the Sea of Marmara, currents are from east to west. The general set of the Aegean and Mediterranean currents is to the south, but there are numerous local variations. In the winter, when southerly winds occur, currents frequently set to the north. Currents are usually stronger around the points or capes of land and in narrow channels.

Winds are normally from the north in summer (they are called "meltem" by the Turks) and from both north and south in winter. However, as with the currents, there are local variations caused by topography and by land and sea breezes.

## THE BOSPORUS

The Bosporus is a channel over two hundred feet deep in places which links the Black Sea with the Sea of Marmara. It is possible to skin dive in this channel, but it is not recommended except for expert divers, accompanied by local divers who know the area, and followed closely by a boat with a man actively keeping track of the divers. There are plenty of fish here but they are spooky and usually hard to approach closely. The current is stiff and great care must be observed because of it. Several divers, including highly trained Navy divers, have died while diving in this waterway. Visibility in the Bosporus ranges from about thirty to thirty-five feet at the Black Sea end to between fifteen and forty feet at the Marmara end.

## SEA OF MARMARA

The Sea of Marmara is a large inland sea connected to the Black Sea by the Bosporus and to the Aegean Sea by the Dardanelles. The best diving sites here are around the Princes Islands and Marmara and adjacent islands.

The Princes Islands, a few miles southeast of İstanbul, can be reached by excursion steamer from the Galata Bridge, İstanbul. There are nine small islands in this group with steep shorelines and rocky offshore patches. The bottom gradually slopes off from depths of five feet or less near shore to deep water from fifty yards to half a mile offshore. There are lobsters, bass, halibut, and occasional schools of dolphins in these waters. In fall and winter, bonito and tuna are seen here.

The best places for lobsters are the waters around Büyük (great) Island and Yassi (flat) Island.

Marmara Island can be reached by excursion steamers of the Turkish Maritime Lines which depart from the Galata Bridge. The island has an irregular, rocky coastline. The bottom drops off sharply from depths of about five feet near shore to over one hundred feet about one hundred to two hundred yards offshore. There are a few smaller islands lying to the south of Marmara which also have interesting underwater terrain. Their coastlines are similar to the Marmara Island coast. Southeast of Marmara there is a large peninsula, Kapidaği Yarimadasi, which is connected to the mainland by a narrow, marshy isthmus. The coast here is also similar to the Marmara Island coast.

## THE AEGEAN COAST

This coastline is a magnificent one for diving—the best in Turkey. It extends southward from the Dardanelles to Gelidonya Point, the eastern entrance to the Gulf of Finike.

There are dozens of ruins of ancient cities in this region, such as Troy, Ephesus, Smyrna, Cnidus, and many others. In some places, the sea bottom is liberally sprinkled with amphorae, the all-purpose containers of ancient Greece and Rome. The water visibility is usually over one hundred feet, except near the mouths of rivers.

Çanakkale is on the southern shore of the Dardanelles, about fifteen miles east of the Aegean end. The ruins of ancient Troy are about fifteen miles southwest of Çanakkale on Hissarlik Hill. Archaeologists have found that this city was inhabited from 3000 B.C. to about A.D. 400. The remains of nine different towns have been discovered, one atop the other. Although this is not a diving site, visiting divers will find Troy a fascinating place to explore. It is necessary to obtain a permit to visit these ruins. It can be obtained from the Governor (Vali) of the Province of Çanakkale, in the city of Çanakkale. Troy is in the zone controlled by the Turkish military authorities. Troy can be reached by paved road from Çanakkale.

The Aegean coast trends south-southwest from the Dardanelles for a little over thirty miles to Baba Point. The shoreline is mostly sandy and muddy here with little of interest for divers except the inland ruins of Troy and the ruins of the ancient city of Alexandria Troas. These ruins are a few miles southwest of Troy near the seaside village of Dalyanoba, which is about fifteen miles south of the Dardanelles. Alexandria Troas was founded by Alexander the Great.

The Gulf of Edremit extends to the east for about fifty miles from Baba Point. The Greek island of Lesbos is just south of Baba Point. The northern shore of the Gulf is low and not too suited for diving. A river discharges into the eastern end of the Gulf. The best diving conditions are on the southeast shore from Boz Point southwest to Eğribucak Point and includes several off-shore rocks and islands, the largest of which is Ali Bey Island. This region is rocky and steep-to with very deep water found close to most shores.

From Eğribucak Point, the coast trends southeast for almost twenty miles to the Baston Islands and is low and sandy and not suited for diving. From the Baston Islands, the shore is steep and indented for about ten miles to the south as far as Kemikli Point. A few offshore rocks and islands fringe this coast. Along most of this portion of the coast, the bottom drops off very sharply.

South of Kemikli Point, Çandarli Bay extends inland for a few miles. The northern and southern shores of this bay are low and marshy. A river discharges into it.

Good diving conditions exist from the southern entrance to Çandarli Bay, at Ilica Point, south to İzmir Bay. In this area is the village of Foca, which was founded in 800 B.C. There is an old Genoese castle on the nearby peninsula.

İzmir is an excellent starting point for exploring the Aegean coast. It was founded by Alexander the Great as ancient Smyrna. Foundation stones excavated in the old city are thought to date from 900 B.C. Ruins of the old marketplace and statues of Poseidon and Demeter can still be seen.

A wreck lies off Yeni Kale (a peninsula about seven miles west of İzmir) in shallow water. It is marked with a buoy.

A large, irregularly indented peninsula extends west and north-west from the southern shore of İzmir Bay. It terminates at Doğanbey Point, at the entrance to Kuşadasi Bay. This entire region is an excellent diving area and features numerous offshore rocks and islets. The Greek island of Khios is across the narrow channel west of this peninsula. Ancient wrecks are found on the shallow reefs here, and fish can be seen in good quantities. This diving area can be reached by boat hired in İzmir.

Doğanbey Point is the northern entrance to Kuşadasi Bay, which extends to the eastward. Dip Point is the southern entrance to this bay. The Greek island of Samos lies just off the southern entrance to the Bay. Two rivers discharge into the Aegean here, the Camburnu and the Küçük Menderes. The best visibility and diving conditions are along the southern shore, from Kavakli Point around Dip Point and east to Incirli Point. The shore here is steep and the water is deep close alongside. Currents are strong in the Samos channel.

Along the northern shore of Kuşadasi Bay, about a mile east of the Camburnu River, is the site of the ancient city of Lebedos, which was a center of ancient Greek drama. Nearby are the ruins of Teos.

At the head of Kuşadasi Bay is the town of the same name. A few miles inland from here, by good paved road, is the town of Selçuk. A short distance south of Selçuk is the house believed to have been the home of Mary, the mother of Jesus. Legend has it that she came here with St. John and spent her last days in the house. Each year it is visited by pilgrims.

The ancient city of Ephesus, once the most important city in the civilized world, can be seen two miles from Selçuk. The best view of the extensive ruins is from the magnificent theater on a hill overlooking the site of the city and the plain beyond. Ephesus was formerly on the seacoast, but silt from the Küçük Menderes has extended the land to the west. Ephesus once had a population of over 300,000. One of the Seven Wonders of the World, the Temple of Artemis, was located here. It has been completely destroyed. Not far from Ephesus is Mount Prion, where ancient tombs were carved into the marble hillside.

From Dip Point south to Tek Ağaç Point, the coastline is low and muddy due to the silty discharge of the Büyük Menderes (the ancient Meander River, from which the word "meander" is derived).

Mandalya Bay extends eastward for about twenty miles, with Tek Ağaç Point on the north and Kizil Point to the south. Diving here is excellent except at the heads of some of the bays, which are sandy.

A short distance inland from Tek Ağaç Point is the town of

Didyma, not far from Altinkum Beach. The ruins here include the remnants of the Great Temple of Apollo, destroyed by an earthquake late in the fifteenth century.

Excellent diving conditions will be found from Kizil Point around an irregularly indented, rocky peninsula to Fener Point and around the shores of Kerme Bay, east of Fener Point. It is on the northern shore of this bay that the town of Bodrum is situated. Bodrum, formerly named Halicarnassus, is rich in history and ancient ruins. The most striking sight is the impressive castle built in the fifteenth century by the Knights of St. John of Jerusalem, from the island of Rhodes. Stones from the Mausoleum, one of the Seven Wonders of the World, were incorporated into the structure of the castle. The Mausoleum no longer exists.

Another place of interest is the Museum of Objects Found in the Sea. This museum, started just a few years ago by the American underwater archaeologist Peter Throckmorton, is in the Knight's Hall of the Crusaders Castle.

Deveboynu Point is at the southern end of the peninsula which separates Kerme Bay from Hisarönü Bay to the south. The extensive ruins of the ancient Greek city of Cnidus, some of them underwater, are to be seen on this point. The Greek islands of Kos, to the northwest, and Nisiros, to the southwest, lie off this point.

Hisarönü Bay extends to the east from Deveboynu Point. This bay is deeply indented and rocky and is excellent for diving. At the heads of some of the bays there are small, sandy beaches. The water is clear and there are quite a few groupers in the area. Boz Point forms the southern entrance to this bay. Extensive ancient ruins are situated just south of this point. Excellent diving will be found off the rocks which fringe Boz Point.

Sombeki Bay lies between Boz Point, to the north, and Kizil Point, to the south. Near the head of this bay is Kizil Island upon which ancient ruins will be found. Diving conditions in Sombeki Bay are excellent and are similar to those described in the last paragraph. Not far from the village of Saranda lie the ruins of an ancient castle.

Alobi Point, the closest cape to the Greek island of Rhodes, is about five miles south of Kizil Point. Atop the point are the ruins of the ancient Greek fortress of Loryma.

From Alobi Point eastward for over fifty miles to Kizil Point (another point of the same name), the rocky, steep, deeply indented coastline offers excellent diving conditions. The town of Marmaris is in this section of the coast.

For about twenty miles southeast of Kizil Point, the coast is low and marshy due to the outflow of a couple of rivers.

At Kurdoğlu Point (at the entrance to Fethiye Bay), the coast becomes steep and rocky. From here to Cape Gelidonya, over one hundred miles to the east, diving conditions are excellent. The exceptions are as follows: (1) An eight-mile stretch of sandy, muddy shore between Zeytin Point and İnce Point where the Esen River (formerly called the Xanthus) discharges muddy water into the sea. In this area the sea is discolored for half a mile or more to seaward. (2) Southeast of the town of Finike is Kum Point. A steep gravel beach extends for about five miles to the northeast from here to the mouth of a lagoon. (3) From Finike eastward for about fifteen miles to Karaoz Bay the shoreline is sandy and the water is discolored from the outflow of two rivers.

A number of ancient ruins are situated in the hundred-mile area just described. The sunken ruins of a city can be seen in a bay which deeply indents the northwest coast of Tersane Island. This island is northwest of the town of Fethiye. In Fethiye, a number of ancient Greek tombs were carved out of the rock face of the cliff near the harbor.

Southwest of the village of Kalkan is İnce Point. The ruins of the ancient Roman city of Patara, including an open theater, can be seen just behind this point. The port of Patara now lies under sand, brought down by the Esen River, and is some distance from the sea.

The village of Kaş is southeast of Patara. The remains of a Greek theater and marketplace can be seen in this village.

The island of Kekova is a few miles east of Kaş. Ucagiz Bay indents the coastline north of this island. A ruined castle is near the eastern entrance to this bay. Inside the castle are the remains of a Greek Theater. Southwest of the castle, close to shore in shallow water, are a number of sunken sarcophagi.

Just east of Kekova is Kim Point. Tot the west of Kim Point are the remains of the Byzantine city of Andriace. To the northeast of Kim Point, near the village of Demre, are the remains of the city of Myra. Turkish legend has it that St. Nicholas (who has evolved into Santa Claus in our current mythology), who was born in Patara, was the Bishop of Myra and lived in the city. The church of St. Nicholas can be seen, although it is pretty well buried by sand.

The remains of a Bronze Age ship, 3200 years old, were brought up from a reef off Gelidonya Point, east of the Gulf of Finike. *The Lost Ships* by Peter Throckmorton gives an interesting and detailed account of this task and of other underwater activities along this coast.

## THE MEDITERRANEAN COAST

The coastline trends north-northeast for over forty miles from Cape Gelidonya to Antalya. The southern portion of this coast is rocky and offers fair diving conditions, although not as good as in the hundred-mile area described previously. For a few miles south of Antalya, the coast is flat gravel and is not suited for diving. A number of archaeological sites can be found in this region.

About fifteen miles north of Cape Gelidonya is Cirali Bay. Here can be seen the ruins of the ancient city of Olympus, once one of the most important cities in the world.

Inland from Olympus, not far from Cirali, is the burning mountain of Chimaera. According to legend, the fire is the flaming tongue of the dragon Chimaera which was killed by a Greek lad named Bellerophon, riding the winged horse Pegasus. Bellerophon later tried to ride Pegasus to Heaven but was thrown off by the divine horse for trying to mingle with the gods. Pegasus went to see Zeus, who put him to work picking up stray thunderbolts, which probably made Pegasus think wistfully of the good old dragon-killing days.

The Roman city of Phaselis, uninhabited for over a thousand years, is situated north of Tekirova, just south of İnce Point. A sunken pier and other artifacts can be seen in the waters here. The ancient city was built on a peninsula, on each side of which is a harbor. Ancient tombs can be seen to the northeast of the main ruins. An aqueduct, temples, a theater, and the ruins of the town can be seen on the peninsula. Cliffs about fifty feet high rim the edge of the peninsula. A swamp lies behind the town.

The best diving near Antalya is around the rocky shore to the east, although there are some caves a short distance east of the eastern breakwater. Antalya is a good-sized town with hotels and other tourist amenities. Quite a few historical sites can be seen in and near the city. Turtles are sometimes seen in the Gulf of Antalya.

Baba Point is a few miles southeast of Antalya. From here for over fifty miles to Kara Point, the shoreline is low and sandy with little of interest to divers except some archaeological remains. Just east of Baba Point a few miles is the site of the ancient port of Laara. It is protected by a breakwater, mostly submerged. A few ruins can be seen ashore.

About thirty miles east of Laara is the town of Selimiye, formerly the ancient city of Side. Here, Greco-Roman ruins cover an extensive area and include a large theater capable of seating fifteen thousand spectators. The remains of an aqueduct, marketplace, and town walls can also be seen. The old port is pretty well silted up now. A village can be seen among the ancient ruins.

From Kara Point, the coast trends for about eighty miles southeast to Anamur Point. The shoreline here is steep, with deep water found close to shore. Ancient ruins can be seen near Alanya, Aydap, and Gazipasa. The remains of an ancient city can be seen atop the bluff at Anamur Point.

The coastline trends eastward for about forty-five miles from Anamur Point to İncekum Point. A sandy beach extends for about ten miles east of Anamur, where the coastline becomes rocky and steep with shoals to seaward for about half a mile. Diving conditions here are good and quantities of groupers can usually be found here. Cyprus is about forty miles south of this part of the coast. On Cape Gilindire, there is a ruined Crusader castle and tower at the end of a small cape. To the east is Cape Agalimani. A ruined Crusader castle is situated on the northern side of this cape and other ruins can be seen on Bagsakada, a small island southeast of the cape.

The coastline between Incekum Point and the Syrian border is indented by Mersin Bay and Iskenderun Bay. The entire region is sandy and uninteresting underwater. Several large rivers discharge into the sea here and the Mediterranean is discolored in places for several miles to seaward. Thus, there is nothing here to especially attract skin divers. However, for those visitors who come to this area anyway, there are a few sites of historical interest.

About fourteen miles northeast of Incekum Point is a ruined ancient castle built on the seashore. The remains of a pier, partially sunken, can be seen. Behind the castle are catacombs and the town walls. West of these relics are the remains of ancient houses hewn out of the rocky hillside. Southwest of the pier is a small islet where the ruins of another castle can be seen. Water depths around the islet are about fifteen feet.

Three miles southwest of the town of Mersin are the ruins of the ancient city of Soli—later known as Pompeiopolis—a very important part of the ancient civilization which once flourished here. The old port is mostly silted over, but some columns, the aqueduct, theater, and road can be seen. Some of these ruins are underwater. The former inhabitants of this city allowed their speech to degenerate into an unintelligible form of Greek which no one else could understand. This condition led to the coining of the word "solecism."

In the Bay of Iskenderun, about ten miles north of the town of Iskenderun, are the remains of an old fort and some houses. The ancient harbor is submerged, but the water is quite dirty and little can be seen underwater.

The town of Iskenderun was founded by Alexander the Great

as Alexandria ad Issum in honor of a military victory over the Persians at Issum, twenty miles to the north. This victory solidified the control of Greek civilization over this part of the world. The city was later named Alexandretta, then İskenderun.

# Chapter 49

# SYRIA

**How to Get There:** By Pan Am Jet Clipper to Beirut Airport, Lebanon, with hired car, taxi, or shared taxi to points in Syria.

**Customs Regulations:** Regulations are subject to periodic change. There is no discernible allowance system and assessments on personal effects are apparently at the whim of the particular customs officer involved. Before visiting this country, check with the Pan Am office or the Syrian Consulate for current regulations, and advice.

**Travel Documents Required:** U.S. citizens must have a passport with a Syrian visa. The Syrian Consulate General is at 527 Madison Avenue, New York.

**Currency:** The Syrian pound is divided into 100 piasters. The exchange rate varies from L.S. 3.80 to L.S. 4.00 to $1.00 U.S.

**Hotels:** On the Mediterranean coast, hotels are limited in number. The best headquarters for divers visiting this country is Latakia (Al Lādhiqūjah). The Casino Hotel is recommended.

**Transportation:** Taxis and hired cars with or without drivers are available in the larger towns. Service (shared) taxis offer intracity and intercity transportation. They operate in the same way as the Dolmus taxis in Turkey—see that chapter for a full description.

**Medical Facilities:** There are three hospitals in Latakia. There are also hospitals in Damascus (Dimashq) and Aleppo (Ḥalab).

**Other Information:** Visitors who have an Israeli visa on their passport will not be allowed into Syria. Arabic and French are spoken by everyone except a few English-speaking Syrians in

Latakia. There are quite a few English-speaking people in Damascus and Aleppo.

Pan Am's agent in Syria is Hitti and Khoury Frères, Sharia al Nasr, Damascus (Tel: 12500). In Beirut, Lebanon, the Pan Am office is in the Pan Am Building, Riad Solh Square (Tel: 21934). Another office is in the Phoenicia Hotel. Tourist information can be obtained from the Arab Information Center, 757 Third Avenue, New York.

## SKIN DIVING INFORMATION

The Syrian coastline is mostly sand and gravel. There is little here to attract a diver except a few ancient ruins along the seashore. Visibility underwater is poor along most of the coast due to the prevailing westerly (onshore) winds and, especially in winter, to the discharge of several rivers. Most of Syria's attractions, such as 6000-year-old Damascus, lie inland.

**Diving Gear for Sale and Rent:** None available. Visitors must bring their own equipment.

**Guides, Boats:** There is no diving business of any kind in Syria except for a few sponge divers on the island of Ruad. These men are the only Syrians who could be of any help as diving guides. Since most of them speak only Arabic, communication is difficult.

Boats can be rented on Ruad and in Latakia. The price is arrived at by bargaining. Do not accept the first price mentioned.

**Compressed Air:** Not available.

**Currents, Winds:** Prevailing winds are from the west except in the winter, when they vary. Frequently (about 75 percent of the time) the coast is subject to a swell from the west, with waves of up to six feet, which makes diving difficult or impossible. It is best to plan diving trips for early morning. The wind usually springs up around 10 or 11 A.M. and increases in strength during the day.

The general set of the current is to the north with a velocity seldom exceeding one knot.

### DIVING SITES

Since conditions along most of the coast are inappropriate for skin diving, only those few rocky areas which may be explored in calm weather are mentioned here.

A few hundred yards north of the entrance to the inner basin in Latakia the shoreline becomes rocky. Rocks fringe the coast for a few hundred yards to the north.

Less than a mile north of Latakia, at El Hamani, the coast is steep and cliffy and the remains of ancient quarries can be seen.

About half a mile north of El Hamani there is a semicircular bay, just south of the cape named Ra's Ibn Hānī. Across the mouth of the bay is a shallow, rocky reef. On the north shore of the bay are the remains of an ancient port, mostly underwater now. Ashore are the ruins of a temple and other buildings.

From Ra's Ibn Hānī north to the Turkish border the coastline is alternately cliffy and low and sandy. Diving conditions in this region are fair, but only in calm weather. Occasional ancient ruins can be seen underwater and ashore. Diving is not permitted near the Turkish border as this area is under the control of the Syrian military authorities.

*Chapter 50*

# LEBANON

**How to Get There:** By Pan Am Jet Clipper from New York to Beirut (Bayrūt) in 13¾ hours. Beirut is linked with most Mediterranean and European ports by steamship and air service.

**Customs Regulations:** Personal clothing and two hundred cigarettes or fifty cigars or 250 grams of tobacco and small quantities of liquor in nonsalable containers will be admitted duty free.

**Travel Documents Required:** U.S. citizens must have a passport with a Lebanese visa and a smallpox vaccination certificate issued within three years. Visas may be obtained at the port of entry or from the Consulate of Lebanon, 9 East 76 Street, New York.

**Currency:** The Lebanese pound (written: L.L.) is exchanged at L.L. 3.00 to $1.00 U.S. There are 100 piasters in a pound. There are no restrictions on importing or exporting any kind of currency.

**Hotels:** There is a wide range of hotels in Beirut, from the elegant Hotel Phoenicia Intercontinental to simple guesthouses. Rates range from about $3.00 to $15.00. Hotels in the smaller towns are more modest in price than those in Beirut. The selection is also smaller.

**Transportation:** Taxis, rental autos, Service (shared) taxis, and city buses are available in Beirut. City buses are efficient and inexpensive—the fare is only 10 piasters. Regular, metered taxis are plentiful. Service taxis operate in the same manner as the Dolmus taxis in Turkey. See the chapter on Turkey for an explanation. The fare from point to point in Beirut, via Service taxi, is 25 piasters per person.

Intercity buses are crowded and not recommended. Intercity Service taxis are the best way of traveling from town to town inexpensively. They depart from the Place des Canons in Beirut. Arrangements for these taxis can be made through your hotel.

**Medical Facilities:** There are several excellent hospitals with English-speaking doctors in Beirut.

**Other Information:** French, Arabic, and English are spoken. The Pan Am offices are in the Pan Am Building, Riad Solh Square (Tel: 21934), and in the Hotel Phoenicia Intercontinental. General tourist information and an up-to-date hotel list, with current rates, can be obtained from the Tourist Counselor of Lebanon, 9 East 76 Street, New York, or from the Lebanese Tourist Office on Rome Street in Beirut.

Lebanon is rich in history and offers many diversions by day and night. It is outside the scope of this book to offer a full description of the points of interest throughout the country. However, the most interesting sights can be listed and very briefly described: (1) The National Museum in Beirut contains an excellent collection of artifacts of ancient civilizations which once existed here. (2) The ruins at Baalbeck, fifty-three miles northeast of Beirut, include the largest Roman temple in the world. An annual music festival is held here. (3) The Grotto of Jeita, twelve miles north of Beirut (open from June 1 to December 15), is a huge, colorful underground cavern with many stalactites and stalagmites. It can be visited by boat. (4) At Byblos (Jubayl), twenty-four miles north of Beirut, there are monuments of several ancient civilizations. (5) Sidon (Saydā), twenty-eight miles south of Beirut, is said to be one of the oldest continuously inhabited cities in the world. Many relics of various cultures which once flourished in this ancient city can be seen. (6) Tyre (Sūr), fifty-two miles south of Beirut, was one of the most powerful cities of the ancient world.

## SKIN DIVING INFORMATION

The best diving spots along the Lebanese coast are in the region from the Casino, north of Beirut, north to a point about three

miles south of Tripoli (Tarābulus). Underwater visibility varies
from ten to a maximum of about sixty feet. The average is about
forty-five feet. Visibility is best in winter.

During the summer the water is warm and a suit is not necessary except for dives lasting for an hour or more. A suit is needed
in winter.

**Laws:** It is unlawful to remove or disturb any ancient artifacts
found on the sea bottom. Spearfishermen should obtain a permit
from the Captain of the Port, rue Foch, Beirut.

**Diving Gear for Sale:** André Cointet, Mécaniques Réunies,
Guiliguian Building, rue Nahr, Beirut, sells and services an excel-
lent selection of top quality French equipment, including Aqua
Lungs. Several sporting goods stores in Beirut have French and
Italian diving gear. The Mediterranean Marine Co., British Bank
of the Middle East Building, Abdel Aziz Street, in Ras Beirut
(Tel: 29-09-74), and Michel Habre Sports, rue Jeanne d'Arc,
Beirut (Tel: 24-79-52), have a good selection.

**Diving Gear for Rent:** Not available.

**Boats:** The St. George's Yacht Club, at the St. George's Hotel,
in Beirut offers yachts and speed boats for hire. The Sporting Club
in Beirut also offers small boats for hire. Along the coastline small
boats can be hired at Tyre (Sūr), Sidon (Saydā), Tabarja, Byblos
(Jubaye) at the Fishing Club, Batroun (Al Batrūn), and Tripoli
(Tarābulus).

**Compressed Air:** André Cointet has a compressor. See "Diving
Gear for Sale."

**Currents, Winds:** Currents set to the north and seldom exceed a
velocity of one knot.

Prevailing winds are from the west or southwest in the summer
and from the south or west in winter. An onshore breeze usually
springs up around 10 A.M. and increases in force until late afternoon.

**Fish:** The usual assortment of Mediterranean fish are found here.
Groupers are the most common game fish and vary in size from
about five to thirty pounds. In this chapter the term "good spearfishing area" is used as a relative term. Due to the unfortunate

practice of some of the Lebanese fishermen of dynamiting the sea for fish, fish are not as plentiful along this coast as they are in other places.

From the Syrian border for several miles to about three miles south of Tripoli, the coast is sandy and offers little of interest to divers. The exception to this is a chain of rocks and small islands which extends northwest of Tripoli for almost four miles. This is the best place near Tripoli for snorkeling and spearfishing.

From Mar Ya'qub Hill, south of Tripoli, southward for about forty miles to the Casino du Liban, the coast is rocky and, in places, steep. This is the best area on the Lebanese coast for snorkeling and spearfishing. Beginners will find several places suitable for shallow-water snorkeling. Shallow water extends seaward for half a mile in most places. Within this area are some historical points of interest.

About seven miles south of Tripoli is the village of Enfe, where Phoenician, Crusader, and Roman ruins can be seen. Enfe is at the northern entrance to Il Hureh Bay, which is rocky along its north shore and sandy along the southern shore. There are freshwater springs of considerable size which discharge volumes of fresh water into the middle of the bay. The village of Chekka is situated at the head of the bay. Amphorae, mostly broken up, have been found in the waters off this village.

The village of Batroun is south of the rocky cape, Ras es Shiga. At Batroun there are ruins of the Roman, Phoenician, and Crusader periods.

The waters off the small village of El Heloue, near Ras Burbara (which is a few miles south of Batroun) are good for spearfishing.

About four miles south of El Heloue is the site of ancient Byblos, now known as Jubayc. The early Greeks used papyrus imported from the Phoenicians of Byblos. Their finished works became known as *biblia* from the name Byblos. Their most important work was the scriptures, which became known by the singular form, *biblia*, which eventually evolved into the word *Bible*. Byblos is said by the Lebanese to be the oldest inhabited town in the world.

In 4000 B.C. the town was commercially important. There are numerous ruins on the site of the ancient city.

Beirut is the port of entry for Lebanon and the logical starting point for most activities. Unfortunately, there is little of interest near the city for skin diving. Between the lighthouse in Ras Beirut and the Sporting Club there are rocks which would look suitable for snorkeling. Unfortunately, several large pipes discharge raw sewage into this area. Snorkelers are advised to stay away from the Pigeon Rocks area, which is along the western shoreline, because water skiers use this area almost daily.

The coast is low and sandy for thirteen miles south of Beirut, as far as Ras Damur. For five and a half miles south of this point the coast is rocky and is suitable for diving. Shallow water extends to seaward for about half a mile.

Saydā, the ancient port of Sidon, is twenty-eight miles south of Beirut. There are many archaeological ruins to be seen, including the remains of medieval block ships in shallow water at the entrance to the ancient harbor.

The ports of Tyre, Sidon, and Byblos were established by the Phoenicians, beginning in about 4000 B.C. The Phoenicians were originally called Canaanites. Eventually, they were referred to as *Phoinikes* by the Greeks (derived from the Greek word *phoinois,* which meant purple) which, in time, evolved into the word *Phoenicians.* The Greek word for purple was used because an important item in Phoenician trade was the purple dye made from the murex shells found near Sidon and Tyre. This dye was so expensive and rare that only the very wealthy could afford to use it. Later the Romans decreed its manufacture to be a royal monopoly and limited its use to the ruling classes. Hence, the term "born to the purple." Those not of the ruling classes caught wearing purple clothing were punished. Near the Castle of St. Louis, on the south side of the port of Saydā, is the Hill of Murex.

The major contribution of the Phoenicians, who ruled these ports for so long, was their alphabet, from which other alphabets are derived.

A short distance north-northwest of the Castle of the Sea in

Saydā is a small island named Ziri. The shoreline is rocky and there is a wreck a short distance east of the north point in about twenty-five feet of water.

The ancient city of Tyre, said to have been established about 2500 B.C., lies about fifty-two miles south of Beirut. In order to dive here, a permit must be secured through the Lebanese Army. Visitors must have their passports with them which are left with the military authorities at the checkpoint just north of Tyre. The passports are returned to their owners upon returning from the city.

The capture of Tyre by Alexander the Great was considered to be one of the famous general's greatest military accomplishments. During his seven-month siege of the Tyrian stronghold, Alexander used military divers to remove obstructions to the port (called boom defenses) which had been placed there by the Tyrians to hinder the movement of his ships. Alexander's divers, then, were the first known Underwater Demolition Team, or "Frogmen."

Tyre was originally an island city connected to the mainland by a temporary bridge which was demolished in times of war. During his siege of the city, Alexander built a permanent causeway to the island fortress. Over the centuries, sand has collected around this causeway with the result that Tyre is now linked permanently with the mainland by a sandy isthmus.

Visitors interested in diving along the coastline from Tyre south to the Israeli border are advised to check with military authorities for the latest regulations concerning travel in this region.

## Chapter 51

# CYPRUS

**How to Get There:** By Pan Am Jet Clipper to Rome, Istanbul, or Beirut with a connecting flight to Nicosia. Cyprus is also linked with most places in Europe and the Middle East by air and sea service.

**Customs Regulations:** Personal baggage and a half pound of tobacco in any form and a bottle of liquor will be admitted duty free.

**Travel Documents Required:** U.S. citizens must have a passport and a smallpox vaccination certificate. A visa is not necessary.

**Currency:** The Cyprus pound is exchanged at £1/- to $2.80 U.S. There are 1000 mils in a pound. Foreign currency can be imported without restriction with the exception of Turkish lire, which must not exceed T.L. 500.

**Hotels:** There are 120 hotels on the island, with a total of 4800 beds. Rates range upward from about $3.00 per day, American plan.

**Transportation:** Taxis, shared taxis, buses, and rental autos provide transportation to all parts of the island. There are one thousand miles of paved roads and two thousand miles of unpaved roads.

**Medical Facilities:** Excellent hospitals with English-speaking doctors are available.

**Other Information:** The official languages are Greek and Turkish, but English is spoken almost everywhere.

Pan Am's Agent for Cyprus is Hull, Blyth Araouzos, Ltd., Metaxas Square, Nicosia. Tourist information and a copy of the pamphlet "Cyprus Hotels Guide," published annually, can be obtained from the Cyprus Tourist Bureau, 26 Evagoras Avenue, Nicosia (Tel: 4000/2153).

## SKIN DIVING INFORMATION

Cyprus is an excellent spot for divers interested in snorkeling over the remains of sunken ports or examining amphorae and other artifacts. The island has been inhabited since about 6000 B.C. and has been ruled by a succession of powers, each of which left traces of its civilization. The island became independent in 1960.

The Cypriots are exceptionally hospitable to foreigners and do their very best to make a visit to their island memorable.

The recommended way of seeing the island, and the diving spots, is by rented car. Rates start at $5.00 per day.

Spearfishing is usually best on the north and east coasts. Visibility is usually better on the south coast (between forty and one hundred feet) than on the north coast (where it varies widely).

The surface temperature of the water varies from 55° in winter to 80° in summer.

The most commonly seen game fish are groupers, dentexes, and gray mullet.

**Laws:** It is unlawful to remove any archaeological remains found on the sea bottom. It is also unlawful to pick up sponges growing on the sea bottom.

From time to time, military authorities declare various parts of the coastline off limits to visitors. To avoid misunderstanding, it is suggested that divers wishing to explore the coastline to any extent get in contact with the Cyprus police or military authorities to learn the current regulations. The British High Commissioner's Office in Nicosia has a map of the island showing the off-limits areas.

**Diving Gear for Sale:** The best selection of diving equipment on the island, and the only professional dive shop, is G. A. Branco Co., P. O. Box 2, Famagusta (Tel: 2365). The Branco brothers are professional divers and maintain a wide stock of French and Italian diving equipment, including spare parts for regulators and spear guns. Their shop is just across the road from the old, walled city of Famagusta (which is currently occupied by Turkish Cypriots).

Snorkeling equipment can be purchased in Famagusta, Nicosia, Larnaca, Limassol, and Kyrenia in sporting goods and toy stores.

**Diving Gear for Rent:** The Brancos will rent aqualungs to divers who can demonstrate ability in scuba diving or who can produce a qualification certificate from a NAUI, YMCA, or other recognized instructor. Rates are low. Group rates are available.

**Guides, Boats:** The R. A. F. Nicosia Sub Aqua Club at the R.A.F. base near Nicosia (Tel: 73122) is an active club which is willing to assist visiting divers whenever possible. Visitors are urged to contact this helpful group.

Another source of assistance and information is the Branco brothers, who are well acquainted with the local waters and can offer whatever help or information desired.

Boats can be rented through the Branco brothers or from fishermen at the larger coastal villages.

**Compressed Air:** G. A. Branco Co., Famagusta.

**Currents, Winds:** Currents are normally weak except around Cape Andreas, the northeastern tip of the island, where they set to the southwest with a velocity of one to three knots.

Winds are mostly from the west in the winter and summer except on the east coast, where there are also winds from the east and the southwest.

NORTH COAST

Cape Arnauti is the northwesternmost part of Cyprus. From here to Cape Kormakiti, several miles to the northeast, the coast is indented by two bays: Khrysokhou Bay and Morphou Bay. Both of these bays are battered by heavy seas for most of the winter and part of the summer. Khrysokhou Bay is rocky except for a sandy stretch at the head of the bay. The water in Morphou Bay is usually murky and unsuitable for diving. The ancient port of Soli can be seen at the head of Morphou Bay, just west of the town of Karavostasi. Here are the remains of the Vouni Palace from the fifth century B.C., together with the ruins of a theater and some ancient tombs.

From Cape Kormakiti the coastline trends in an east-northeast direction for over one hundred miles. Most of this coast is rocky and steep-to, with some sandy beaches at the heads of some of the bays. There are three particularly good portions of this coast for spearfishing. The first area extends from about four miles south of Cape Kormakiti, north to the Cape and east for about eight miles to a point about a mile east of the village of Orga. Access to this area is by boat rented in Kyrenia or another coastal village. The next spearfishing area extends from just east of Kyrenia eastward for about twenty miles to a point about four miles east of Stazousa Point. The third area is from Plakoti Cape eastward for twenty-five miles to Cape Andreas, the northeastern tip of the island.

Several ancient wrecks have been found around Cape Kormakiti and between the villages of Vavilas and Kyrenia.

Perhaps the best spot on the north for shallow-water snorkelers is Akhiropietos Point. Here, shallow water extends northward of the point for about a mile. Groupers are found here among the rocks. Just west of the point is Lambousa, where many Roman and pre-Roman ruins have been discovered.

Kyrenia has an exceptionally attractive harbor where small boats can be rented for approximately $1.15 per hour. There is a Crusader castle near the harbor. There are six hotels in the town which range in rates from less than $7.00 per day, American plan, for the deluxe Dome Hotel to about $4.50, American plan, for the modest Bosfor Hotel.

Dhavlos is a small resort town about forty miles east of Kyrenia, also on the north coast. There are two small hotels in the town, Louis Hotel and Tony's Hotel, where room and all meals cost less than $4.00 per day. Dhavlos makes another convenient headquarters for divers who want to explore the north coast.

Eight miles east of Dhavlos is Yioti where some ancient tombs can be seen, carved out of the rock.

About four miles northeast of the town of Yialousa is Ayios

Thyrsos reef. This is a good spot for beginners as well as deep-diving scuba divers. Up to about fifty yards offshore, the rocky bottom is ten to twenty feet deep and is very good for snorkeling. Scuba divers will have to swim out about one hundred yards offshore, where the bottom drops off to depths of one hundred feet or more. Spearfishing, especially for groupers, is very good here.

About three miles north of the town of Rizokarpaso is Ayios Philon, where divers can explore the partially sunken remains of an ancient port.

Cape Andreas is the northeasternmost point of the island. On the north shore, near the cape, are a number of ruins and tombs. It was near here that an earthquake toppled the Temple of the God of the Sea into the sea many years ago. Traces of this temple can still be seen in fairly shallow waters.

## EAST COAST

Famagusta is the best base for divers interested in exploring this coast. Boats and the services of the Branco brothers dive shop are available here.

From Cape Andreas for almost fifty miles southwest to the village of Boghaz, spearfishing conditions are good. The coastline is mostly rocky, with a few sandy beaches. The mountains protect this stretch of coastline from the prevailing westerlies.

A short distance north of Famagusta is the ancient city of Salamis, which was destroyed by an earthquake in A.D. 342. There are a great number of ruins ashore, and quite a few in the shallow water offshore. Quite a few ancient wrecks have been found in the nearby water. About half a mile offshore there is a reef about seventy-five feet deep where fish are plentiful.

The best spearfishing area close to Famagusta is on the eastern sides of the small offshore islands. Depths here vary from awash to about thirty feet. Just off the main harbor of Famagusta, a number of amphorae can be seen. A Roman wreck lies ten feet deep just outside the harbor.

In four of the five acts of *Othello*, the setting is Famagusta. In

Shakespeare's play, Othello was transferred from Venice to Cyprus as commander of the island. Othello's Tower can be seen in the town.

A lovely beach extends for over five miles south of Famagusta. South of the beach, the shoreline is rocky and indented with small bays as far south as Cape Greco, the southeastern extremity of the east coast. Several ancient wrecks have been found off the cape.

At times the waters around Cape Greco have been placed off limits by military authorities. Visitors should find out the current situation here before entering these waters. If a red flag is displayed from the Cape Greco lighthouse, it indicates that artillery practice is scheluled for the day and that it is dangerous to enter the water near the cape.

### SOUTH COAST

From Cape Greco west to Cape Pyla, the coast is rocky and is fringed with offshore rocks. Snorkeling and spearfishing conditions are good here. This diving area is reached by boat from Famagusta, Dhekelia, or Larnaca.

From Cape Pyla east to the town of Dhekelia, the coast is less steep and fewer fish are seen than in the area to the east.

From Dhekelia east and south to Cape Kiti the coast is mostly low and sandy except for a few offshore rocks just north of Cape Kiti. The eastern face of Cape Kiti is rocky and fair amounts of fish, as well as some ancient wrecks, are to be seen here.

It is over forty miles from Cape Kiti to Cape Gata, on the southeastern tip of the Akrotiri Peninsula. The entire stretch of coastline is low and sandy and offers little of interest to divers except for a two-mile stretch of cliffy shoreline west of Petounda Point and a four-mile stretch of rocky shore just west of Cape Dolos. In this last-named area, spearfishing conditions are good and some ancient Greek wrecks can be explored in the shallow water.

The Akrotiri Peninsula is an excellent spot for snorkeling, spearfishing, or exploring for ancient wrecks. A cliff extends for six miles from Cape Gata west to Cape Zevgari. The best diving is along this southern face of the peninsula and a mile or so north of each cape on the eastern and western shores of the peninsula. A rocky spit extends to seaward from Capes Gata and Zevgari, with depths of fifteen to twenty feet for five hundred yards offshore.

The rest of the south coast is alternately sandy and rocky, with mediocre diving conditions. The best place for diving on the south coast west of the Akrotiri Peninsula is around Cape Aspro, where the coast is cliffy with fringing rocks in the offshore waters. The ancient city of Curium is situated at the head of Episkopi Bay, near the village of Episkopi. This city was settled in Neolithic times and was continuously inhabited until the fourth century, when it was destroyed by an earthquake. A Christian basilica and a Greco-Roman theater are the principal remnants of the city.

Paphos Point is the western tip of the south coast. The nearby town of Paphos is famous chiefly because of the legend that it was here that the goddess Aphrodite was born. There are extensive ruins all around the present village, indicating that the ancient city was one of importance. Divers can explore the sunken Phoenician harbor on the southeastern side of Paphos Point. Several ancient, amphorae-laden wrecks have been discovered in the surrounding water.

### WEST COAST

Because the prevailing winds are from the west, this coast is buffeted by heavy seas for much of the year. The result is that little diving can be done here. During periods of calm weather, the best spearfishing is found from Cape Paphos north to about a mile beyond Cape Drepanum. Rocks fringe most of this shoreline and shallow water is found close to shore. The best access is by boat rented in Paphos.

# *Chapter 52*

# ISRAEL

**How to Get There:** By Pan Am Jet Clipper from New York to London, Paris, Rome, Vienna, or Istanbul with connecting flight to Tel Aviv. Israel is also linked by air and sea to most large cities in Europe.

**Customs Regulations:** Personal belongings, 250 cigarettes or 250 grams of tobacco, and gifts up to a value of $40.00 will be admitted duty free.

**Travel Documents Required:** U.S. citizens must have a passport. A visa is issued free of charge upon entering Lod Airport in Tel Aviv. A smallpox vaccination certificate is required unless visitors have resided for more than fourteen days in the United States, Canada, or a European country immediately before arriving in Israel.

**Currency:** The Israeli pound (written: I.L.) is exchanged at I.L. 3 to $1.00 U.S. There are 100 agorot in a pound. There are no restrictions on the importation of foreign currency. A maximum of 100 Israeli pounds, in one- and five-pound notes, may be imported.

Visitors are issued a Currency Exchange Form upon entering the country. This form must be kept until departure and all currency transactions must be entered on it. Foreign currency may be exchanged only at banks, hotels, or other agencies authorized to accept foreign currency. Upon departure from Israel the Currency Exchange Form is returned to Israeli officials. At this time a maximum of I.L. 900 (equivalent to $300.00 U.S.) may be reconverted from Israeli currency into foreign currency.

**Hotels:** There are 212 Government-approved hotels in Israel. Accommodations for all budgets and tastes are available, from the elegant and luxurious Caesarea Golf and Beach Hotel, in Caesarea, to modest and inexpensive guesthouses. Visitors can make arrangements through the Israel Government Tourist Offices to stay on a kibbutz, one of the cooperative farms that dot the countryside.

**Transportation:** Taxis, trains, buses, rented cars, and airplanes provide internal transportation in Israel. Shared taxis, called "Sherut taxis," can be used for intercity trips. Arrangements for Sherut trips can be made by the hotels.

**Medical Facilities:** There are several modern hospitals with English-speaking doctors. The Jewish equivalent of the Red Cross, Magen David Adom, maintains the following telephone numbers to be used in a medical emergency: Eilat 2333; Tel Aviv 64333; Haifa 3335; and Jerusalem 25111.

**Other Information:** Hebrew is the national language, but English is spoken everywhere.

Visitors wishing to go to Jordan from Israel, or to Israel from Jordan, must do so through the Mandelbaum Gate in Jerusalem. Application must be made forty-eight hours in advance and can be made through most tourist offices and hotels. The gate is open daily from 8 A.M. to 8 P.M. Only one crossing is permitted by Jordanian authorities.

General tourist information and a copy of the pamphlet "Israel Tourist Hotel Rates" can be obtained from the Israel Government Tourist Information Offices at 574 Fifth Avenue, New York; 5 South Wabash Avenue, Chicago; or 615 South Flower Street, Los Angeles.

Except for a few restaurants and clubs, everything, including public transportation, closes down for the Jewish Sabbath from Friday at sundown until Saturday at sundown. It is best not to plan to get anything done or to go anywhere on Saturday except in a rented car.

The Pan Am office is at 38 Achad Ha'am Street in Tel Aviv (Tel: 64422).

## SKIN DIVING INFORMATION

There are two centers of diving in Israel: Caesarea, on the Mediterranean coast, north of Tel Aviv, and Eilat, on the Gulf of Aqaba, an arm of the Red Sea. The attraction of diving in the Caesarea area is in exploring the extensive ruins of ancient civilizations, some of them two thousand years old. The attractions of the Red Sea are, thanks to Captain Jacques Cousteau's award-winning film *World Without Sun,* world famous: exceptionally clear, warm water; beautiful underwater formations; and exotic species of fish —all within a few minutes' snorkeling distance from the shore.

Visitors to Israel are strongly urged to sample both types of diving. The addresses of the dive centers and details of their operations are given below.

A unique opportunity to participate in underwater archaeological excavations is offered by the Undersea Explorers Society of Israel. Each year the society undertakes an underwater survey project of various sunken ports. If visiting divers can spend a minimum of four days with this group, they may participate in these ventures. This offer is for qualified scuba divers only. Arrangements must be made in advance by writing to Mr. Elisha Linder, Secretary, Undersea Explorers Society of Israel, Kibbutz Ma'agan-Michael, Hacarmel, Israel.

Underwater visibility at Caesarea varies with the season. The best visibility, from forty to sixty feet, is from mid-September through November. From December through April, visibility is generally twenty to thirty feet. From April through June, visibility improves to about forty feet. In July and August, and sometimes into September, the northgoing tide brings up silt from the Nile River. The result is poor visibility. It is hoped that this problem will be minimized when the Aswan Dam is completed.

In the Red Sea, underwater visibility is excellent the year around. Most of the time it exceeds one hundred feet and, in summer, approaches 150 feet.

**Laws:** Israeli law prohibits the removal of ancient artifacts, such as amphorae, from the sea. It is also illegal to remove coral from the sea. In the Red Sea, it is forbidden to shoot small reef fish. Only game fish may be shot.

**Diving Gear for Sale and Rent, Instruction, Trips, Guides, Boats, and Compressed Air:** Diving gear is expensive in Israel and rental equipment at Caesarea and Eilat is inexpensive. Visitors can bring their own snorkeling equipment if they prefer or they can rent it. Scuba equipment rental rates are low.

*Tel Aviv:* Morris Greenberg, 83 Shalma Road (Tel: 82-47-25), has an exceptionally good selection of Spanish and French diving equipment for sale. Rental equipment is not yet available here. Compressed air is available.

*Caesarea:* The Caesarea Diving Center (Tel: 80-81 Binyamina) is a completely equipped dive shop operated by ex-Israeli UDT divers. Basic equipment is offered for sale. Snorkeling and scuba gear can be rented here. Scuba instruction (in English or Hebrew), boats, guides, compressed air, and trips to diving spots along the coast are available here at moderate cost. A one-man recompression chamber is maintained by the diving center. Fourteen divers can be equipped at a time. Larger parties can be accommodated with advance notice.

*Eilat:* Arthur Gross, who was the first professional diving guide in Eilat, operates Dagit Sport Shop, which is in the New Commercial Centre, opposite the downtown terminal of Arkia Airways (Tel: 2343 or 2505). Snorkeling equipment is for sale here. Gross specializes in snorkeling tours and offers instruction in English, German, French, and Hebrew. He provides transportation for his clients to and from their hotels. Scuba trips can also be arranged.

Raffi Nelson also offers snorkeling trips for novices or experienced snorkelers. His headquarters is a small house trailer on Coral Beach.

The most complete diving center in Eilat is Aqua Sport Red Sea Diving Centre, Ltd., on Coral Beach, P. O. Box 300 (Tel: 2877). This center is also operated by ex-Israeli Navy UDT divers. Instruction (in English, Hebrew, French, German, and Swedish), rentals, night diving, boats, compressed air, and guide service are offered by this group. Special rates for large parties are offered. The diving center will supply electricity and water to visiting divers who want to camp out on the beach. Aqua Sports has two compressors, a recompression chamber, and 28 scuba units (14 single tanks and 14 doubles).

**Currents, Winds:** In the Mediterranean the ocean current sets to the north, but seldom exceeds one knot. From July through mid-September, the outflow of the Nile River tends to accelerate the current slightly.

Except in winter, when occasional gales occur, the weather is usually fairly calm. A sea breeze usually springs up around 10 A.M., increases in force until 2 P.M., then tapers off.

Winds and current are seldom strong enough at Eilat to interfere with diving.

## THE MEDITERRANEAN COAST

South of Tel Aviv the coast is edged with sand dunes, and there is little of interest for divers in the offshore areas. There are a few ruined cities along the coast, the best known of which is Ashkelon (Migdal Ashqelon), now a beach resort. Herod the Great is said to have been born here.

From Tel Aviv north for about twenty-seven miles the coast is alternately cliffy and sandy. There is little of interest in this region, except for a few offshore rocks. The bottom is mostly sandy.

Caesarea is the nearest point to Tel Aviv of interest to skin divers. This city was built by King Herod in honor of Augustus Caesar in 10 B.C. At one time there were 125,000 residents in the city. Now, after having been occupied by the Phoenicians, Greeks, Romans, Arabs, Turks, and Crusaders, the ancient city is being revived as a tourist center. Huge marble columns, an ancient racetrack, an open theater, and broken pieces of pottery can be seen everywhere—mute evidence of the city's former grandeur.

The Caesarea Hotel (Tel: 063-8191) is the most luxurious hotel in the area and provides daily shuttle service to the diving center and the beach. Israel's only championship golf course is adjacent to the hotel. Other accommodations can be found at the Semadar Villa Hotel (Tel: 063-8167). A nearby kibbutz operates a modest motel-type inn from May to October, the Kayit Veshayit Resort (Tel: 063-8161).

The Caesarea Diving Center is situated within the Crusader walls in the ancient port. Herod's ancient port is completely submerged and huge columns, building stones, stone anchors, amphorae, and coins can be seen here. The diving center operates two outboard-powered Zodiac boats for trips up the coast to other diving spots. Depths within the harbor are a maximum of thirty-six feet. Also within the Crusader walls, near the Diving Center, are a discothèque and an outdoor restaurant.

A few miles north of Caesarea is Kibbutz Ma'agan-Michael. This is the home of the Underseas Explorers Society of Israel and the Kibbutz Diving Club, who have established a museum of the many ancient relics discovered in the nearby waters. A small island just off the kibbutz is used for spearfishing.

From the kibbutz north to Haifa the coast is mostly sandy except for a rocky stretch extending north of the town of Dor for a few miles to Atlit. Just north of Dor there are foundation stones, tombs, and other artifacts. There are some submerged ruins at Atlit as well as some ruins ashore. Offshore, there are three small islands for exploration.

North of Atlit, off the village of Tiral Karmel, is Tire Reef which has a least depth of about fifteen feet. The reef parallels the coast a few hundred yards offshore for about two miles.

Tell es Samak is a cape on the northwestern tip of Haifa. Carmel Reef, with a least depth of about fifteen feet, lies less than a mile north-northwest of this point. Another offshore reef, Spartan Reef, lies about the same distance northwest of the cape named Ras el Kurum. It is best to plan on diving on these reefs early in the morning, before the sea breeze commences. A stiff breeze can cause quite a surge here.

Haifa is at the southern end of the Bay of Acre and the town of Acre is at the north end. Acre has been fought over and ruled by Greeks, Romans, Persians, Venetians, Crusaders, and Saracens. Consequently, a considerable number of artifacts, up to Napoleon's time, can be found in the surrounding waters. Napoleon failed in his efforts in 1799 to take the city from the Pasha, el Jazzar. Napoleonic cannon balls are among the items salvaged from the sea here.

A more or less continuous reef with an average depth of twenty-five feet parallels the coast from about the center of the Bay of Acre north for about seven miles. About five and a half miles north of Acre, there is a 146-foot, light yellow cement water tower near the beach. About a mile off the beach, on the reef, west-northwest of the tower is a wreck. It is about eight feet to the top of this sunken vessel. About one and a half miles north of the wreck, there are some above-water rocks where spearfishing is pretty good, especially for groupers. The resort town of Tel Achziv is on the coast northeast of these rocks. Visibility is as much as seventy-five to eighty-five feet around these rocks in late fall/early winter.

All the diving areas mentioned above can be reached in day trips from Caesarea. There are no facilities for scuba divers along this coast except at Caesarea.

## THE RED SEA COAST

The Red Sea coast of Israel is slightly less than seven miles long and is bordered by Egypt to the west and Jordan to the east. Eilat first became a port under King Solomon's reign. It was here that the Queen of Sheba landed while on her way to visit Solomon. King Solomon's copper mines, north of Eilat, are once again being worked and can be visited by daily command car trips from Eilat. Three neighboring countries, Jordan, Egypt, and Saudi Arabia, can be seen from Eilat.

Eilat can be reached by road or by air from Tel Aviv. The diving conditions here are superb and novices will find this area an excellent one in which to learn snorkeling or scuba diving. There are eleven hotels of various types. The Government Tourist Information Office is in the New Commercial Centre next to Dagit Sport Shop (Tel: 2268).

The western third of the shoreline has been declared a nature reserve. Here the coral reef is less than one hundred yards from the beach. Spearfishing or removal of coral or seashells in this area is prohibited. The reserve is well marked with signs at frequent intervals along the beach. The western two-thirds of the shoreline may be used for spearfishing, although the removal of coral is prohibited here also. Coral reefs are a short distance offshore from the eastern edge of the reserve east as far as the old harbor. From the old harbor east to the Israeli/Jordan border, the bottom is mostly sandy, with little coral.

Because the reef is so close to the beach, a boat is usually not necessary. However, boats can be rented if needed.

The reef extends to seaward for about 200 to 250 yards. Depths vary from one to 150 feet.

There are two recompression chambers in Eilat. One is maintained by Aqua Sports, the other by the Israeli Navy.

The Eilat Diving Club established and maintains the Marine Museum of Eilat. This well-laid-out and neatly kept museum is near the Ophir Hotel and is well worth a visit, especially by divers. There are exhibitions of marine fossils, seashells, and hydroarchaeological antiquities, as well as a collection of Red Sea fish in aquarium tanks.

# BIBLIOGRAPHY

**Diving Manuals:**

Ciampi, Elgin, *The Skin Diver*, The Ronald Press Co., New York, 1960.

Davis, Sir Robert H., *Deep Diving and Submarine Operations*, fifth edition, St. Catherine Press, Ltd., London, 1955.

Lee, Owen M., *Complete Illustrated Guide to Snorkel and Deep Diving*, Doubleday & Co., Inc., New York, 1965

U. S. Navy, *U. S. Navy Diving Manual*, Navy Department, Washington, D.C.

**Underwater Archaeology:**

Dumas, Frédéric, *Deep Water Archaeology*, translated by Honor Frost, Dufour Editions, Chester Springs, Pa., 1962.

Frost, Honor, *Under the Mediterranean*, Prentice-Hall, Inc., Englewood Cliffs, N.J., 1963.

Peterson, Mendel, *History Under the Sea*, Smithsonian Institution, Washington, D.C., 1965.

Throckmorton, Peter, *The Lost Ships*, Atlantic, Little, Brown, Boston, 1964.

**Underwater Photography:**

Brundza, Paul, and Walter Starck, *The Art of Underwater Photography*, Chilton Books, Philadelphia, Pa., 1966.

Tzimoulis, Paul, and Henry Frey, *Camera Below*, Association Press, New York, 1967.

**History and Adventure:**

Cousteau, Capt. Jacques Y., with James Dugan, *The Living Sea*, Harper and Row, New York, 1963.

Cousteau, Capt. Jacques Y., with Frederic Dumas, *The Silent World,*
Harper and Bros., 1953, New York.

Cousteau, Capt. Jacques Y., ed. by James Dugan, *World Without
Sun,* Harper and Row, New York, 1965.

Dugan, James, *Man Under the Sea,* Harper and Row, New York, 1965.

Dugan, James, with Richard Vahan, *Men Underwater,* Underwater
Society of America, Chilton Books, Philadelphia, Pa., 1966.

Gaddis, Vincent, *Invisible Horizons,* Chilton Books, Philadelphia, Pa.,
1965.

Gilpatric, Guy, *The Compleat Goggler,* Dodd, Mead & Co., with the
*Skin Diver* Magazine, 1957.

Haas, Hans, *We Come from the Sea,* Doubleday & Co., Inc., New
York, 1959.

Link, Marion C., *Sea Diver,* Holt, Rinehart & Winston, New York,
1959.

Potter, John S., with John Nathan, *The Treasure Divers of Vigo Bay,*
Doubleday & Co., Inc., New York, 1958.

Taillez, Capt. Philippe, *To Hidden Depths,* William Kimber & Co.,
London, 1954.

**Marine Life:**

Buchsbaum, Ralph, and Lorus J. Milne, *The Lower Animals,* Doubleday & Co., Inc., New York, 1960.

Herald, Earl S., *Living Fishes of the World,* Doubleday & Co., Inc., New
York, 1961.

LaMonte, Francesca, *Marine Game Fishes of the World,* Doubleday
& Co., Inc., New York, 1952.

Wagner, Robert, and R. Abbott, eds., *Van Nostrand's Standard Catalog
of Shells,* D. Van Nostrand Co., Inc., Princeton, N.J., 1964.

**Magazine:**

*Skin Diver* Magazine, Petersen Publishing Co., 5959 Hollywood Blvd.,
Los Angeles, California. Issued monthly.